PORTLAND FAMILY ADVENTURES

Portland

Family

ADVENTURES

City Escapades, Day Trips,
Weekend Getaways, and Itineraries
for Fun-Loving Families

JEN STEVENSON

SASQUATCH BOOKS
SEATTLE

Printed in the United States of America

Published by Sasquatch Books
21 20 19 18 17   9 8 7 6 5 4 3 2 1

Editor: SUSAN ROXBOROUGH
Production editor: EMMA REH
Cover design: ANDREW BROZYNA
Interior design: TONY ONG
Maps: Copyright © 2017 DIGITAL VECTOR MAPS
Copyeditor: LAURA WHITTEMORE

Library of Congress Cataloging-in-Publication
Data is available.

ISBN: 978-1-63217-099-6

Sasquatch Books
1904 Third Avenue, Suite 710
Seattle, WA 98101
(206) 467-4300
www.sasquatchbooks.com
custserv@sasquatchbooks.com

CONTENTS

INTRODUCTION

Rain or shine (and be prepared for plenty of the former!),
Portland, Oregon, is a year-round playground for the whole
family. This beautiful, friendly, oh-so-green-in-every-way Pacific
Northwest city has earned its reputation as one of the country's
food, coffee, and outdoor-recreation meccas, and its laid-back,
fleece-swathed natives are always up for an adventure . . . so
hopefully you are too!

This book's designed to take your family on a grand tour
of all things Portland, from waterfall-splashed hiking trails and
world-famous rose gardens, to kindie-rock concerts and puppet-
theater productions, to local produce-packed farmers' markets
and the best family-owned pizza, ice cream, and doughnut shops
(because you've got to keep your energy up as you explore!).

And whether you're on a family vacation, or just rainy-day
lockdown, this book's here to help you find something fun to do,
anytime, anywhere. After all, one of the reasons so many people
choose to raise their brood in Portland is because there's such a
rich kid culture—whether they're into the arts, music, food, crafts,
sports, science, or all of the above, they'll find plenty of outlets for
their interest and like-minded new friends to share it with.

Getting around the city is a breeze; Portland has some of the
best public transportation in the country and is world-renowned
for its dedication to building safe and convenient bike lanes.
Driving is easy too—just avoid the traffic-clogged freeways by taking
alternate routes, and explore the city's patchwork of unique, artsy,
and sometimes downright quirky neighborhoods in the process.
Wandering through Portland's interesting neighborhoods is
actually the best possible way to experience the real city.

Speaking of which, here in Portland, supporting local
businesses is right up there with recycling, bike riding, and
urban chicken-keeping, so with a few exceptions, you won't
find chain restaurants or stores in this guide. You *will* find a
delightful cross section of restaurants, coffeehouses, pizzerias,
bowling alleys, galleries, bookstores, and scores of other
exceptional locally owned establishments.

Now those rain boots were made for walking, so let's go!

HOW TO USE THIS GUIDE

Whether you need something to do, something to eat, or somewhere to use the loo, *stat*, consider this guide your very own pocket concierge as you and your family explore every nook and cranny of this charming city, from Goose Hollow to Grant Park and Sellwood to the South Waterfront.

Each destination within comes with all the necessary accoutrements—address, phone number, website, pricing, and insider tips about don't-miss details and discounts. Do remember that while this information was accurate as of the book going to press, things can change in the blink of an eye, so always double-check the facts before you go.

Part 1 of the book highlights the city's top attractions, then presents an array of kid-friendly destinations organized by the experience that they offer—be it a train ride, rainy-day refuge, or farmers'-market shopping spree. Part 2 leads you on an insider's romp through the city, neighborhood by neighborhood, pointing out the most unique sights, shops, and snack stops as only a local would experience them. Part 3 is your definitive guide to all the best restaurants, pizzerias, ice-cream parlors, sweet shops, and food carts this dining-savvy city has to offer, while Part 4 gets you out of your usual routine, with a variety of day and weekend trips for the whole family.

When you're packing, be it for a weekend trip or day about town, keep in mind that the weather here is notoriously fickle, and while you might wake up to bright sunlight, by lunch you could very well be slogging through a torrential downpour, and vice versa. Wear sturdy, water-resistant footwear, layer like the locals (i.e., T-shirt, Henley, flannel, fleece), and consider keeping a lightweight waterproof coat within reach at all times. But should you get caught without the proper gear, no worries—one of Portland's many virtues is its lack of sales tax, so shop away!

And finally, don't forget to have fun, make memories, and share your favorite finds with friends!

KEY

This guidebook is broken up into four main sections. In addition to listing full contact information for every business, restaurant, and attraction mentioned, several sections also include the following **icons to help guide your travels**, indicating **general pricing information** and **suggested age ranges** for each activity, as well as insights on great **rainy-day spots**, **birthday-party places**, and **nearby playgrounds**, should little ones get a case of the wiggles while you're out and about.

PRICING INFORMATION

FREE!	Free
$	Under $10 per person
$$	Under $20 per person
$$$	$20 and up per person

RECOMMENDED AGE RANGE

ALL AGES	Fit for everyone, from babes in arms to budding teenagers
AGES 0–2	Great for babies and toddlers
AGES 3–5	Well suited to the preschool crowd
AGES 6–9	Perfect for elementary-age kids
AGES 10–14	Tops for tweens or teens

OTHER HANDY NOTES

🛒	Stroller-friendly
☂	Just right for rainy days
🧑‍🤝‍🧑	Near a playground
✕	Near a restaurant
🎁	Good for parties

PART 1:

OUT & ABOUT

In this section you'll find over two hundred things for the kiddos to do, broken out by type of activity. From animal parks to bookstores, toy shops to xylophone lessons, if there's something fun to be done in Portland, it's here.

First up, the top-tier local to-dos, those quintessential Portland museums, parks, gardens, markets, and other attractions that are on every visitor's list, and rightfully so. After that, delve a little deeper according to what your kids' interests are—activities are listed by category, with all necessary contact information. Just be sure to check websites or Facebook pages for updated hours and pricing before you go, so there aren't any unexpected surprises.

Itineraries that correspond to your child's age will help you to plan a rainy-day romp or ways to beat the heat on a sweltering summer day, and if you're just visiting the city, there are itineraries to help you prioritize your time, whether you've got a few hours, a day, or the whole weekend.

All you have to do is have fun!

CITY HIGHLIGHTS

The Ultimate Portland Bucket List

Whether you're a Stumptown native or just dropping into town for a whirlwind weekend, here are the city's top family-friendly attractions, from OMSI (Oregon Museum of Science and Industry) to the Oregon Zoo. These top fifteen "bucket list" sights are first organized geographically, then expanded upon individually in the Activities section (page 4).

CITY CENTER

Like Baby Bear's bed, Downtown Portland is just the right size—not too big, not too small—which makes for easy navigation *and* efficient exploring. Even if you never leave the city's center, you can still experience over half of its major attractions, either on foot or via the easy-to-use Portland Streetcar (page 8) and MAX light-rail system (page 5).

In the heart of Downtown you'll find "Portland's living room," bustling **(1) Pioneer Courthouse Square** (page 77); drop into the visitor center for city info and insights, then calculate how far you are from home (be it Timbuktu or Tipperary) using the Milepost sign.

Portland's past and present merge in Old Town/Chinatown, a beautiful if slightly gritty historic neighborhood that was Portland's original city core. Pass through the ornate Chinatown Gate at NW 4th Avenue and Burnside, and take a turn around the oasis-like **(2) Lan Su Chinese Garden** (page 32), then share a pot of oolong in the ornate two-story teahouse. While the Old Town hood is a diamond in the rough, with many exciting projects and developments in the works, it is also home to many of the city's homeless and, at night, supports a robust bar scene. Simply be aware and use your best judgment while navigating this priceless piece of Portland history!

Let the family bibliophiles loose in world-famous **(3) Powell's City of Books** (page 38) for a few hours, or if it's Saturday or Sunday, walk down to **(4) Tom McCall Waterfront Park** (page 54) and wander around the **(5) Portland Saturday Market** (page 78), a merry mishmash of arts-and-crafts vendors, food booths, and live entertainment.

Walking through Downtown's scenic maple- and elm-lined South Park Blocks, you can't miss the stately front doors of the **(6) Portland Art Museum** (page 93). Founded in 1892, PAM's the oldest art museum on the West Coast and home to more than forty-two thousand objets d'art, so take your time admiring them before enjoying a snack break at the museum café.

Every Saturday, rain or shine, the **(7) Portland Farmers Market** (page 84) sets up shop on the beautiful Portland State University campus, with nearly two hundred local vendors selling everything from juicy just-picked Hood strawberries and farmstead cheeses to wood-fired pizza and wedges of homemade pie.

And no family trip to Portland would be complete without a day well spent at the **(8) Oregon Museum of Science and Industry** (page 66). OMSI's sprawling, enthralling riverfront complex hosts hundreds of natural-science and technology exhibits and labs, a planetarium, a four-story-screen IMAX theater, and the USS *Blueblack*, famous for its cameo in Paramount's *The Hunt for Red October*.

PARKS & REC

One of Portland's greatest (and greenest) virtues is vast, verdant **(9) Forest Park** (page 68), a 5,172-acre public park that dominates the city skyline for nearly 8 miles, has upwards of 70 miles of hiking and biking trails, and is home to hundreds of wildlife species. Adjacent Forest Park, just west of Downtown, is wondrous **(10) Washington Park** (page 210), where you'll find no shortage of epic city sights. Stop to smell the nearly seven hundred varieties of roses at the **(11) International Rose Test Garden** (page 32), and take a serene stroll through the **Portland Japanese Garden** (page 33), which, while lovely any time of year, is particularly stunning in the fall, when the Japanese maples work their magic.

Down in the southwest corner of the park, the **(12) Oregon Zoo** (page 9), **(13) Portland Children's Museum** (page 64), and **(14) World Forestry Center** (page 69) are all mere steps from each other, and at nearby **(15) Pittock Mansion** (page 77), you can tour the regal former home of *Oregonian* publisher Henry Pittock, snap selfies with one of the best views in the city, and picnic on the grand back lawn.

ACTIVITIES

ALL ABOARD
If things that go zoom float your kids' boat, here's a roundup of Portland's trams, trains, and trolleys.

BY BOAT

Portland Spirit
DOWNTOWN
SW Naito Pkwy. and SW Salmon St.
503-224-3900
www.portlandspirit.com
FREE! $$$ ALL AGES ✕

Cast off with your little mateys on the *Portland Spirit*, which sails from a dock near the Salmon Street Springs fountain (page 49) and cruises the Willamette River on several types of tours, from the basic sightseeing cruise to lunch, brunch, and dinner cruises. The accommodating crew runs an onboard Sailor Training program, where junior sailors learn about the ship and take home an honorary Captain's Certificate.

Willamette Jetboat Excursions
HOSFORD-ABERNETHY
1945 SE Water Ave.
503-231-1532
www.willamettejet.com
$$$ ALL AGES

For a wet 'n' wild Willamette River adventure, book one of these thrilling jet-boat adventure tours that skims the river at speeds up to 50 miles an hour (complete with 360-degree turns). Along the way, see a variety of wildlife, ogle opulent riverfront mansions, and get a floating history lesson about Portland and its beautiful bridges from the fun, friendly guides. If you have an adventurous toddler, opt for the one-hour tour; kids 3 and under ride free.

BY BUS

TriMet Buses
VARIOUS ROUTES THROUGHOUT THE CITY
Ticket office at 701 SW 6th Ave.
503-238-7433
www.trimet.org/bus
$ ALL AGES 👶

Efficient and easy to use, Portland's TriMet buses converge at
the central downtown bus mall near Pioneer Courthouse Square
(page 77) and serve the entire Portland Metro area via nearly
eighty bus lines.

Insider tip: Plan your route on the website, and take advantage of
the real-time Transit Tracker—text a bus stop's custom code to 272-
99 to find out exactly when your mass-transit chariot will arrive.

BY TRAIN

Amtrak's Union Station
OLD TOWN/CHINATOWN
800 NW 6th Ave.
800-872-7245
www.amtrak.com
FREE! ALL AGES 👶

Situated on the fringe of Old Town/Chinatown, this grand historic
railway station seems frozen in time. Take a turn around the quiet,
marble-lined interior (bonus: there's a public restroom in the south
hall), then walk up the ramp toward the Broadway Bridge and
snap a selfie with the clock tower's landmark *Go By Train* sign.

MAX
VARIOUS ROUTES THROUGHOUT THE CITY
701 SW 6th Ave.
503-238-7433
www.trimet.org/max
$ ALL AGES 👶

For older, slightly more jaded riders, the Metropolitan Area
Express light-rail system is just a way to get to work, but kids

see the magic in this everyday people mover. From the airport, board the Red Line to Downtown; if you're already Downtown and want to explore, hop the Orange Line to Milwaukie. It passes over Tilikum Crossing, the first major US bridge to accommodate public transportation, cyclists, and pedestrians, but no cars.

Molalla Train Park
MOLALLA
31803 S. Shady Dell Rd.
503-829-6866
www.pnls.org
FREE! ALL AGES 👶

Every Sunday afternoon May through October, this nonprofit train park gives little locomotive enthusiasts the ride of their lives on a nearly mile-long loop of 7.5-inch track. It's about a forty-five-minute drive from Portland proper, so BYO lunch; there's a pretty first-come-first-served picnic area.

Mount Hood Railroad
HOOD RIVER
110 Railroad St.
800-872-4661
www.mthoodrr.com
$$$ ALL AGES 🍴

From midspring through October, this handsome historic train trundles through the scenic Hood River Valley, affording riders views of Mt. Hood usually reserved for postcards. The regular route starts at Hood River depot and pauses in picturesque Odell for a thirty-minute layover, while on Saturdays, spaghetti-Western-loving riders can take the Western Train Robbery Tour. In winter, there's nothing quite as festive as the Polar Express—pajama-clad little ones sip cocoa and cookies and write letters to Santa on their way to the "North Pole."

Oregon Rail Heritage Center
HOSFORD-ABERNETHY
2250 SE Water Ave.
503-233-1156
www.orhf.org
FREE! ALL AGES 👶

Browse railroad memorabilia and admire the three lovingly restored vintage engines on display at the ORHC, whose mission is to preserve and share the legacy of Portland's historic steam locomotives. In December, the center operates the Holiday Express, a festive twinkle-lit forty-five-minute round-trip train ride that leaves from Oaks Park and travels along the Willamette River.

Zoo Railway

WASHINGTON PARK
4001 SW Canyon Rd.
503-226-1561
www.oregonzoo.org/visit/washington-park-and-zoo-railway
$-$$ ALL AGES ✖

One of the highlights of any Oregon Zoo trip is a ride on the Zoo Railway, which chugs around the park perimeter. The railway is the last operating railroad in the country that still offers mail service, and any mail deposited on zoo grounds or trains is hand-canceled with the historic Washington Park and Zoo Railway stamp, so consider mailing those vacation postcards here.

BY TROLLEY

Big Pink Hop-On Hop-Off Trolley

DOWNTOWN
780 SW Broadway
503-241-7373
www.graylineofportland.net
$$-$$$ ALL AGES

All aboard this bubblegum-tinted trolley, which makes a ninety-minute loop around the city, stopping at fourteen major points of interest, from the Rose Garden to the Portland Art Museum. The day pass lets you hop on and off at will, with the trolley revisiting each stop every hour. If you enjoy the ride, the same company also runs a charter tour of the scenic Columbia River Gorge. Kids under 5 ride free.

Portland Aerial Tram
SOUTH WATERFRONT
3303 SW Bond Ave.
503-865-8726
www.gobytram.com
$ ALL AGES 🚼 ✕

Built to ferry riders from the South Waterfront to Oregon Health
& Science University's campus atop Marquam Hill (a.k.a. Pill
Hill), the aerial tram offers soaring city views and a stomach-
flipping dip and sway that will elicit delighted gasps. Stay up top
and explore the campus, then come back down and grab lunch
at the nearby food-cart pod. Check the calendar for the tram's
monthly family fun days, which include themed activities, arts
and crafts, and photo ops.

Portland Streetcar
VARIOUS ROUTES THROUGHOUT THE CITY
1031 NW 11th Ave.
503-238-7433
www.portlandstreetcar.org
$ ALL AGES 🚼

Not only a fun way to explore some of the city's most beautiful
neighborhoods by rail, the streetcar also makes convenient
stops right in front of several prime kid-friendly attractions, like
Powell's City of Books (page 38), Jamison Square (page 49), the
Saturday Portland Farmers Market at Portland State University
(page 84), and the Portland Aerial Tram (above). Most stops are
covered, and real-time reader boards help antsy riders count
down their wait.

ANIMAL ATTRACTIONS

Whether they're nuts about newts or head over heels for horses, your little animal lover will go ape over these creature-centric destinations.

FLOCKS, FARMS & ZOOS

Audubon Society of Portland
FOREST PARK
5151 NW Cornell Rd.
503-292-6855
www.audubonportland.org
FREE!-$$$ AGES 6-9 AGES 10-14

Sign the family bird lover up for one of this marvelous organization's birding and natural history classes, or grab your binoculars and join a morning birdsong walk. The society also offers nature-based winter break, spring break, and summer camps for kids in grades 1 to 12, some of which stick around Portland; others venture to such exotic locales as Beverly Beach State Park and the San Juan Islands.

Oregon Zoo
WASHINGTON PARK
4001 SW Canyon Rd.
503-226-1561
www.oregonzoo.org
$-$$ ALL AGES 🛒 ✕ 🎒

With 64 acres of animal, reptile, and insect exhibits, the zoo offers endless entertainment. It also hosts spring break and summer camps, Zoo Snooze overnighters, and the epic holiday ZooLights spectacular. Taking your whole herd can get pricey, so mark the calendar for the second Tuesday of the month, when admission drops to $4. Kids 2 and under are always free.

Swift Watch

NORTHWEST

1445 NW 26th Ave.

503-292-6855

www.audubonportland.org

FREE! ALL AGES 🚼

Come early September, Northwest Portland goes on high bird alert, as Vaux's swifts congregate at Chapman Elementary School in preparation for their long flight south for the winter. Every evening at dusk, they swarm overhead, then dive into the chimney to commence the evening's roost, inciting a dramatic bird tornado that earns oohs and aahs from even the most seasoned viewer.

Insider tip: It's free to watch from the school-yard hill—spread a blanket and break out the swifts-watching snacks.

Wildwood Farm Sanctuary

NEWBERG

15481 NE North Valley Rd.

www.wildwoodfarmsanctuary.org

$ ALL AGES 🚼

May through October this bucolic Willamette Valley animal sanctuary hosts special events, monthly public tours, and volunteer work parties every other Sunday for children of all ages (accompanied by a parent). Kids muck stalls; clean pastures; and feed, groom, and socialize the farm's furry residents, while parents' help is much appreciated with repair and building projects.

PONY EXPRESS

Once Upon a Horse

NEWBERG

35525 NE Kramien Rd.

503-502-1719

www.onceuponahorse.com

$$$ AGES 3-5 AGES 6-9 AGES 10-14 👫

For an excellent introduction to the world of horses and riding, this Newberg farm offers hourly English- and Western-style riding instruction to kids as young as 2. Besides petting, riding, and carrot feeding, lessons cover horse language, grooming, and safety. Come summer, the farm offers an intimate two-person weekday horse camp that ends with a parents' show and pizza party.

Oregon Dream Ponies
NEWBERG
16725 NE Hillside Dr.
503-710-2092
www.oregondreamponies.com
$$$ AGES 3-5 AGES 6-9 AGES 10-14 🎁

Tucked away in the Willamette Valley wine country, 5-acre Taylor Hillside Farm & Ranch hosts pony rides and parties, A Day on the Ranch experiences, and Pony Palooza—a two-hour pony extravaganza involving pony petting, pony riding, pony pictures, pony crafts, a trick show, and obstacle races (schedule in advance).

Quarry Ridge Farm
BATTLE GROUND
25604 NE Manley Rd.
360-909-8605
www.quarryridgefarm.com
$$$ AGES 3-5 AGES 6-9 AGES 10-14 🎁

Saddle up for Quarry Ridge's riding academy, where kids of all ages can learn to ride, starting at $45 per lesson. Schedule a pony birthday party for up to fifteen kids, or sign them up for summer camp, where they learn horse science, safety, care, and riding, *and* get a dip in the farm pool.

Stafford Hills Equitation
WEST LINN
705 Rosemont Rd.
503-723-4468
www.staffordhills.org
$$$ AGES 6-9 AGES 10-14 🎁

Wednesdays during the school year Stafford Hills holds hourly riding lessons for kids age 8 and up in the afternoon and evening and in the morning during summer. Learn everything from grooming and riding to how to halter, lead, and tack up a horse; don't be surprised if kiddos come home begging to take vaulting lessons, because when you're young, performing gymnastics moves on the back of a cantering horse seems like the best idea ever.

FISHING TRIP
The **Oregon Coast Aquarium** (2820 SE Ferry Slip Rd.; 541-867-3474; www.aquarium.org) is a two-and-half-hour drive west to the coastal town of Newport, but giving the kiddos a glimpse of life underwater is worth the trek. (Make a weekend out of it with the **Central Oregon Coast** itinerary on page 254.) Explore exhibits on everything from shipwrecks to jellyfish; watch the sea otter feeding; and tour the seabird aviary, garden, and interpretive estuary trails. Snack-wise, there's an on-site café and coffee bar, but if the weather's nice, pack a lunch and plunk down at the outdoor picnic tables.

BE A SPORT
From smacking Ping-Pong balls to climbing the walls (literally), these sporty spots will get heart rates up *and* help burn off all that pesky excess energy.

ARCHERY

Trackers PDX
BROOKLYN
4617 SE Milwaukie Ave.
503-345-3312
www.trackerspdx.com
$ AGES 6-9 AGES 10-14

If you've got a wannabe Katniss or Gale begging to learn archery, take them to this outdoor education program's all-ages open archery-range sessions, held several times weekly, with no experience or registration required. BYO gear, or rent it for $5.

BOWLING

AMF
RICHMOND
3031 SE Powell Blvd.
503-234-0237
www.amf.com/location/amf-pro-300-lanes
$ AGES 3-5 AGES 6-9 AGES 10-14 🛒 ⬆ ✕ 🎁

This old-school alley has a whopping thirty-six lanes, plus an arcade, so make an afternoon of it with lunch at notoriously kid-friendly Hopworks Urban Brewery (page 199) across the street, followed by a few games. The early bird gets the bowling ball on Sundays—games are $1.99 before 12 p.m.

Grand Central Bowl
BUCKMAN
808 SE Morrison St.
503-236-2695
www.thegrandcentralbowl.com
$ AGES 6-9 AGES 10-14 🛒 ⬆ ✕ 🎁

This big, modern, Inner Southeast bowling alley boasts twelve lanes *and* an upstairs game room stuffed with Pop-A-Shot, Skee-Ball, air hockey, shuffleboard, and four-way Pac-Man. During summer, kids bowl free until 5 p.m. every day.

Kellogg Bowl
MILWAUKIE
10306 SE Main St.
503-659-1757
www.kelloggbowl.com
$ AGES 3-5 AGES 6-9 AGES 10-14 🛒 ⬆ ✕ 🎁

Sleepy small-town-esque Milwaukie is home to two classic bowling alleys, and this one charms with twenty-four old-fashioned wooden lanes and a retro feel. Snacks are limited, but you can call neighboring Pietro's Pizza (503-659-7770; www.pietrosrestaurants.com) for lane-side delivery. Sign your peewee bowler up for the Kids Bowl Free program and get free weekly bowling passes May through September.

Milwaukie Bowl

MILWAUKIE

3056 SE Harrison St.

503-654-7719

www.milwaukiebowl.com

$ AGES 3-5 AGES 6-9 AGES 10-14 🎳 ↑ ✕ 🎁

This cheery Milwaukie bowling alley is just the place to work on your game after the Sunday farmers' market. Or have your kiddo's Glow in the Dark birthday party here. The alley's Saturday-morning junior leagues welcome players as wee as 3, a.k.a. the Bumper Thumpers.

Sunset Lanes

BEAVERTON

12770 SW Walker Rd.

503-646-1116

www.sunsetlanes.com

$ AGES 3-5 AGES 6-9 AGES 10-14 🎳 ↑ ✕ 🎁

Opened in 1963, this beloved bowling alley has kept up with the times—for a guaranteed game, you can reserve lanes online before leaving the house or school yard. Come summer, sign your bowling newbie up for the 8 for 8 Learn to Bowl program: for $8 a week, they'll get eight weeks of hands-on coaching and twice-weekly league play.

SuperPlay

BEAVERTON

9300 SW Beaverton-Hillsdale Hwy.

503-292-3523

www.superplayor.com

$ AGES 3-5 AGES 6-9 AGES 10-14 🎳 ↑ ✕ 🎁

With a twenty-four-lane bowling alley, 3,200-square-foot laser-tag arena, *and* forty-game arcade, this popular Beaverton hangout leaves kids wanting for nothing—there's even a kids' menu with chicken strips, pizza, and burgers when they need to refuel. On Sunday mornings, be a baller for a dollar from 10 a.m. to 12 p.m.

Tigard Bowl
TIGARD
11660 SW Pacific Hwy.
503-639-2001
www.tigardbowl.com
$ AGES 3-5 AGES 6-9 AGES 10-14 🎳 ⛵ ✗ 🎁

This is the place to be on Saturday nights at 6 p.m., when this old-school alley's Glow in the Dark bowling kicks off with laser lights, cosmic fog, and neon balls. Bowling birthday parties start at the lanes, then move into nearby Pizza Caboose pizzeria (11670 SW Pacific Hwy.; 503-620-1400). The Kingpins junior league meets Saturday mornings, and all ages play Sunday evenings.

MINIATURE GOLF

Eagle Landing
HAPPY VALLEY
10220 SE Causey Ave.
503-698-7888
www.theaerieateaglelanding.com
$-$$ AGES 3-5 AGES 6-9 AGES 10-14 🎳 🎁

This genteel thirty-six-hole mini golf course, tucked into a peaceful Happy Valley housing development, is dotted with impeccably maintained lawns, waterfalls, Japanese maples, and burbling fountains, leaving you feeling like you've had an invigorating nature hike, not necessarily the usual sensation associated with a game of family mini golf. Kiddos might also be keen on the nine-hole dedicated soccer golf course—cleats allowed!

Family Fun Center
29111 SW Town Center Loop W
503-685-5000
www.fun-center.com/public/wilsonville
$ AGES 3-5 AGES 6-9 AGES 10-14 🛒 ⬆ ✕ 🎁

There isn't much you *can't* do at this Wilsonville fun farm—there's a zip line and rock wall, batting cages and bumper cars, plus an eighteen-hole miniature golf course. Afterward dig into the Moose-Sized pizza meal, then hit the arcade. On Tuesdays from 12 to 8 p.m., it's just $12 for unlimited laser tag, playground access, Cyber Coaster rides, and video games.

Glowing Greens

BEAVERTON

DOWNTOWN

3855 SW Murray Blvd.   *509 SW Taylor St.*
503-520-1586   *503-222-5554*
www.glowinggreens.com
$-$$ AGES 3-5 AGES 6-9 AGES 10-14 🛒 🎁

If not for the pirate standing guard outside, you'd walk right by this trippy underground 3-D, glow-in-the-dark, pirate-themed mini golf course, located right in Downtown Portland. Bigger kids will find the whole affair captivating, but little ones might be freaked out by the dark digs and animatronic creature features. With ID, play for free on your birthday, or celebrate with a group in the adjoining Party Zone. The Beaverton sister course is alien themed.

Oaks Park Mini Golf
SELLWOOD
7805 SE Oaks Park Way
503-233-5777
www.oakspark.com
$ AGES 3-5 AGES 6-9 AGES 10-14 🛒 ✕ 🎁

Between the amusement park, skating rink, and picnic area, you could spend all day at Oaks Park, but if time's short, putter around the links. This eighteen-hole course is as pretty as a picture, with its old-growth oaks, lush grass, and expansive views of the Willamette River. Groups rates are available for fifteen or more mini golfers, or go big and rent out the entire course for up to thirty players.

Safari Sam's
SHERWOOD
16260 SW Langer Dr.
503-925-8000
www.jungleoffun.com

$ AGES 3–5   AGES 6–9   AGES 10–14   🛒 🍗 ✕ 🎁

Safari Sam's rules of the jungle are simple—kids have to wear socks, and pretty much anything else goes. The indoor amusement park, which caters mostly to the 12-and-under crowd, has a jungle gym, bounce house, sports gym, game room, *and* a relaxed eighteen-hole glow-in-the-dark mini golf course populated by faux palm trees and neon geckos. There's a full menu of reasonably priced junk food, plus beer and wine for Mom and Dad.

Tualatin Island Greens
TUALATIN
20400 SW Cipole Rd.
503-691-8400
www.tualatinislandgreens.com

$ AGES 3–5   AGES 6–9   AGES 10–14   🛒 ✕ 🎁

The eighteen holes on this pastoral course are modeled after some of the most famous holes in the world, complete with sand bunkers and water hazards, which make for a surprisingly challenging game—wear short sleeves because you'll probably be fishing for balls. After you've played through, head over to the Island Grill for the daily happy hour (2–6 p.m.), when cheese nachos are only $3 and burgers are $5.

PING-PONG

Pips & Bounce
BUCKMAN
833 SE Belmont St.
503-928-4664
www.pipsandbounce.com
$-$$$ ALL AGES   🛝 ☂ ✗ 🎁

With ten tables, one hundred paddles, and over one thousand balls, this brothers-owned Buckman Ping-Pong parlor is ready for action and welcomes the under-21 crowd until 9 p.m. on weekdays, 7 p.m. on weekends. They're happy to help plan a Ping-Pong party, and they have a fun in-house café menu, with everything from quesadillas and nachos to rice bowls and mochi.

Insider tip: Table time is half off on Mondays, all day.

ROCK CLIMBING GYMS

The Circuit Bouldering Gym

KERNS	SOUTHWEST	TIGARD
410 NE 17th Ave.	*6050 SW Macadam Ave.*	*16255 SW Upper Boones Ferry Rd.*
503-719-7041	*503-246-5111*	*503-596-2332*

www.thecircuitgym.com
$$ AGES 3-5 AGES 6-9 AGES 10-14   🛝 ☂ 🎁

One of this rock gym's coolest features is the dedicated kids' bouldering area, with multiple walls sporting a wide variety of handholds, slides, and a slackline. Birthday parties are invariably a hit and accommodate a wide age range, since every child can climb (or just watch) at their own pace. To take things to the next level, sign up for an after-school climbing club (ages 4-10), the Circuit Breakers youth bouldering team (age 9 and up), or the weeklong summer Camp Rockstar.

Portland Rock Gym
LOWER BURNSIDE
21 NE 12th Ave.
503-232-8310
www.portlandrockgym.com

$$ AGES 3-5 AGES 6-9 AGES 10-14 🛒 ⬆ ✗ 🎁

BYO monkeys anytime to this big LoBu rock gym, and climb
together or drop them off at an after-school program or camp.
Postclimb, slip upstairs to beautiful Prasad East café (page 188);
the kids' menu is both healthy and fun, with ants on a log,
strawberry chia pudding, and hot chocolate with coconut milk.

Stoneworks Climbing Gym
BEAVERTON
6775 SW 111th Ave.
503-644-3517
www.belay.com

$$ AGES 3-5 AGES 6-9 AGES 10-14 🛒 ⬆ 🎁

With 34-foot climbing walls, high-ball bouldering to 20 feet,
and an autobelay dedicated just to kids, there's plenty for
your mini mountain goat to do here. The kids' climbing team
(ages 9–19) is one of the best in the country, and Stoneworks'
birthday parties go over big. Morning climbing camp runs all
summer and covers bouldering, autobelaying, and top roping.

SKATEBOARDING

Commonwealth Skateboarding
BUCKMAN
1425 SE 20th Ave.
503-208-2080
www.commonwealthskateboarding.com

$-$$ AGES 6-9 AGES 10-14 ⬆ ✗ 🎁

Tucked into a former stone-cutting warehouse, this
4,500-square-foot indoor skate park has a double pocket
bowl, mini ramp, bank, and small street section with a mix of
rails, boxes, and pole jams, plus a retail shop. Daily general

sessions are all ages, but from 10 a.m. to 12 p.m. on Saturdays, the space is reserved for the 14-and-under crowd, making it a good time to bring your skateboarding novice.

If seeking spots to skate and shred snow, find **roller and ice rink** details in **Thrills & Chills** (page 71), and a weekend's worth of fun on the slopes in the **Mt. Hood** getaway guide (page 247).

Skate Like a Girl
VARIOUS LOCATIONS
www.skatelikeagirlpdx.com
FREE! AGES 6–9 AGES 10–14

___

This neat nonprofit empowers girls through skateboarding and works to build an inclusive skateboarding community via lessons, beginner and intermediate clinics, and ladies' nights. Check the calendar for Saturday Sessions, when you can drop kids at Glenhaven Skate Park at 9 a.m. and pick them up by 12 p.m., and a trained coach is on hand to supervise and instruct.

BEST BIG SCREENS
Upgrade from tiny smartphone screens to the silver screen with these budget-friendly theaters, outdoor drive-ins, and city-sponsored free family movie nights.

BUDGET THEATERS

Academy Theater
MONTAVILLA
7818 SE Stark St.
503-252-0500
www.academytheaterpdx.com
$ AGES 3–5 AGES 6–9 AGES 10–14

___

Movies are $4 or less at this beloved vintage Montavilla movie theater, plus they offer in-theater babysitting, making it both a family *and* a date-night destination. The food's great too; the Academy partners with neighborhood eateries to offer Flying Pie pizza (available gluten free with forty-five minutes' notice), Miyamoto sushi, and Bipartisan Cafe (page 205) baked goods, and there are ten local microbrews on tap. On Double Feature Mondays, see two consecutive movies for $6 ($4 for kids), while Two-For-Tuesday nights are BOGO.

Avalon Theatre and Wunderland
SUNNYSIDE
3451 SE Belmont St.
503-238-1617
www.wunderlandgames.com
$ AGES 3-5 AGES 6-9 AGES 10-14

Tucked away in a nondescript brick building across from the Historic Belmont Firehouse (page 80), the Avalon Theatre is a wealth of affordable fun. The second-run movie theater plays family flicks for a few dollars, while the Wunderland arcade boasts over one hundred games. On Tantalizing Tuesdays, movies are $2, and game room admission is only $1 on Wunderful Wednesdays. Wunderland also has locations in Beaverton, Milwaukie, and Gresham, and the latter two have laser-tag arenas for kids 7 and up (ages 5–6 allowed with a parent). For more on Wunderland arcade, see page 60.

Hollywood Theatre
HOLLYWOOD
4122 NE Sandy Blvd.
503-281-4215
www.hollywoodtheatre.org
$ AGES 3-5 AGES 6-9 AGES 10-14

The Hollywood's stunning facade is an excellent lesson in Spanish Colonial Revival architecture, and its classics-filled calendar is an excellent lesson in film history. While movies are mostly adult oriented, Saturday and Sunday afternoons are reserved for Family Pictures, with admission reduced to $6 for adults and $3 for kids 12 and under.

Laurelhurst Theater
KERNS
2735 E. Burnside St.
503-232-5511
www.laurelhursttheater.com
$ AGES 3–5 AGES 6–9 AGES 10–14 🛒 ☂ ✕

Kids are welcome up until 5:30 p.m. at this historic East Burnside
theater, where moviegoers 12 and under get tickets for a scant $2
(everyone else gets them for $3). Proudly boasting five-minute
previews and no commercials, the Laurelhurst also has a full menu
of pizza, salads, and snacks made fresh daily by its sister café.

McMenamins

CONCORDIA (KENNEDY SCHOOL)	RICHMOND (BAGDAD)
5736 NE 33rd Ave.	*3702 SE Hawthorne Blvd.*
503-249-7474 ext. 4	*503-249-7474 ext. 1*
FOREST GROVE (GRAND LODGE)	ST. JOHNS
3505 Pacific Ave.	*8203 N. Ivanhoe St.*
503-992-9533	*503-249-7474 ext. 6*
NORTHWEST (MISSION)	TROUTDALE (EDGEFIELD)
1624 NW Glisan St.	*2126 SW Halsey St.*
503-249-7474 ext. 5	*503-249-7474 ext. 2*

www.mcmenamins.com/theaters
$ AGES 3–5 AGES 6–9 AGES 10–14 🛒 ☂ ✕

Nobody makes going to the movies more fun than McMenamins,
and many of its historic properties—which range from a
former Northeast Portland schoolhouse turned hotel to a

turn-of-the-century county poor farm converted into a gorgeous rural resort—are equipped with a vintage movie theater (Kennedy School, Edgefield, Grand Lodge), and some are a vintage movie theater (Mission, Bagdad, St. Johns). Several screen second-run movies at a very nice price ($2–$4), and while the food's pretty average, kids dig it—after all, what more could you want at the movies than hot pizza, heaping burgers, and fresh popcorn?

Valley Cinema Pub

BEAVERTON

9360 SW Beaverton-Hillsdale Hwy.
503-296-6843
www.valleycinemapub.com

$ AGES 3-5 AGES 6-9 AGES 10-14 🛝 ⛷ ✕ 🎁

The only small-box theater from the 1960s still in operation, Beaverton's Valley Cinema screens recently released films for a flat $4.75, payable in cold hard cash only. Kids are allowed until 8 p.m., when the theater goes 21 and up, and the snack selection includes nachos, popcorn, six kinds of Pizza Schmizza, and candy, plus various adult beverages.

FLICKS ALFRESCO

99W Drive-In

NEWBERG

3110 Portland Rd.
503-538-2738
www.99w.com

$ ALL AGES ✕

A historic treasure passed down through three family generations, this wine-country drive-in is the last of its kind in the area. It's about a forty-five-minute drive from Portland proper, and it's best to arrive early, as lines to enter can be long, and movies often sell out on summer weekend evenings. There's a snack shack on the premises but outside food is allowed, so pack a car picnic.

Flicks on the Bricks
DOWNTOWN
701 SW 6th Ave.
503-223-1613
www.thesquarepdx.org
FREE! AGES 3-5 AGES 6-9 AGES 10-14

Come summertime, the city turns Pioneer Courthouse Square (page 77) into a huge outdoor movie theater every Friday night from 7 to 11 p.m., screening fun films like *Raiders of the Lost Ark* and the *Grease Sing-A-Long* for a throng of thousands, with live entertainment beforehand. Movies are free; just BYO popcorn, sweet treats, lawn chairs, and blankets and pillows to cushion the brick steps.

Movies in the Park
VARIOUS LOCATIONS
www.portlandoregon.gov/parks/69554
FREE! ALL AGES

Long, warm summer nights in Portland are local legend, and one of the best ways to enjoy them is with a picnic dinner, pile of pillows and blankets, and movie in the park. Several times weekly, June through September, the city projects free family films in various parks, so be sure to attend your home hood screenings, and maybe check out a few unfamiliar parks as well.

CRAFTY KIDS
Whether the medium is clay, canvas, or chocolate, these art studios, craft centers, and culture clubs will stoke your prodigy's creative fires.

CERAMICS & POTTERY

Carter & Rose
RICHMOND
3601 SE Division St.
503-729-8677
www.carterandrose.com
$-$$$ AGES 6-9 AGES 10-14

A purveyor of exquisite ceramic homewares, jewelry, and other handmade goods, this Southeast studio also holds all-ages open clay sessions twice a week, and spring and summer art camps for kids 7 and up, which cover everything from pet portraits and piñatas, to clay bird feeders and collages.

CeramiCafe

BEAVERTON
14600 SW Murray Scholls Dr.
503-590-8510
www.ceramicafenw.com

CLACKAMAS
12056 SE Sunnyside Rd.
503-698-5411

$-$$$ AGES 3-5 AGES 6-9 AGES 10-14 ⬆ 🎁

With a motto that puts perfectionists at ease ("You don't have to be a Monet to create a masterpiece"), these paint-your-own art lounges are a fun way to create a keepsake. While ceramics are the main attraction here, they do take five days to glaze and dry, so if that won't go over well with your instant-gratification-seeking little artist, consider making a mosaic instead.

Mimosa Studios

VERNON
1718 NE Alberta St.
503-288-0770
www.mimosastudios.com

$-$$$ ALL AGES 🛒 ⬆ ✕ 🎁

This sweet Alberta Street ceramics studio lets kids choose from over two hundred pieces of unfinished pottery, then provides stencils, idea books, tools, and paints so they can go to town. They also host unique birthday parties and fun special events like Moms & Mimosas, where moms come in with their little ones (ages 0-5) for pottery painting, snacks, and, of course, mimosas.

CRAFTS OF ALL KINDS

100th Monkey Studio

BUCKMAN
1600 SE Ankeny St.
503-232-3457
www.the100thmonkeystudio.com

$-$$$ AGES 6-9 AGES 10-14 🛒 ⬆ 🎁

In this Southeast studio's fine-art workshops, kids age 7 and up experiment with everything from binding their own sketchbook and drawing with pastels, to abstract expressionism and color field painting.

Collage

RICHMOND	SELLWOOD	VERNON
3701 SE Division St.	*7907 SE 13th Ave.*	*1639 NE Alberta St.*
503-477-8804	*503-777-2189*	*503-249-2190*

www.collagepdx.com

$$ AGES 3-5 AGES 6-9 AGES 10-14

One of those shops you could spend hours and probably your life savings in, Collage provides kids with endless inspiration as they freak out over the thousands of arts-and-craft supplies (there's an entire *wall* of washi tape). Shop staff is also happy to offer recommendations for art studios and classes.

Confection Crafts

BOISE

3936 N. Williams Ave.
503-505-0481
www.confectioncrafts.com

$$$ AGES 6-9 AGES 10-14

Owned and operated by a former pastry chef to the stars, this confections studio holds private workshops ideal for older kids (age 8 and up) interested in the culinary arts, especially those who watch the Cooking Channel's *Unique Sweets*. Kids learn serious technique, like tempering chocolate, manipulating modeling chocolate, and decorating with edible gold and all-natural sprinkles and candies.

The Craft Factory

MULTNOMAH VILLAGE

7832 SW Capitol Hwy., Suite B
503-577-4310
www.craftfactorypdx.com

$-$$ AGES 0-2 AGES 3-5 AGES 6-9

Perfectly positioned in picturesque Downtown Multnomah Village, within a block of a bookshop, candy shop, and toy shop, this bright studio hosts a variety of crafting classes, from seasonal specials like embellishing a lucky clover, to Friday morning's Toddler Time arts-and-crafts session.

Independent Publishing Resource Center

HOSFORD-ABERNETHY

1001 SE Division St.

503-827-0249

www.iprc.org

FREE!-$$$ AGES 6-9 AGES 10-14 ☂ ✗

Perfect for budding authors, artists, and designers, the IPRC invites kids ages 8–18 to join everything from Intro to Letterpress workshops to Open Collage night. They also host a bimonthly meeting of the Kids Comics and Drawing Club, an informal drop-in session where kids bring their pens, ideas, and favorite new comics, and the IPRC provides the paper, supplies, and socializing.

Multnomah Arts Center

HILLSDALE

7688 SW Capitol Hwy.

503-823-2787

www.multnomahartscenter.org

$-$$$ AGES 3-5 AGES 6-9 AGES 10-14 🚼 ☂ 🏠

Offering visual arts, performing arts, and literary arts classes to kids age 3 and up, Portland's *other* MAC club is a phenomenal resource for exposing kids to all types of artistic experiences, from painting and sculpting to dance, music, and dramatic play.

Portland Child Art Studio

NORTHWEST

1819 NW Everett St., Suite 204

971-200-7554

www.portlandchildart.org

$-$$$ AGES 3-5 AGES 6-9 AGES 10-14 🚼 ☂ 🏠

Your future Matisse is in good hands at this darling Alphabet District art studio, which teaches drawing, painting, printmaking, sculpture, clay, papier-mâché, and more to kids age 3 and up. On Fridays and Saturdays, drop in to Open Studio, where kids make as much art (and mess) as they want, with unlimited supplies, for a nominal fee.

Smartypants
OVERLOOK
5512 N. Montana Ave.
503-477-8884
www.smartypantspdx.com
$$ ALL AGES 🛒 ⬆ 🎁

At this anything-goes NoPo art studio and play space, kids ages 1–10 are urged to "make a beautiful mess" with a wide variety of art supplies and sensory stations, and *you* don't have to clean up! Sign up for weekly classes, like sensory arts for 2- to 4-year-olds, or painting, clay, and recycled materials for 5- to 10-year-olds. Every Wednesday morning, join the Story+Art Time session, where kids hear an educational story, then do an art project based on the themes, characters, and illustrations in the book.

CURTAIN TIME
Watch your favorite book characters step off the page and onto the stage, soak in Shakespearean sonnets, play with puppetry, or laugh out loud at these theater and improv outlets.

COMEDY & IMPROV

ComedySportz Improv 4 Kids
NORTHWEST
1963 NW Kearney St.
503-236-8888
www.portlandcomedy.com
$-$$$ AGES 3–5 AGES 6–9 AGES 10–14 🛒 ⬆ 🎁

For the family comic, ComedySportz hosts a special Sunday Improv 4 Kids show geared for the 12-and-under set, with kid-friendly games and suggestions, lots of audience participation, and a postshow meet-and-greet. If your birthday boy or girl is keen on comedy, book a birthday party package with an improv workshop.

MAINSTREAM THEATERS

Oregon Children's Theatre

DOWNTOWN   KERNS
1111 SW Broadway   1939 NE Sandy Blvd.
Phone number for both: 503-228-9571
www.octc.org
$-$$$ AGES 3-5 AGES 6-9 AGES 10-14 🚌 ⬆ ✗

Junie B. Jones, James and the Giant Peach, Bad Kitty—kids' favorite characters fly off the pages and onto the stage at this sweet little theater. Most shows are suitable for 4 and up, but the theater's Young Professionals Company—a year-long teen acting program—also presents shows exploring serious themes like peer pressure and the power of rumors.

Insider tip: Newbies, ask about the First Timer/First Saturdays special, when kids' first tickets to a play's first Saturday performance are $5.

NW Children's Theater & School

NORTHWEST
1819 NW Everett St.
503-222-2190
www.nwcts.org
$$-$$$ AGES 3-5 AGES 6-9 AGES 10-14 🚌 ⬆ 🎪

Four shows a year are produced here, from adaptations of classics like *Alice in Wonderland* to new works *Shrek: The Musical*. Occasionally a production is more serious in nature and best for an older crowd, but most are silly and fun enough to entertain kids as young as four. NWCT also runs one of the biggest theater schools on the West Coast, offering an impressive list of classes for kids ages 3-17, ranging from basic Acting Essentials to Shakespeare's Villains.

KIDS' SHOWS & STORYTELLING

Penny's Puppet Productions
VARIOUS LOCATIONS
503-282-9207
www.pennypuppets.com
$-$$$ AGES 3-5

Peppy puppeteer Penny Walter's shows are geared for the pre-K to 3rd-grade set, but even adults will be charmed by her thoughtful productions, and if you're planning a puppet-themed birthday party, Penny will bring the stage to you.

Shaking the Tree Theatre
HOSFORD-ABERNETHY
823 SE Grant St.
503-235-0635
www.shaking-the-tree.com
$$$ AGES 3-5 AGES 6-9 AGES 10-14

Covering rich and varied works of literature, like Rudyard Kipling's *Just So Stories* and the Norwegian folktale collection *The Troll with No Heart in His Body*, this Southeast theater company offers weekly afternoon classes for kids and teens ages 5-14, with a live performance on the last day.

Tears of Joy Theatre
HOSFORD-ABERNETHY
1444 SE Hawthorne Blvd.
503-248-0557
www.tojt.org
$$$ AGES 3-5 AGES 6-9 AGES 10-14

These gorgeous puppet productions enchant kids of all ages—and adults too—as they perform stringed renditions of classics like *The Jungle Book* and *Three Billy Goats Gruff*. The theater's popular summer camps, for kids ages 5-14, are rich cultural experiences, with weeklong forays into folklore, fables, and different types of mask and puppet making, and a Friday-night performance at the end.

GATHER IN THE GARDEN

Take a nature walk, stop and smell the rose bushes (all ten-thousand-plus of them), and get your hands dirty at these community gardens and farm camps.

BOTANICAL GARDENS

Crystal Springs Rhododendron Garden

EASTMORELAND
5801 SE 28th Ave.
503-771-8386
www.crystalspringsgarden.org
FREE!-$ ALL AGES

From Downtown, it's a fifteen-minute drive to this oft-overlooked botanical garden, a beautiful spot for a walk even when its namesake florals aren't in bloom. Kids will love the bridges, secret hiding places, duck pond, and its assertive residents. Admission is $4, but on Mondays, Tuesdays, and before 10 a.m. or after 6 p.m. Wednesdays through Sundays, it's free.

Elk Rock Garden

SOUTHWEST
11800 SW Military Ln.
503-636-5613
www.elkrockgarden.org
FREE! ALL AGES

Part of a historic riverfront estate in Dunthorpe, about a twenty-minute drive from Downtown, this elegant, uncrowded English-style garden is worth the effort of finding it. Wind your way through the wisteria- and lilac-lined pathways, admire the Willamette River and Mt. Hood views, and visit the resident fish, sometimes without seeing another soul.

The Grotto

MADISON
8840 NE Skidmore St.
503-254-7371
www.thegrotto.org
FREE!-$ ALL AGES

Renowned for its Christmas lights festival, this Catholic shrine and sanctuary's 62 acres of serene forest and gardens make it a must-visit the other eleven months of the year too. Walking around the lower garden, Grotto, chapel, and visitor center is always free; touring the upper level is $6 (children under 6 free) and well worth it—the mile-long walking path, lushly landscaped botanical garden, and spectacular views are priceless.

International Rose Test Garden
WASHINGTON PARK
400 SW Kingston Ave.
503-823-3636
www.portlandoregon.gov/parks/finder/index
.cfm?action=viewpark&propertyid=1113
FREE! ALL AGES

No Rose City visit is complete without the actual roses, nearly seven hundred varieties of them, all sequestered in this Washington Park garden dreamscape. Get lost in the rows of rose varietals, enjoy dramatic views of Downtown and Mt. Hood, gobble a hot dog at the Olympia Provisions frankfurter cart, then run laps around the grassy amphitheater. If you're on a garden crawl, the Portland Japanese Garden is steps away. Or catch the free shuttle up to the Oregon Zoo (page 9), Portland Children's Museum (page 64), and World Forestry Center (page 69).

Lan Su Chinese Garden
OLD TOWN/CHINATOWN
239 NW Everett St.
503-228-8131
www.lansugarden.org
$ ALL AGES

An oasis of serenity and craftsmanship hidden in the center of Chinatown, this exquisite botanical garden was constructed by Chinese artisans from Portland's Chinese sister city, Suzhou. Wander around at your own pace or join one of the several daily forty-five-minute docent-led tours, and don't leave without enjoying tea and moon cakes in the two-story teahouse, a.k.a. the Tower of Cosmic Reflections. Kids 5 and under are free.

Portland Japanese Garden

WASHINGTON PARK

611 SW Kingston Ave.

503-223-1321

www.japanesegarden.com

$ ALL AGES

Just across the street from the International Rose Test Garden (opposite page), this impeccably groomed 5.5-acre sanctuary is dotted with koi ponds, statuary, a life-size Zen garden, and stunning water features. The garden is beautiful any time of year, but autumn is particularly spectacular; try staging a family Japanese maple scavenger hunt, and plan on taking *lots* of pictures of the brilliantly colored foliage. Kids 5 and under are free.

COMMUNITY PATCHES & HANDS-ON GARDENING

City of Portland Community Gardens

VARIOUS LOCATIONS

www.portlandoregon.gov/parks/39846

$$-$$$ ALL AGES

You may not have space for a home garden, but with over fifty community gardens sprinkled throughout the city, kids can still experience the thrill of growing their own food via the Portland Community Gardens program. Some gardens are full (if so, put your name on the waiting list), but if you aren't too picky about location, open plots can be had by checking the city website and filling out a Garden Plot Request Form. (While you're there, check the events calendar for free gardening workshops.)

Food Works

SAUVIE ISLAND

4625 N. Trenton St.

503-927-0820

www.villagegardens.org/food-works

FREE! AGES 10-14

Made up of a remarkable group of 14- to 21-year-olds who plan, plant, harvest, and care for a 1-acre certified organic farm on

Sauvie Island, Food Works grows its own produce, then sells it to local grocery stores and donates it to the community via its free farmers'-market stand. In spring and summer, it hosts volunteer work parties every Saturday from 10 a.m. to 2 p.m.—kids help with seeding, planting, weeding, and other farm chores.

Kruger's Farm Camp
SAUVIE ISLAND
17100 NW Sauvie Island Rd.
503-621-3489
www.krugersfarm.com
$$$ AGES 6-9 AGES 10-14

Take that common summer sentiment "go outside and play" to a whole new level at this popular Sauvie Island farm's summer day-camp series, where kids ages 6–12 attend weeklong sessions covering topics like organic gardening and composting, survival skills, and canning and outdoor cooking.

Portland Nursery
MT. TABOR
5050 SE Stark St.
503-231-5050
www.portlandnursery.com

POWELLHURST
9000 SE Division St.
503-788-9000

FREE!-$ AGES 3-5 AGES 6-9 AGES 10-14

Green thumbs rule at this marvelous century-old nursery, where you'll find everything from tiny garden tools to every seed under the sun. You can also sign up for interactive kids' classes, like building a fairy garden or designing a terrarium. Every October, the Mt. Tabor location hosts an epic apple festival, with apple tastings, cider pressing, caramel apples, and a kids' tent with puppet shows and pumpkin carving.

Sauvie Island Center
SAUVIE ISLAND
13901 NW Howell Park Rd.
503-341-8627
www.sauvieislandcenter.org
FREE!-$$$ ALL AGES

The Sauvie Island Center's mission is to educate kids about food, farming, and the land by way of its beautiful organic farm and the adjoining 1,200-acre Howell Territorial Park. Get involved by encouraging teachers and schools to schedule a field trip, signing up for the summer farm camp, and attending special events like the Pollination Celebration, barn dance, and fall open house.

GET INVOLVED

Whether giving used books a new home, playing with puppies, or packing meals for families in need, these community organizations will help teach kids the joys of giving back.

Children's Book Bank
KERNS
1728 NE Glisan St.
503-616-3981
www.childrensbookbank.org
FREE! AGES 6–9 AGES 10–14

Every year, the book bank accepts thousands of new and gently used donations, then distributes them to kids who aren't lucky enough to have a home library. Donations are always welcome, and the bank also relies heavily on volunteers to clean, repair, sort, and deliver books. Kids as young as 6 can get involved at the book-sprucing-up level, working in groups to clean covers, erase scribbles, and tape torn pages before books are delivered to their new home.

Hands On Greater Portland
DOWNTOWN
619 SW 11th Ave.
503-200-3355
www.handsonportland.org
FREE! AGES 3–5 AGES 6–9 AGES 10–14 ☂

When crazy family schedules don't allow for a regular volunteer gig, carve out a few hours for one of Hands On's "done-in-a-day" opportunities. There are tons of activities for kids as young as 4, like sorting and packaging supplies for families in need, creating care packages for foster children, and helping at an urban farm.

Oregon Food Bank

SUNDERLAND

7900 NE 33rd Dr.

503-282-0555

www.oregonfoodbank.org

FREE! AGES 6–9 AGES 10–14 ☂

A great way for families to work together to help other families, the food bank welcomes volunteers age 6 and up for two- to three-hour shifts spent repacking and labeling foods like rice, pasta, and produce into family-size bundles. As an added bonus, everyone gets to wear a hairnet, which is always good for a giggle.

Oregon Humane Society

SUNDERLAND

1067 NE Columbia Blvd.

503-285-7722

www.oregonhumane.org

$$$ AGES 10–14

Ideal for the family animal lover, OHS's youth volunteer program works with 12- to 17-year-olds, who commit to either a one-time after-school shift helping animals develop social skills, or to the long-term program, which requires a regular six-month commitment. Every other week, kids walk, bathe, groom, socialize, and clean up after pets and help with various jobs around the shelter. Just don't be surprised if you end up gaining a few furry new additions to the family.

GET LOST IN A BOOK

Peruse a picture book, track down your favorite YA author's newest novel, sit still for story time (or don't, if you're at Story & Stroll), and start a lifelong love affair with the library.

BOOKSTORES

A Children's Place

SABIN

1423 NE Fremont St.

503-284-8294

www.achildrensplacebookstore.com

$ ALL AGES 🛒 ⛱ ✕

The oldest independent bookstore in Portland, this darling destination is both bookstore and community hub. Book hounds should join the Frequent Buyers Club to get store credit for every fifteen books bought, and story-time lovers should mark the calendar for Thursdays at 10:30 a.m.

Annie Bloom's Books

MULTNOMAH VILLAGE

7834 SW Capitol Hwy

503-246-0053

www.annieblooms.com

$ ALL AGES 🛒 ⛱

This beloved Multnomah Village bookshop has impeccable taste in children's literature, so trust its picks and stock up accordingly, then coddle the resident feline, Molly, who maintains her own list of favorite reads, which she helps promote by sitting next to them in the front window.

Green Bean Books

VERNON

1600 NE Alberta St.

503-954-2354

www.greenbeanbookspdx.com

$ ALL AGES 🛒 ⛱ ✕

Browse this darling Alberta Street bookshop's shelves of classics, bestsellers, and Newbery winners; flip through the latest board books; and then settle in for the weekly story time. Watch for special events like multicultural sing-alongs, Read to a Dog signups, and author visits. Afterward perhaps pay a visit to nearby Candy Babel (page 225) or Salt & Straw (page 231). Just a thought.

Powell's City of Books

PEARL DISTRICT

1005 W. Burnside St.

800-878-7323

www.powells.com

$ ALL AGES 🚼 ☂ ✗

The name says it all, and while Powell's has several stores throughout the city, the Downtown Portland mothership must be seen to be believed, with 68,000 square feet of books and more than a million titles. It's a common occurrence for readers to disappear inside for a few hours before reemerging with an armload of new additions to the home library.

Insider tip: The story-time calendar is second to none, so check who's reading before you go.

LIBRARIES

Multnomah County Library

VARIOUS LOCATIONS THROUGHOUT MULTNOMAH COUNTY

503-988-5342

www.multcolib.org

FREE! ALL AGES ☂

There's nothing like your neighborhood library, and hopefully you visit often, but if an incentive's needed, check the awesome citywide story-time schedule—it's chock-full of literary opportunities for kids of all ages, from Book Babies, to Tiny Tots, to Preschool Sensory Storytime. If your children are in a language immersion program, they can attend in a variety of languages, including Russian, Mandarin, Cantonese, and Spanish.

ONE-OF-A-KIND STORY TIMES

Story & Stroll

SOUTHWEST

11321 SW Terwilliger Blvd.

503-636-4398

www.tryonfriends.org

FREE! AGES 0-2 AGES 3-5 AGES 6-9 🚼 🏃

Hosted by Tryon Creek State Park (page 70), this free Friday-morning program takes 2- to 6-year-olds (although all are welcome) on an hour-long interactive jaunt integrating nature exploration, outdoor play, art, literature, and movement, with cute themes like My Five Senses and Some Smug Slug. The weekly stroll is first come, first served; register in the nature center a half hour beforehand.

Story Time with Olive & Dingo
VARIOUS LOCATIONS
www.oliveanddingo.com
$ AGES 0-2 AGES 3-5 🛒 👕 🎁

Nobody works the toddler crowd quite like Olive and Dingo, veterans on the clown circuit. This quirky local duo sets up shop at various kid-friendly venues around town and works its zany magic—storytelling, singing, cracking jokes, painting faces, and twisting balloons.

GO, TEAM
Whatever your sport of choice, Portland's on it—cheer alongside chainsaw-wielding soccer mascot Timber Joey, watch the roller skates and elbows fly at Oaks Park, and see if blood really *does* bounce on ice at the Winterhawks Skating Center.

BASEBALL

Portland Pickles
LENTS
4727 SE 92nd Ave.
503-775-3080
www.portlandpicklesbaseball.com
$-$$ AGES 3-5 AGES 6-9 AGES 10-14 🛒 ✕

Cheer alongside mascot Dillon the Pickle as Portland's very own summer collegiate wood-bat league plays ball at old-fashioned

Walker Stadium in Lents. An enthusiastic hometown crowd fills the bleachers and packs the outfield's lush berm—bring blankets, chairs, and snacks, and be sure to get your picture snapped with Dillon before the night's through.

BASKETBALL

Portland Trail Blazers
LLOYD DISTRICT
1 N. Center Ct. St.
503-797-9619
www.nba.com/blazers
$-$$ ALL AGES 🛒 ↑ ✕

From October to May, Portland's beloved Blazers whip their loyal hometown crowd (the team holds the record for most consecutive sold-out home games) into a frenzy of cheers and "We are Rip City!" chants that kids find fascinating (or overwhelming, you be the judge). For most games, nosebleed seats are as low as $12, and children 2 and under are free. To avoid game-day traffic, take the MAX (page 5)—it stops right at the stadium, as does the Portland Streetcar (page 8).

COLLEGIATE SPORTS

Portland State Vikings
GOOSE HOLLOW
1844 SW Morrison St.
503-725-3307
www.goviks.com
$$$ ALL AGES 🛒 ✕

There's nothing like a football game on a crisp fall night, so come September, take the family to cheer on the hometown team, which plays through November. Vikings home games are played a mile from the university, at Providence Park, and while the parking situation isn't quite as dire for Vikings games as it is for Timbers games (page 42), it's still a good idea to take the MAX.

HOCKEY

Portland Winterhawks
LLOYD DISTRICT

300 N. Winning Way
503-238-6366
www.winterhawks.com

$$ ALL AGES 🛒 ⚓ ✗

If someone's gotten ahold of *The Mighty Ducks* DVD and has the hockey bug, get tickets to see Portland's official hockey team in action at the Moda Center or Veteran's Memorial Coliseum. Or sign up for time on the ice at the Winterhawks Skating Center in Beaverton, where the team practices—skating lessons are available for kids as young as 3, while the three-level youth hockey series enrolls kids age 6 and up (more details on page 74).

HORSE RACING

Portland Meadows
EAST COLUMBIA

1001 N. Schmeer Rd.
503-285-9144
www.portlandmeadows.com

FREE! AGES 3–5 AGES 6–9 AGES 10–14 🛒 ✗

Very young kids might not see the allure of watching horses run in circles, but older kids get caught up in the excitement of the chase, even if they can't bet on the outcome. Racetrack food is also pretty thrilling, with various cafés slinging hot dogs, burgers, ice-cream sandwiches, nachos, and hot chocolate. Parking is free, or take the MAX Yellow Line (page 5); it's a fifteen-minute walk from the station to the track. The racing season is October through February.

ROLLER DERBY

Rose City Rollers
SELLWOOD
7805 SE Oaks Park Way
www.rosecityrollers.com

$$ AGES 3-5 AGES 6-9 AGES 10-14 🛒 ☂ 👫 ✖

Punny team names, snazzy outfits, flying elbows, and high-speed turns and tumbles—few spectator sports are as entertaining as roller derby, and the teams know it and put on a show from January to June. Watch a bout at Oaks Park, then meet the players, snap photos, and collect autographs afterward. Kids might even be inspired to join the junior derby—girls 12–17 can try out for the Rosebuds, while 7- to 12-year-olds have a shot at the Rose Petals.

SOCCER

Portland Thorns
GOOSE HOLLOW
1844 SW Morrison St.
www.timbers.com/thornsfc

$$ ALL AGES 🛒 ✖

Sharing Providence Park with the Timbers from March to September, Portland's professional women's soccer team commands a strong following of its own, but tickets are nonetheless much cheaper and easier to come by than Timbers' tickets, so you'll still get a great game, just with more money leftover to spend at the concessions stand.

Portland Timbers
GOOSE HOLLOW
1844 SW Morrison St.
503-553-5555
www.timbers.com

$$$ ALL AGES 🛒 ✖

Timbers fans suffer no shortage of team spirit, and when the MLS Cup–winning team plays at Providence Park from March to

October, the whole town knows it. Wrap everyone in their green-and-gold scarves and waterproof parkas, rehearse your favorite Timbers Army chants, and join the soccer-obsessed throngs as they cheer, clap, and stomp. Snap selfies with burly lumberjack mascot Timber Joey, who ambles through the crowd revving his chainsaw. And because this is Portland, even the stadium food is a notch above normal, with local favorites like Bunk Sandwiches and Pacific Pie Company (page 189) on the menu.

Insider tip: Avoid traffic tangles by parking downtown and walking or taking the MAX (page 5).

HITTING THE HIGH NOTES

Whether you prefer the musical stylings of Mozart or Mr. Ben, be your venue of choice a concert hall or pizza parlor, and should your budget be a zillion dollars or zero, tune into these jazzy venues and activities.

MUSICAL ACTIVITIES

Micah and Me
VARIOUS LOCATIONS
www.micahandmerocks.com
FREE!–$ ALL AGES 🚼 ⛵ 🎁

Let the kiddos rock out at these fun musical movement shows, a.k.a. dance parties, geared for kids ages 0–8 and held at different locations around town. They also teach a weekly group ukulele class for kids 8 and up, Just Uke It, at the Northeast Community Center, and can be booked for private parties as well.

Mississippi Pizza Pub
BOISE
3552 N. Mississippi Ave.
503-288-3231
www.mississippipizza.com/events
$ AGES 0–2 AGES 3–5 🚼 ⛵ ✕ 🎁

Every Monday night at this cheerful Mississippi Street pizza parlor, beloved local performer Mr. Ben breaks out his guitar and ukulele and wows his adoring audience with covers of hits like "The Itsy Bitsy Spider" and "The Wheels on the Bus," as well as original material like "My Bicycle," a catchy educational ode to helmet safety. The pizzeria also hosts children's performers every Wednesday and Thursday at 5 p.m. and Saturdays at 4 p.m.

Multnomah Arts Center
HILLSDALE
Contact information on page 27
$-$$$ AGES 3-5 AGES 6-9 AGES 10-14 🚼 ☂ 🎒

From piano to percussion, this Southwest Portland art center offers a wide variety of affordable musical lessons for kids age 5 and up, plus group sing-alongs for the toddler and pre-K set, and a youth chorus that teaches singing technique, note reading, and the principles of pitch and rhythm.

Music Together of Portland
VARIOUS LOCATIONS
503-236-4304
www.musictogether-pdx.com
$$$ AGES 0-2 AGES 3-5 🚼 ☂

Based on the belief that kids should be exposed to many musical experiences from the get-go, this early childhood music program brings infants, toddlers, preschoolers, and kindergartners together to sing and dance in perfect (or sort of perfect) harmony. Attend a free demo class before signing up for the ten-week term, which at around $100–$150 per child is significantly cheaper than what a spring term's going to cost you in 12–18 years.

The Old Church
DOWNTOWN
1422 SW 11th Ave.
503-222-2031
www.theoldchurch.org
FREE! AGES 0-2 AGES 3-5 AGES 6-9 🚼 ☂ ✕

A nonprofit, this beautiful historic, nonreligious concert-and-event venue works with various Portland music organizations and independent artists to produce eight Little Ears music, storytelling, and theatrical performances a year, all of which are free to attend—check the calendar for dates.

Oregon Symphony Young People's Concerts & Kinderkonzerts
DOWNTOWN
1037 SW Broadway
503-228-1353
www.orsymphony.org
$-$$$ ALL AGES 🚼 ☂ ✗

Especially designed for kindergarten through 8th grade, these fifty-minute performances by the acclaimed Oregon Symphony, in Downtown's regal Arlene Schnitzer Concert Hall, are an experience to remember.

Poa Café
BOISE
4025 N. Williams Ave.
503-954-1243
www.poacafe.com
$ ALL AGES 🚼 ☂ ✗

This hip, super-kid-friendly North Portland café hosts weekly kids' events, from the ever-popular musician Mr. Ben to the enthusiastic dancing, drumming, and storytelling of performance artist Habiba Addo.

Portland School of Music and Dance
ELIOT   NORTH TABOR
120 NE Knott St.   *205 NE 50th Ave.*
503-287-5028   *503-444-0775*
www.portlandmusicanddance.com
$$$ AGES 3–5 AGES 6–9 AGES 10–14

If there's a budding Benjamin Grosvenor in the family, sign him or her up for piano lessons at this music-and-dance studio. Kids as young as 3 can take group or individual lessons, and while the studio specializes in piano, it also offers instruction in guitar, strings, drums, and composition. If you've got more of a mover than a finger shaker, try the ballet, jazz/tap, or creative movement classes.

Portland Youth Philharmonic

VARIOUS LOCATIONS

503-223-5939

www.portlandyouthphil.org

$$$ AGES 6-9 AGES 10-14 🛒

Founded in 1924, Portland Youth Philharmonic—whose members range in age from 7 to 23—was the country's first youth orchestra, and it's still wowing audiences and inspiring future youth musicians nearly a century later. It plays around a dozen concerts a year (check its website for calendar dates and tickets), and watch for its free preview concerts.

Red Yarn Productions

VARIOUS LOCATIONS

www.redyarnproductions.com

$-$$$ ALL AGES 🛒 🌳 🎭

Local folk-music performer and puppeteer Andy Furgeson has earned quite a following with his upbeat folk-rock performances and creative sets. Andy performs regularly around town at venues like Mississippi Pizza Pub (page 43) and Village Ballroom, both solo and with his five-piece Red Yarn Band. While shows are designed for kids ages 2–9, toddlers will be fascinated, and so will adults.

OUTDOOR INSTRUMENTALS

Concerts in the Park

VARIOUS LOCATIONS

www.portlandoregon.gov/parks/69555

FREE! ALL AGES 🛒 👫 ✕

Akin to popular Movies in the Park (page 24), this city-sponsored summer concert series runs July through August, with family-friendly performances nearly every night of the week in a different park. Shows start at 6:30 p.m., but arrive early with family, friends, and a picnic. If you pedal over, take advantage of the free bike-valet service.

Kruger's Farm Summer Concerts

SAUVIE ISLAND

17100 NW Sauvie Island Rd.

503-621-3489

www.krugersfarm.com/events-programs/summer-concerts

$ ALL AGES 🚲 ✕

Bring a picnic dinner to these Thursday-night concerts at Kruger's beautiful Sauvie Island farm, but don't worry too much about dessert—you can buy fresh fruit from the farm stand or queue up at the cotton-candy booth.

Zoo Concerts

WASHINGTON PARK

4001 SW Canyon Rd.

503-226-1561

www.zooconcerts.com

$$$ ALL AGES 🚲 ✕ 🎁

It's an unforgettable experience, sitting on a blanket on the zoo amphitheater lawn, rocking out to Pink Martini as the elephants gently trumpet in the background. Tickets often sell out, so don't dally, and they include zoo admission, so come early and hang out with the animals. Outside food and beverages aren't permitted; parking gets crowded; so consider taking the MAX (page 5) from Downtown, and remember to pack a light coat as nights can get chilly.

MAKING WAVES

When the summer heat hits and sitting in front of the open fridge or eating ice chips isn't quite cutting it, take your sweaty Bettys and Bradleys to one of these pools, spray parks, or splash pads.

BEACHES

Sauvie Island

www.sauvieisland.org

$ ALL AGES

Only fifteen minutes from Downtown, step into small-town life on sleepy Sauvie Island, a bucolic blend of family farm stands, berry patches, and livestock-dotted fields. Follow the road to Collins Beach, a popular stretch of riverfront that gets busy during summer, so come early for a good parking and sand spot (remember to buy a parking pass from one of the markets en route). Part of the beach is clothing optional, so you may find yourself giving an impromptu anatomy lesson.

BOATING

Alder Creek Kayak, Canoe, Raft & SUP

JANTZEN BEACH	LAKE OSWEGO	TUALATIN
200 NE Tomahawk Island Dr.	14110 Stampher Rd.	5855 SW Nyberg Ln.
503-285-0464	971-313-4781	503-691-2405

www.aldercreek.com

$$ AGES 3-5 AGES 6-9 AGES 10-14

With three Oregon locations on the Columbia, Tualatin, and Willamette Rivers, this paddle sports shop owns the state's largest fleet of rental kayaks, canoes, and stand-up paddleboards. It also has a full calendar of events, camps, and classes for the whole family.

FOUNTAINS, SPRAY PARKS & WADING POOLS

Bill Naito Legacy Fountain

OLD TOWN/CHINATOWN

2 SW Naito Pkwy.

www.portlandoregon.gov/parks/42348

FREE! ALL AGES

This Old Town fountain near the Burnside Bridge is just the spot to end a summer day's stroll through Tom McCall Waterfront Park (page 54). For extra credit, start at the Salmon Street Springs (opposite page) and see if you can get to the Naito fountain before your swimsuit dries.

Caruthers Park Fountain

SOUTH WATERFRONT

3508 SW Moody Ave.

www.portlandoregon.gov/parks/42348

FREE! ALL AGES 🛒 ✕

Set amidst the South Waterfront skyscrapers, Elizabeth Caruthers Park is a peaceful spot to cavort in the splash pad, then roll around in the lust grass to dry off before grabbing cheeseburgers at nearby Little Big Burger (page 199), PB&J doughnuts at Blue Star Donuts (page 228), or Baked Oregon brownie sundaes at What's the Scoop? (page 232).

Jamison Square

PEARL DISTRICT

810 NW 11th Ave.

www.portlandoregon.gov/parks/42348

FREE! ALL AGES 🛒 🏃 ✕

Of course kids love this pretty Pearl District park—it's got totem poles, a grassy knoll, lots of dogs ambling around, a hot-dog cart, Cool Moon Ice Cream (page 229) across the street, and arguably the coolest fountain in town—a long stone staircase that transforms into a mini waterfall and wading pool when the weather warms. The summer crowds get thick, so go early or be prepared for the pandemonium.

Salmon Street Springs

DOWNTOWN

SW Naito Pkwy. and SW Salmon St.

www.portlandoregon.gov/parks/42348

FREE! ALL AGES 🛒

Just the thing after a hot stroll through Tom McCall Waterfront Park (page 54), this popular downtown fountain is a feat of engineering, with 185 water jets controlled by an underground computer that constantly changes the water flow's pattern. Babies can dip their toes while bigger kids run through the jets, and even bigger kids can stand in the spray and look blasé about the whole thing.

Teachers Fountain
DOWNTOWN
815 SW Park Ave.
www.portlandoregon.gov/parks/42348
FREE! ALL AGES 🚼 ✕

If you're downtown doing some shopping or sightseeing or food-cart-hopping and want to cool hot feet on the fly, try this placid Director Park fountain. Very baby- and toddler-friendly, and rarely occupied (oddly enough, the suits who eat lunch in the park don't tend to dip), the fountain has a few gentle jets and eight water-circulating "burbles."

SWIMMING POOLS & WATER PARKS

Mt. Scott Indoor Pool
MT. SCOTT
5530 SE 72nd Ave.
503-823-3183
www.portlandoregon.gov/parks/60939
$ ALL AGES 🚼 ⛱ 👪 🎁

Shrieks and screams are a common reaction to the Mt. Scott Community Center's indoor pool and water park, and that's before the kids even hit the water. Fair enough, one look at this Playmobil set come to life and thrill levels go through the roof—there's a corkscrew waterslide, current channel, vortex, rope swing, basketball hoop, interactive play structure, and shallows for your toddler. The center also offers swimming lessons for all ages.

Sellwood Outdoor Pool
SELLWOOD
7951 SE 7th Ave.
503-823-3679
www.portlandoregon.gov/parks/61026
$ ALL AGES 🚼 👪 🎁

Mixing historic charm and modern amenities like slides, a play structure, and zero depth entry for tots, this cool pool draws a crowd from all over town. June through September, it offers swimming lessons for all ages and open play every afternoon; during the last week of August, it hosts the wildly popular Sellwood Dive-In movie—where you watch a family flick from the comfort of your floatie *in the pool*.

Wilson Outdoor Pool
HILLSDALE
1151 SW Vermont St.
503-823-3680
www.portlandoregon.gov/parks/61027
FREE!-$ ALL AGES 🚼 🏊 🍴

Open from mid-June to mid-August, this awesome outdoor pool at Hillsdale's Wilson High School is nothing but fun, with two pools, a lazy river, a 120-foot waterslide, spray jets, a diving board, a frog kiddie slide, and a basketball hoop. There's a shallow area for little ones and less confident swimmers, which is a relatively safe place from which to observe the controlled chaos.

Wings & Waves Waterpark
MCMINNVILLE
500 NE Captain Michael King Smith Way
503-434-4180
www.evergreenmuseum.org/waterpark
$$-$$$ ALL AGES 🚼 ✈ ✕ 🍴

A most unusual water park, Wings & Waves is not only located inside a Willamette Valley airplane hangar, but also has a waterslide coming out of a real Boeing 747 perched on the roof. The ten slides range from easy for the wee ones, to hair raisers that will satisfy the family stuntman. Visit the many interactive exhibits about water and its critical role, and the adjoining aviation museum, which has the original *Spruce Goose* parked *inside*.

PARKS & PLAYGROUNDS

There's a park in practically every Portland nook and cranny, so after the kids have tired of your neighborhood playground, make a game of trying a new one every week using the city's park finder: www.portlandoregon.gov/parks/finder.

DIG!

Portland Children's Museum's Outdoor Adventure
WASHINGTON PARK
4015 SW Canyon Rd.
503-223-6500
www.portlandcm.org/exhibits/outdoor-adventure
$$ AGES 0-2 AGES 3-5 🚌 🧗 ✕ 🎁

Located in the Portland Children's Museum in Washington Park, this 1.3-acre alfresco exhibit is one of the best playgrounds around, albeit with an entry fee ($10.75, under 1 free). It's structures, from tumbling blocks woven out of vine maple to piles of logs in the DIY fort section, are made with all-natural materials. There's a creek for experimenting with dams and waterspouts, a grassy meadow for cloud watching, and a dig pit that kids love to sink their hands (and hopefully not teeth) into.

Westmoreland Park
SELLWOOD
7530 SE 22nd Ave.
www.portlandoregon.gov/parks/57822
FREE! ALL AGES 🚌 🧗 🎁

Giant Westmoreland Park has a little bit of everything—baseball diamonds, tennis courts, picnic tables, streams, and ponds; it's even home to the Portland Lawn Bowling Club. Little ones will love the all-natural teaching playground and its boulders, blocks, sticks, stumps, sand, and, come summertime, water pumps. Geese love this park too, so watch where your wee one's waddling.

LOOK!

Mt. Tabor Park
MT. TABOR
SE 60th Ave. and Salmon St.
www.portlandoregon.gov/oni/article/418024
FREE! ALL AGES 👶 🚶 🎁

Popular with neighborhood folk, runners, and stair climbers (the summit stairway has 282 steps), Mt. Tabor Park gets major kid points for having a top-notch playground *and* for being atop a dormant volcano, which means stunning city views. On Wednesdays, the park is closed to cars, so your little one has the run of the place. Hiking trails crisscross the park; take one or explore them all, whatever the group's attention span allows for.

RUN!

The Fields Park
PEARL DISTRICT
1099 NW Overton St.
503-823-7529
www.portlandoregon.gov/parks/finder/index
  .cfm?action=viewpark&propertyid=1448
FREE! ALL AGES 👶 🚶 🎁

This bright, open Pearl District park makes up for what it lacks in shade with a huge grassy field perfect for running wild in, plus it's got a playground, picnic tables, restrooms, and an off-leash dog park. The park hugs the railroad tracks, and your junior train enthusiast will be mesmerized by the Amtrak passenger trains and seemingly endless freight trains that rumble past.

Peninsula Park
PIEDMONT
700 N. Rosa Parks Way
503-823-3620
www.portlandoregon.gov/parks/60415
FREE! ALL AGES 👶 🚶 🎁

Home to Portland's original rose garden, this elegant, old-fashioned park covers over 16 acres, from the French-style garden to the Italian villa-style community center. Kids love splashing around in both the pool and rose-garden fountain, crawling all over the playground, and running rampant in the wide grassy fields. And unlike its more famous siblings, this rose garden is rarely overrun with flower gawkers, so you can spread a picnic blanket right in the grassy aisles, inches from the blooms.

Tom McCall Waterfront Park
DOWNTOWN
Naito Pkwy. between SW Harrison St. and NW Glisan St.
www.portlandoregon.gov/parks/finder/index
.cfm?action=viewpark&propertyid=156
FREE! ALL AGES

Comprising 30 acres running right along the Willamette, this former freeway turned downtown park is a major city attraction, home to a popular riverfront bike-and-walking path, nearly 2 miles of grassy pastures, the Salmon Street Springs (page 49) and Bill Naito Legacy (page 48) fountains, Portland Saturday Market (page 78), the Japanese American Historical Plaza and cherry tree grove (page 80), and countless festivals, from Bite of Oregon to the annual Portland Rose Festival.

SLIDE!

Sellwood Park
SELLWOOD
SE 7th Ave. and Miller St.
www.portlandoregon.gov/parks/finder/index
.cfm?propertyid=666&action=viewpark
FREE! ALL AGES

There's so much happening at Sellwood Park it's hard to decide where to start—at the big, shady playground; old-timey community center; pool; tennis courts; or beach? Stay awhile, then hop down to Oaks Park (page 72) for rides, roller skating, and mini golf.

Washington Park Playground

WASHINGTON PARK

South of the International Rose Test Garden on SW Sherwood Blvd.

www.portlandoregon.gov/parks/finder/index
.cfm?&propertyid=841&action=viewpark

FREE! AGES 0-2 AGES 3-5 🚼 🏃

Between the Oregon Zoo (page 9), Portland Children's Museum (page 64), International Rose Test Garden (page 32), Portland Japanese Garden (page 33), and miles of hiking trails, it's easy to forget that Washington Park has a good old playground too (the biggest in town!), with plenty of slides and swings, a sand pit, and picnic tables.

SWING!

Laurelhurst Park

LAURELHURST

3756 SE Oak St.

www.portlandoregon.gov/oni/article/418026

FREE! ALL AGES 🚼 🏃 ✕ 🎒

This superb Southeast park's paved walking path winds through nearly 27 acres of lush forest and past a pretty duck pond, playground, and picnic area, with dozens of grassy blanket-friendly alcoves along the way. BYO lunch and badminton and make an afternoon of it, or after your walk and/or playground and swing set session, wander west through elegant Laurelhurst to Staccato Gelato (page 232).

PEDAL POWER

Portland's a two-wheelin' kinda town, and here are some of the best urban trails, indoor tracks, and group rides, plus bike rental and tour info.

INDOOR TRACKS

The Lumberyard
MADISON
2700 NE 82nd Ave.
503-252-2453
www.lumberyardmtb.com
$$ AGES 3-5 AGES 6-9 AGES 10-14 🚲 ⛵ ✗ 🎪

As much fun as you can have indoors on two wheels, this bike park's four color-coded tracks accommodate everyone from beginners to riders who can do air flips, plus there's a mountain bike trail. BYO bike or rent one, and helmets are required at all times. After a hard ride, relax with a pizza at adjoining Pulehu Pizza (www.pulehupizza.com). If your kiddos have the bike bug, sign them up for private lessons at the after-school Shred Academy (ages 4-14), Balance Bike Camp, or one of the weeklong spring break and summer camps.

> **RIDE ON**
> To expand your biking horizons, consult Travel Oregon's comprehensive **Ride Oregon** website (www .rideoregonride.com), which lists every mountain bike ride, road route, and bicycle event imaginable.

Springwater Corridor
HOSFORD-ABERNETHY
SE 4th Ave. and SE Ivon St.
www.portlandoregon.gov/parks/article/145158
FREE! ALL AGES 🚲 🚶

This is an excellent extension to an Eastbank Esplanade ride. The entrance to Springwater Corridor is slightly south of OMSI (page 66); just follow the signs. This 3-mile stretch south to Sellwood is flat, easy, and terrifically scenic, with Willamette River views and quiet stretches of wetlands and forest. Stop at Oaks Bottom Wildlife Refuge (page 70) along the way, and at the south end, have a picnic at Sellwood Park, then hit the rides, rink, or mini golf course at Oaks Park. Or head east when you hit SE Spokane Street and wheel around the quiet residential streets of Sellwood.

RENTALS & TOURS

Cycle Portland Bike Tours

OLD TOWN/CHINATOWN

117 NW 2nd Ave.

844-739-2453

www.portlandbicycletours.com

$-$$$ ALL AGES

It's only fitting to tour one of the country's best bike cities on two wheels, and this Old Town company will rent the bikes and provide the maps necessary to take a self-guided tour; or sign up for its Essential Portland Tour, an easygoing two-hour, 7-mile ride suitable for kids 10 and up (must also be 4 feet 10 inches tall).

Pedal Bike Tours

OLD TOWN/CHINATOWN

133 SW 2nd Ave.

503-243-2453

www.pedalbiketours.com

$$$ ALL AGES

Patient, knowledgeable guides and fun, interactive routes make this Old Town bike shop's tours a sound pick for pedaling around town with kids. For a Portland 101 ride, take the Historic Old Town Tour, a 9-mile meander through Downtown and along the river. You'll want to take the brewery tour sans kids, but the 5-mile Food Carts Tour is perfect for short legs and attention spans, with five food-cart snack stops. If you'd rather plot your own path, the shop has very reasonable rental rates.

RIDE-ALONGS

Providence Bridge Pedal
DOWNTOWN
503-281-9198
www.providence.org/bridge-pedal
FREE!–$$ ALL AGES

Mark your calendars for this perennially popular annual August ride, which closes off nearly all of Portland's major bridges to cars and opens them to bikers. The eight- and ten-bridge routes are best left to the experienced riders, but the six-bridge route is appropriate for older kids, and the wobbly wheeled 3-mile Kids Pedal is perfect for little ones, plus it's free!

Sunday Parkways
VARIOUS LOCATIONS
www.portlandoregon.gov/transportation/46103
FREE! ALL AGES 🚼 🛝 ✕

May through September, the city hosts five monthly family bikes rides that loop through the East, North, Northeast, and Southeast sectors, as well as Sellwood and Milwaukie. Big, boisterous party zones are set up at various parks along the way, with food booths, activities, live music, fun freebies, and, perhaps most entertaining of all, free Zumba classes. Routes range from 7 to 10 miles, and while mostly flat, there are occasional hilly sections. Local bike shops offer assistance with flats and other fixes at various intervals, but packing a patch kit or portable pump is a good idea. Stick a picnic in your pack, or if you want to ride fancy-free, bring cash and hit up the various food vendors.

URBAN TRAILS

Eastbank Esplanade
BUCKMAN
SE Water Ave. and SE Taylor St.
www.portlandoregon.gov/parks/finder/index
    .cfm?&propertyid=105&action=viewpark
FREE! ALL AGES 🚼 ✕

Stretching from the Hawthorne Bridge to the Steel Bridge, this 1.5-mile paved path is mostly flat, with a few metal ramps that little ones might need to walk their bikes up. Along the ride, stop and check out the twenty-two interpretive panels about the river, the bridges, and east-side development. At SE Taylor Street, the Esplanade connects to the Inner Southeast Industrial district through a (pretty gritty) parking lot; ride up and get a snack at Water Avenue Coffee (1028 SE Water Ave.) or noodles and homemade Twinkies at Boke Bowl (page 212).

RAINY-DAY ROMPING

When the rain won't relent and the natives are getting restless, slip on boots and slickers and make a run for the nearest indoor playground, trampoline park, community center, or vintage arcade.

ARCADES & BOARD GAMES

Ground Kontrol

OLD TOWN/CHINATOWN

511 NW Couch St.

503-796-9364

www.groundkontrol.com

$ AGES 6-9 AGES 10-14 🎋 ✗ 🎁

From Frogger and Tetris to Dance Dance Revolution, this dim, screen-lit Old Town arcade will instantly enthuse your otherwise indifferent family gamer. Besides the nearly one hundred classic arcade games, it's also got the largest pinball room in the region and a menu littered with joyful junk foods like nachos, grilled cheese, and corn dogs, alongside more virtuous eats like hummus and vegan chili. The arcade is all ages until 4:30 p.m., 21 and up after 5 p.m.

Interactive Museum of Gaming and Puzzlery

BEAVERTON

8231 SW Cirrus Dr.

503-469-9998

www.imogap.org

FREE!-$ AGES 3-5 AGES 6-9 AGES 10-14 🎋 🎁

Board-game enthusiasts will go bananas at this hands-on board-game "museum," where the shelves are piled with over five thousand games and puzzles that you can play at your leisure. It's a few dollars to play for the day, or donate a new or gently used board game in lieu of the fee.

Wunderland

BEAVERTON

17235 NW Corridor Ct.

503-626-1665

GRESHAM

140 NW Burnside Rd.

503-328-8496

www.wunderlandgames.com

MILWAUKIE

11011 SE Main St.

503-653-2222

SUNNYSIDE

3451 SE Belmont St.

503-238-1617

$ AGES 6-9 AGES 10-14 🍴 ✖ 🎁

Besides movie theaters and a bevy of nickel arcade games (over a hundred at each location), these affordable family fun centers also have laser tag arenas at the Beaverton and Gresham sites (age 7 and up; 5- and 6 year-olds can play if accompanied by a parent), plus fun arcade-appropriate snacks like slushies, kettle corn, and ice cream. Get dollar-game room admission on Wunderful Wednesdays, and $3 laser tag games on Thrilling Thursdays.

INDOOR SPORTS

G6 Airpark

HAZELWOOD

10414 SE Washington St.

503-255-3334

www.g6portland.com

$$ ALL AGES 🛒 🍴 🎁

It's love at first sight for your little leaper at this indoor trampoline park, which boasts wall-to-wall trampolines with an open jump area, trampoline dodgeball, a basketball dunk station, and a "trick zone." The official age limit is "If you can walk, you can bounce," but there's a separate jumping area for kids age 8 and under. Save money with daily half-price matinee jumps from 3 to 5 p.m. and Sunday Funday specials from 5 p.m. to close.

JJ Jump

CLACKAMAS

9057 SE Jannsen Rd.

503-723-3600

www.jjjump.com

$ ALL AGES 🛒 🎪 🎁

Fun to say, fun to visit, JJ Jump has 12,000 square feet of bounce houses, bounce slides, and a zip swing and climbing wall, plus games and party rooms. Check the calendar for time and age restrictions; some open play times are age 7 and under, others are 4–15. Socks are required and are available for the sockless for a dollar.

Punch Bowl Social

DOWNTOWN

340 SW Morrison St.

503-334-0360

www.punchbowlsocial.com/location/portland

$-$$ ALL AGES 🛒 🎪 🍴 🎁

Occupying the entire third floor of Pioneer Place mall, just below the movie theater, this leather armchair- and antler-studded hangout has a decidedly mature feel but does welcome kids of all ages until 10 p.m. nightly. Inside, find bowling lanes, private karaoke rooms, Ping-Pong, corn hole, marbles, darts, foosball, shuffleboard, and an '80s arcade scattered throughout the labyrinthine space.

Sky High Sports Trampoline Park

TIGARD

11131 SW Greenburg Rd.

503-924-5867

www.por.skyhighsports.com

$$ ALL AGES 🛒 🎪 🍴 🎁

Pull on socks, sign the liability waiver, and get ready to go sky high at this Tigard trampoline park, where kids can bounce freestyle, play pickup trampoline dodgeball, dive into the foam pit, and then, once they've had their fill of being airborne, hit the ground for pizza and Dippin' Dots at the café, followed by a few games of air hockey in the arcade.

PLAY SPACES

Indoor Playground at Mittleman Jewish Community Center
HILLSDALE
6651 SW Capitol Hwy.
503-244-0111
www.oregonjcc.org
$ AGES 0-2 AGES 3-5 🛒 🌂 🏃

From September through May, drop in to the Mittleman Jewish Community Center's indoor playground on Mondays, Wednesdays, and Fridays from 10 a.m. to 12 p.m., when the center hosts open play for kids ages 6 months to 5 years—there are tons of toys, gymnastics equipment, and a trampoline. Members are free; nonmembers are $5.

Mt. Scott Community Center
MT. SCOTT
5530 SE 72nd Ave.
503-823-3183
www.portlandoregon.gov/parks/60409
$ ALL AGES 🛒 🌂 🏃 🎒

Not all community centers are created equal, and this one's straight-up awesome, with a gym and basketball court; weight room; roller rink; playground; and indoor pool with a waterslide, current channel, and rope swing. There's also every kind of kids' class under the sun, from Baby Sing-a-longs and Little Picassos "messy art," to badminton, bouldering, and gymnastics.

Playdate PDX
NORTHWEST
1434 NW 17th Ave.
503-227-7529
www.playdatepdx.com
$-$$ ALL AGES 🛒 🌂 🏃 ✕ 🎒

BOREDOM BEATERS

As a wise philosopher, or maybe just the internet, once said, "Only the boring are bored." This list of offbeat local to-dos will help kiddos to never be boring or bored.

1. Climb a dormant volcano (Mt. Tabor Park, page 53).
2. Meet a Malayan sun bear (Oregon Zoo, page 9).
3. Locate Portland, *Maine*, on the Milepost sign (Pioneer Courthouse Square, page 77).
4. Munch moon cakes in the Tower of Cosmic Reflections (Lan Su Chinese Garden, page 32).
5. Browse the world's biggest indie bookstore (Powell's City of Books, page 38).
6. Smell nearly seven hundred kinds of roses (International Rose Test Garden, page 32).
7. Earn the high score on Donkey Kong (Ground Kontrol, page 59).
8. Waterslide out of a rooftop Boeing 747 (Wings & Waves Waterpark, page 51).
9. Scarf Scooby Snacks in a $2 movie (McMenamins, page 22).
10. Become a junior ranger (Tryon Creek State Park, page 70).
11. Take the tram to Pill Hill (Portland Aerial Tram, page 8).
12. Ride the Looping Thunder Roller Coaster (Oaks Park, page 72).
13. Visit the world's smallest park (Mill Ends Park, page 76).
14. Join a Pokémon League (Cloud Cap Games, page 88).
15. Slurp a bug sundae (FreakyButTrue Peculiarium and Museum, page 164).
16. Play pirate-themed, glow-in-the-dark mini golf (Glowing Greens, page 16).
17. Skateboard in an old stone-cutting warehouse (Commonwealth Skateboarding, page 19).
18. Peer through a submarine periscope (OMSI, page 66).
19. Perfect your toe jumps (Lloyd Center Ice Rink, page 72).
20. Find the city's oldest tombstone (Lone Fir Cemetery, page 75).

Kids (up to 12) go nuts for this three-story, four-slide indoor playground castle, while parents appreciate the adjoining café and the separate toddlers' area. Every Friday at 6:30 p.m., catch the free puppet show, and come summer, sign the kids up for Player's Club, an all-week, all-day camp featuring a variety of educational crafts, games, and open play. Socks required!

The Playground Gym

LLOYD DISTRICT

505 NE Grand Ave.
503-235-7529
www.theplaygroundgym.com

PORTSMOUTH

5215 N. Lombard St.
503-894-8503

$-$$ ALL AGES 🛒 ☂ 🏃 🎁

For kids ages 1–12, these popular kids' gyms host daily first-come-first-served open play (max twenty-five kids). If you're on the fence about signing up for regular classes, try one out for free. And if you need a date night, sign up for Parents' Night Out—an evening of open gym play, skill-building activities, games, pizza, and a movie for 5- to 12-year-olds, held every second and last Friday.

Portland Children's Museum

WASHINGTON PARK

4015 SW Canyon Rd.
503-223-6500
www.portlandcm.org

$$ AGES 0–2 AGES 3–5 AGES 6–9 🛒 ☂ ✕ 🎁

Neighboring the zoo, this lively museum is all about hands-on entertainment—kids weigh their stuffed animals in the pet hospital, demolish walls and install plumbing in the construction zone, and get creative in the clay studio. Check the calendar for daily special activities, sign up for kids' yoga or Zumba, or snag a spring break or summer camp spot. Budgeteers, admission is free every first Friday from 4 to 8 p.m.

Southside Swap & Play
WOODSTOCK
5239 SE Woodstock Blvd.
971-266-3023
www.southsideswapandplay.org
$ ALL AGES 🚼 ⛲ 🏃

Sporting 3,000 square feet of indoor play space designed for kids up to 10 years old, this Woodstock community hub is divided into The Forest—with play structures, a climbing wall, and tons of toys—and The Meadow, where toddlers and small children enjoy a wooden play structure and playhouse, activity tables, musical instruments, and a toddler roller coaster. There's also the Nest classroom, with an arts-and-crafts area, library and reading nook, and baby corner. Prospective members can attend a biweekly tour, then stay afterward and play.

Woodlawn Swap 'n Play
WOODLAWN
704 NE Dekum St.
503-269-4943
www.woodlawnswapnplay.org
$ ALL AGES 🚼 ⛲ 🏃 ✕ 🎁

This Woodlawn play space brings parents and kids together to play, swap toys and clothing, and attend regular musical events like Mr. Ben and Red Yarn concerts. If interested in membership, attend one of the weekly open play sessions, or check out one of the Family Concert Series events.

SCIENCE & TECH
Climb through a submarine, then see the stars at OMSI, count the propellers on the original Spruce Goose, or build a robot at these top tech and science spots.

SCIENCE

Oregon Museum of Science and Industry
HOSFORD-ABERNETHY
1945 SE Water Ave.
503-797-4000
www.omsi.edu
$$ ALL AGES 🚼 👆 ✗

OMSI is a curious mind's mecca, and kids will spend hours crawling, waddling, skipping, and flinging themselves from one exhibit to another. There's also a four-story-screen IMAX theater, planetarium, submarine, laser light show, and, when all that excitement evokes hunger pangs, a cafeteria with some serious culinary chops—hence the towering gas-powered pizza oven and fancy cupcake case.

TRANSPORTATION & TECH

Engineering for Kids
VARIOUS LOCATIONS
503-330-8781
www.engineeringforkids.com/location/portlandmetro
$$$ AGES 3-5 AGES 6-9 AGES 10-14

Devoted to getting kids excited about engineering, this educational program for kids 4 and up makes tricky subjects fun, whether it's teaching them how to overcome engineering challenges like designing fully functioning robotic models using Lego robotics, or creating their own video game. Classes are held after school at various Portland elementary schools, or book a Saturday series or camp (scholarships available).

Evergreen Aviation & Space Museum
MCMINNVILLE
500 NE Captain Michael King Smith Way
503-434-4180
www.evergreenmuseum.org
$$ ALL AGES 🚼 👆 🏃 ✗ 🎁

Not many museums can say they have the original *Spruce Goose* aircraft parked in the middle of the building; in fact, only this one can. Located about an hour outside of Portland, this glassed-in airplane hangar houses a beautiful aviation and space museum featuring fully restored military planes and booster rockets, as well as the one-of-a-kind Wings & Waves Waterpark (page 51). Outside food isn't allowed, but there are three on-site cafés.

Oregon Rail Heritage Center
HOSFORD-ABERNETHY
Contact information on page 6
FREE! ALL AGES

Kids who are fascinated by things that go chugga will love this Inner Southeast locomotive museum's 20,000-square-foot enginehouse, where they can get up close with the historic locomotives, pore over the exhibits' meticulously arranged maps and photos, and pepper the cheerful volunteers with technical questions to their hearts' content. On Saturday afternoons, take the $5 forty-five-minute round-trip train ride to Oaks Bottom Wildlife Refuge (page 70); if available, request to ride in the cab.

TAKE A HIKE
From deep dark forests to blooming botanical gardens, getting out into nature was never so easy—just close your eyes and point to one of these pretty parks, then hit the trail.

IN CITY TRAILS & NATURE CENTERS

4T
DOWNTOWN
www.4ttrail.wordpress.com
FREE! ALL AGES

This unique half-day hike involves four modes of transportation—train, trail, tram, and trolley. Download the detailed route and map on the city's website, then start your trek downtown by catching the MAX train to Washington Park and alighting near the Oregon Zoo (page 9). Follow the 4T trail to Council Crest Park, then Oregon Health & Science University, where you'll hop the Portland Aerial Tram (page 8) down to the South Waterfront. Catch the Portland Streetcar trolley (page 8) back downtown, and you've hit all four Ts. You can also do the 4T in reverse, but do remember that while the tram is free on the way down, it's $4.50 per person going up.

Forest Park
NORTHWEST
NW 29th Ave. and Upshur St.
www.portlandoregon.gov/parks/article/151164
FREE! ALL AGES

Portland's crown jewel, Forest Park is one of the first things you'll notice about the city skyline: a great *green* 5,172-acre swath of protected land riddled with hiking and biking trails. The park's Wildwood Trail meanders for 30 miles, but you can pick it up at many different points in Northwest Portland—download the trail map on the Portland Parks website to plan a hike that fits your family.

Hoyt Arboretum
WASHINGTON PARK
4000 SW Fairview Blvd.
503-865-8733
www.hoytarboretum.org
FREE! ALL AGES

A 189-acre sanctuary set within Washington Park, the arboretum has 12 miles of hiking trails and is home to more than two thousand species of plants and trees. The visitor center is open most days; pop inside and browse the exhibits, then get a Meet the Trees children's activity map, which details three different hikes, plus all the types of vegetation to look out for.

Insider tip: Come April, on Saturdays at 12 p.m., a volunteer leads a ninety-minute, all-ages guided hike ($3 donation appreciated).

Ladybug Nature Walks

VARIOUS LOCATIONS

www.portlandoregon.gov/parks/64625

$ AGES 0-2 AGES 3-5 🚼 🚶

Led by a trained preschool naturalist, these slow-paced guided nature walks teach kids ages 2–5 about the local flora and fauna, bodies of water, insects, plants, and animals in a fun and engaging way. Walks are held every Friday morning from mid-February through early November, rain or shine, in various city parks; drop in anytime, no reservation needed. Most are stroller-friendly too; just check the schedule for details.

Mt. Tabor Park

MT. TABOR

Contact information on page 53

FREE! ALL AGES 🚼 🚶 🎁

This nearly 200-acre Southeast park, set atop a dormant volcanic cinder cone, is laced with both paved and natural hiking trails that wind around four open reservoirs, bypass a sizable playground and picnic area (and restrooms), and culminate in breathtaking panoramic views at the top. On Wednesdays, the park is car free, turning the roads into stroller- and bike-friendly—if quite hilly—footpaths.

World Forestry Center

WASHINGTON PARK

4033 SW Canyon Rd.

503-228-1367

www.worldforestry.org

$ ALL AGES 🚼

Planted deep in Washington Park, steps from the Oregon Zoo (page 9) and Portland Children's Museum (page 64), this 20,000-square-foot museum is a temple to all things tree related, where kids can learn about various international forests and ecosystems, take a raft ride, check out Peggy the Train, and meet a 5,000,000-year-old petrified stump.

Leach Botanical Garden's Honeybee Hikes
PLEASANT VALLEY
6704 SE 122nd Ave.
503-823-9503
www.leachgarden.org
$ AGES 0–2 AGES 3–5

This lush Pleasant Valley botanical garden is open every day
but Monday for unguided visits, but each Wednesday morning
at 10 a.m., it hosts a delightful Honeybee Hikes series for
nature-loving youngins ages 2–5. Kids explore the grounds,
look for wildlife, work in the Discovery Garden, listen to stories,
and do crafts, all for a nominal fee (adults and nonwalking
siblings are free).

Oaks Bottom Wildlife Refuge
SELLWOOD
SE 7th Ave. and Sellwood Blvd.
www.portlandoregon.gov/parks/finder/index
    .cfm?propertyid=490&action=viewpark
FREE! ALL AGES

Saved from an ugly landfill fate by the city in 1969, this beautiful
141-acre marshland area and wildlife refuge is a prime spot for
bird-watching, and great blue heron sightings are common thanks
to its proximity to Ross Island rookeries. Walk the easy 2-mile
loop trail, stopping to look for salamanders in Tadpole Pond, and
see how many mallards, coots, woodpeckers, and widgeons you
can spot (or just say five times fast). Biking is permitted in Oaks
Bottom, and the Springwater Corridor bike path (page 56) runs
along its western edge, so bring your wheels.

Tryon Creek State Park
SOUTHWEST
11321 SW Terwilliger Blvd.
503-636-9886
www.tryonfriends.org
FREE! ALL AGES

Just fifteen minutes from Downtown lies this 658-acre forest straight out of Jurassic Park, where friendly visitor-center staff is happy to help you choose a hiking loop that meets your kids' ability and interest level. Attend family-friendly events like Story & Stroll (page 38) and the annual Trillium Festival, or sign up for a summer day camp or junior ranger program. Parking is limited, so go early or prepare to circle a few times. There's also a 3-mile paved bike trail, so bring the bikes.

THRILLS & CHILLS

Channel your inner Tarzan, practice your triple Lutz (or maybe just practice staying upright) on the ice, or eat a corn-dog combo then ride the roller coaster—it's a thrill a minute at these amusement parks, adventure courses, and skating rinks.

ADVENTURE THRILLS

Pumpkin Ridge Zip Tour
NORTH PLAINS
22616 NW Pumpkin Ridge Rd.
971-371-3895
www.pumpkinridgeziptour.com
$$$ AGES 6-9 AGES 10-14 🎒

About a half-hour drive from the city, in scenic North Plains, this two-hour tour crosses seven zip lines and three suspension bridges, letting kids age 8 and up experience life in the magical, mystical Pacific Northwest forest canopy.

Tree to Tree Adventure Park
GASTON
2975 SW Nelson Rd.
503-357-0109
www.tree2treeadventurepark.com
$$$ ALL AGES 🎒

An hour outside Portland, in the wilds of wine country, Tarzan it up at this aboveground playground, where you'll travel tree to tree via suspension bridges, tightropes, and nineteen zip lines, plus tackle over sixty treetop obstacles. Kids 7 and up can do the full aerial course, while little ones age 2 and up can frolic around the Adventure Village tree fort. If your tweens and teens can't get enough of life in the canopy, sign them up for a summer adventure camp (ages 10–14).

AMUSEMENT PARKS & RIDES

Oaks Park
SELLWOOD
7805 SE Oaks Park Way
503-233-5777
www.oakspark.com
$-$$ AGES 3-5 AGES 6-9 AGES 10-14

There's something inherently endearing about this old-timey amusement park, which occupies a prime piece of riverfront real estate along the Springwater Corridor. There are over twenty low-key rides, and while many appeal to a younger crowd, there's still enough thrill for older kids thanks to rides like the stomach-churning Disk'o and Looping Thunder Roller Coaster. There's plenty of carnie food available, from corn dogs to cotton candy, or BYO and eat in the gorgeous grassy picnic area.

ICE & ROLLER RINKS

Lloyd Center Ice Rink
LLOYD DISTRICT
953 Lloyd Center
503-288-6073
www.lloydcenterice.com
$ AGES 3-5 AGES 6-9 AGES 10-14

When it opened in 1960, the Lloyd Center Ice Rink was the first shopping center ice rink in the world, and it's hosted many celebrity skaters over the years, including infamous Olympian Tonya Harding, who started skating there at age 3. Skaters of all ages frequent the ice, but it's a kid's world here—take group or

individual lessons, play broomball, dance across the ice at Rock
'n' Skate, or sign up for the Summer "Kool" Kamp.

Mt. Scott Community Center Skate Rink
MT. SCOTT
5530 SE 72nd Ave.
503-823-3183
www.portlandoregon.gov/parks/article/450408
$ AGES 3-5 AGES 6-9 AGES 10-14 🚼 👕 🏃 🎁

Like this supercool Southeast community center didn't have
enough going for it with its next-level indoor pool, ball courts,
indoor preschoolers park, arts and sports classes, and fitness
center, they also have a skating rink in the basement, with open
skate offered several days a week for $4-$5 per person (skate
rentals are a dollar).

Oaks Park Roller Rink
SELLWOOD
7805 SE Oaks Park Way
503-233-5777
www.oakspark.com/roller-skating.html
$ AGES 3-5 AGES 6-9 AGES 10-14 🚼 👕 ✕ 🎁

This historic rink tucked inside popular Oaks Park (opposite
page) is one of the largest in the country and delights kids with
its rocking tunes, snack bar full of sweets and treats, and good
old-fashioned four-wheeled fun. There's something for all ages
on the calendar, from the morning Preschool Play and Skate
sessions, featuring Chipper the Squirrel, to the all-ages speed
skating and roller derby classes.

Sherwood Ice Arena
SHERWOOD
20407 SW Borchers Dr.
503-625-5757
www.sherwoodicearena.com
$ ALL AGES 🚼 👕 ✕ 🎁

This NHL-size ice arena is home to the Northwest's largest
adult hockey program, but it's also quite kid-friendly too, with

daily open skate, Stick Time sessions most days of the week, and Friday-night family pickup sessions. Check the website for admission coupons and skating lesson discounts.

Winterhawks Skating Center

BEAVERTON

9250 SW Beaverton-Hillsdale Hwy.

503-297-2521

www.winterhawksskatingcenter.com

$ AGES 3-5 AGES 6-9 AGES 10-14 ☂

Work up a sweat on the ice at this Beaverton skate center, where the Portland Winterhawks hockey team practices. Every afternoon, the rink holds an open skate session, and skating lessons are available for kids as young as 3, while the three-level youth hockey series enrolls kids 6 and up.

Snowboarding, skiing, sledding, tubing, snowball fighting, and sitting by the lodge fireplace with hot cocoa are just an hour's drive from Portland; get your guide to a super snow day at **Mt. Hood** on page 247.

TIME TRAVEL

History is all around you here in Portland, from the Benson Bubbler water fountains and Beverly Cleary Sculpture Garden to the famous White Stag neon sign that watches over Downtown.

ATTRACTIONS & LANDMARKS

Benson Bubblers

VARIOUS LOCATIONS

www.portlandoregon.gov/water/article/352768

FREE! ALL AGES 🚼 ✗

Bubbling and burbling with fresh, clean Bull Run water from 6 a.m. to 11 p.m. every day, these iconic four-bowl drinking fountains date back to 1912, when prominent local businessman

Simon Benson gave the city of Portland $10,000 to install twenty beautiful bronze drinking fountains. Over the years, more were added, and the grand total today stands at fifty-two, plus seventy-four one-bowl fountains. See how many you can spot and sample from as you travel around the city.

Beverly Cleary Sculpture Garden

GRANT PARK

NE 33rd Ave. and NE US Grant Pl.

www.portlandoregon.gov/parks//finder/index
.cfm?action=viewpark&propertyid=167

$-$$$ ALL AGES 👶 🧒

Fans of Ramona, Henry, and Ribsy will delight at this Grant Park fountain's trio of bronze statues, lovingly cast by local artist Lee Hunt to honor one of Portland's most beloved authors. Kids can read the Beverly Cleary book titles from the granite plaques around the fountain, then head to the library and check out the ones they haven't read yet. Or download the library's Walking With Ramona map (https://multcolib.org/sites/default/files /Cleary%20Map_2016.pdf), a walking tour that includes book settings like Klickitat Street, as well as Cleary's childhood home and school.

Lone Fir Cemetery

BUCKMAN

SE 26th Ave. and SE Washington St.

503-224-9200

www.friendsoflonefircemetery.org

FREE! ALL AGES 👶

A fascinating—and very, very quiet—spot for a walk, this beautiful Buckman cemetery is the resting place for over twenty thousand Portlanders going back nearly 200 years. For kids interested in the history of its (often remarkable) residents, docents offer monthly guided history, art, and epitaph tours; check the website for details. On Halloween, spooky story and history buffs alike will love the Tour of Untimely Departures, where guides lead groups through the candle-lit tombstones, telling ghostly stories of the mysterious means by which inhabitants ended up there.

Mill Ends Park

DOWNTOWN

SW Naito Pkwy. and SW Taylor St.

www.portlandoregon.gov/parks/finder/index
.cfm?&propertyid=265&action=viewpark

FREE! ALL AGES

It's easy to miss this Portland park—after all, according to Guinness World Records, it's the smallest park in the world, measuring a whopping 452 square inches. Located right in the middle of busy SW Naito Parkway, the park is treated with great affection by city residents, who, since its founding in 1948 by late newspaper columnist Dick Fagan, have accessorized it with everything from a miniature Ferris wheel to a butterfly garden.

Oregon Holocaust Memorial

WASHINGTON PARK

SW Washington Way and SW Wright Ave.

www.portlandoregon.gov/parks/finder/index
.cfm?action=viewpark&propertyid=1330

FREE! AGES 6–9 AGES 10–14

A heartbreaking reminder of the atrocities of the Holocaust, this Washington Park memorial will incite somber conversations with children old enough to grasp the implications of the bronze shoes, glasses, and suitcase carefully scattered on the pavement.

Pioneer Courthouse

DOWNTOWN

700 SW 6th Ave.

503-833-5305

www.pioneercourthouse.org

FREE! AGES 3–5 AGES 6–9 AGES 10–14

Many people, locals included, have no idea that Downtown's regal Pioneer Courthouse is open to the public for free self-guided tours every weekday during business hours. Enter off SW 6th Avenue; go through security; collect a tour brochure from the clerk's office; and set off to see the historic lobbies and courtrooms, judges' chambers, library, and cupola.

Pioneer Courthouse Square

DOWNTOWN

701 SW 6th Ave.

503-223-1613

www.thesquarepdx.org

FREE! ALL AGES 🛒 ✕

Also known as "Portland's living room," this one-square-block brick plaza in the center of Downtown always has something fun on the books, hosting hundreds of events a year, like the summertime Festival of Flowers and Flicks on the Bricks (page 24), as well as public festivals, a farmers' market, and the city's Christmas tree lighting ceremony. Even when nothing's happening, it's worth a visit, if just to check out the Milepost sign and bronze *Umbrella Man.*

Pittock Mansion

FOREST PARK

3229 NW Pittock Dr.

503-823-3623

www.pittockmansion.org

$ ALL AGES ☂

This stately historical hideaway has some of the city's best views and most interesting history, and kids will be fascinated by the old-fashioned decor, plumbing, and toy collection. Pack a posttour picnic, spread a blanket on the back lawn, and throw your own mini garden party after touring the main house and caretaker's cottage. Kids 5 and under are free.

Portlandia

DOWNTOWN

1120 SW 5th Ave.

FREE! ALL AGES 🛒 ✕

Long before the TV show came along, the most famous statue in the city, the lovely *Portlandia,* has stood watch over SW 5th Avenue, trident in hand. Made of copper by renowned sculptor Raymond Kaskey, *Portlandia* is the second-largest statue of her kind in the country—trumped only by the Statue of Liberty—and had to be floated into the city via the Willamette River, on a barge. Perched above the Portland Building, the 36-foot statue is free for viewing anytime.

Portland Saturday Market
OLD TOWN/CHINATOWN
2 SW Naito Pkwy.
503-241-4188
www.portlandsaturdaymarket.com
FREE! ALL AGES 🚼 ✕

While browsing and buying locally made crafts and curios are the main draw at this nearly 50-year-old riverfront market, even those with limited shopping attention spans will be spellbound by the eclectic street performers, live music, and snow-cone stand.

Simon Benson House
DOWNTOWN
1803 SW Park Ave.
www.pdx.edu/profile/visit-simon-benson-house
FREE! ALL AGES 🚼 ✕

The former home of early twentieth-century Portland pillar Simon Benson, a wealthy logger and philanthropist (and donor of the aforementioned Benson Bubblers, page 74), this richly detailed Queen Anne–style mansion was rescued from condemnation in the late 1990s, relocated five blocks to the Portland State University campus, lovingly renovated, and now serves as the PSU Alumni Association's headquarters. Walk by when visiting the Portland Farmers Market (page 84) on Saturday; it anchors the northwest corner of the market.

Skidmore Fountain
OLD TOWN/CHINATOWN
Betweem W. Burnside St. and SW Ankeny St. at Naito Pkwy.
www.portlandoregon.gov/parks/42348

A good historic tour destination on its own, or coupled with a visit to the Portland Saturday Market (page 78), this grand bronze fountain is the city's oldest work of public art; erected in 1888 to serve as a drinking fountain for both people and horses, at one point it had tin cups dangling from the lion heads at the base, for communal use.

St. Johns Bridge
ST. JOHNS
8600 NW Bridge Ave.
www.portlandoregon.gov/parks/finder/index
.cfm?&propertyid=97&action=viewpark

Bridges abound in Stumptown, but there's something special about the St. Johns, which at 408 feet (thanks to the two Gothic towers), is the city's tallest bridge and somewhat of a local celebrity, having appeared in TV shows, movies, and even a comic book. Cross in a light fog for the spookiest effect, and to see its magnificent underbelly, stroll the lovely river-hugging Cathedral Park (page 118), especially in fall, when the grassy grounds explode into color and the mild weather is picnic perfect.

Vietnam Veterans of Oregon Memorial
WASHINGTON PARK
4000 SW Canyon Rd.
www.portlandoregon.gov/parks/finder/index
.cfm?&propertyid=835&action=viewpark
FREE! AGES 6–9 AGES 10–14 🛒

This visually arresting curved black granite wall in Washington Park is engraved with the names of all Oregon residents who either died in the Vietnam War or are listed as missing in action. There's also a written history of both the war and parallel local events, which is an interesting lesson in wartime contrasts.

White Stag Sign
DOWNTOWN
70 NW Couch St.
FREE! ALL AGES

One of the most famous and photographed Portland landmarks, this iconic historic neon sign depicting a stag leaping over the state sits atop the White Stag Building, which overlooks the Burnside Bridge, so your best view is from either Tom McCall Waterfront Park or the bridge, driving/walking west. Come Christmas, the stag's nose glows red, à la Rudolph.

HISTORICAL MUSEUMS

Historic Belmont Firehouse
SUNNYSIDE
900 SE 35th Ave.
503-823-3615
www.friendsofportlandfire.org/belmont-learning-center
FREE! ALL AGES 🚼 🍼 ✕ 🎎

Drop in to this handsome historic Belmont Street firehouse on weekly Open House Wednesdays and monthly Safety Saturdays from 9 a.m. to 3 p.m., for a free tour of the Safety Learning Center and Fire Museum's hands-on exhibits and equipment— see an 1860s hose cart and vintage steam-pumper fire engine, experience the fire-truck simulator, slide down a fire pole, and watch a fire safety video.

Insider tip: Your future family firepeople can even hold their birthday party here!

Japanese American Historical Plaza and Museum
OLD TOWN/CHINATOWN
121 NW 2nd Ave.
503-224-1458
www.oregonnikkei.org
FREE!-$ AGES 6-9 AGES 10-14 🚼

A profound and sobering history lesson, this stone monument in the midst of Portland's waterfront cherry-tree grove was designed to raise awareness of what Japanese Americans endured during World War II incarcerations, and the meaning and value of freedom for all. To continue the conversation, visit the Japanese American History Museum up the street, where kids can view exhibits detailing the challenges and contributions of Oregon's Nikkei community.

Kidd's Toy Museum
BUCKMAN
1300 SE Grand Ave.
503-233-7807
www.kiddstoymuseum.com

FREE! ALL AGES ☂

A labor of love for devoted toy collector Frank Kidd, who owns the auto-parts business next door (hence the collection's strong leaning toward toy planes, trains, and automobiles), this nondescript museum also houses one of the most comprehensive mechanical-bank collections around. If you're in the neighborhood, knock and wait for an answer; if you're making a special trip, call before you go.

The Oregon Historical Society
DOWNTOWN
1200 SW Park Ave.
503-222-1741
www.ohs.org

FREE!-$$ ALL AGES 🚌 ☂

From Lewis and Clark to landmark legislation, most every detail of this great state's history can be found in this venerable museum's carefully curated exhibits and research library. Located on a quiet corner in the scenic South Park Blocks, the museum is open daily and free to Multnomah County residents.

Oregon Maritime Museum
DOWNTOWN
198 SW Naito Pkwy.
503-224-7724
www.oregonmaritimemuseum.org

FREE!-$ ALL AGES ☂

Nautically inclined kids will love the novelty of this floating museum—it's located on the steam sternwheeler *Portland*, moored on the Willamette River in Tom McCall Waterfront Park. They'll also dig the hands-on Children's Corner, where they can blow a ship's whistle, operate a governor, and play with a model ship. Just a few steps west of the museum, find the Battleship Oregon Memorial, which showcases the mast of the historic battleship USS *Oregon*.

Portland Puppet Museum

SELLWOOD

906 SE Umatilla St.

503-233-7723

www.puppetmuseum.com

FREE! ALL AGES 🌂

Set in a turn-of-the-century Sellwood storefront and run by two master puppeteers, this exquisitely detailed homage to puppetry maintains rotating exhibits that feature all types of shadow, string, rod, and hand puppets and teaches puppet history as well as the value of good craftsmanship and unlimited creativity.

Stark's Vacuum Museum

KERNS

107 NE Grand Ave.

503-232-4101

www.starks.com/vacuum-museum

FREE! AGES 3-5 AGES 6-9 AGES 10-14 🌂

Tucked into a corner of longstanding Stark's Vacuums since the 1970s, this ode to the largely unsung hero of household chores features hundreds of vintage vacuums dating back to the 1800s and made of everything from wood to cardboard. Store staff is happy to show you around and ply curious kids with fun, quirky vacuum factoids.

TO MARKET, TO MARKET

Portland's farmers markets are one of the most delicious ways to experience this food-loving city—they're stocked with the region's freshest produce, there's always a live musician or two for entertainment, and the locals you meet are as kind as can be. Kids of all ages are welcomed, plied with tasty samples, and invited to attend special events and classes (check market calendars for details). Most markets close in the bleak winter months, but from late spring through fall, there's a market to visit every day of the week except Friday. Happy shopping!

MONDAY

Pioneer Courthouse Square
June–September
www.portlandfarmersmarket
.org/our-markets/pioneer
-courthouse-square

TUESDAY

Lloyd Center
Year-round
www.lloydfarmersmkt.net

Oregon Health & Science University
June–September
www.ohsu.edu/farmersmarket

WEDNESDAY

Beaverton
June–August
www.beavertonfarmers
market.com

Kenton
June–September
www.portlandfarmersmarket
.org/our-markets/kenton

Moreland
May–October
www.morelandfarmers
market.org

People's Food Co-op
Year-round
www.peoples.coop/farmers
-market

Shemanski Park
May–November
www.portlandfarmersmarket
.org/our-markets/shemanski
-park

THURSDAY

Cully
June–September
www.cullyfarmers
market.com

Northwest
June–September
www.portlandfarmersmarket
.org/our-markets/northwest

SATURDAY

Beaverton
February–November
www.beavertonfarmers
market.com

Hillsboro
April–October
www.hillsboromarkets.org

Hollywood
Year-round
www.hollywoodfarmers
market.org

Lake Oswego
May–October
www.ci.oswego.or.us
/parksrec/lake-oswego
-farmers-market

Oregon City
Year-round
www.orcityfarmers
  market.com

Portland State University
Year-round
www.portlandfarmersmarket
  .org/our-markets/psu

St. Johns
June–December
www.stjohnsfarmers
  market.org

SUNDAY

Hillsdale
Year-round
www.hillsdalefarmers
  market.com

Irvington
June–October
www.irvingtonfarmers
  market.org

King
May–November
www.portlandfarmersmarket
  .org/our-markets/king

Milwaukie
May–October
www.milwaukiefarmers
  market.com

Montavilla
May–October
www.montavillamarket.org

Tigard
April–October
www.tigardfarmers
  market.org

Woodstock
June–October
www.woodstock
  marketpdx.com

CREAM OF THE CROP
Every Saturday, rain or shine, the **Portland Farmers Market** (SW Park St. and SW Montgomery St.; www.portlandfarmersmarket.org/our-markets/psu) sets up at Portland State University, bringing together more than two hundred vendors from all over the region. Browsing the booths, kids learn about the importance of seasonal produce from the farmers who grew it, sample to their hearts' content, and munch on everything from breakfast burritos and biscuits and gravy to homemade Oregon berry pie. Come summer, take advantage of the kids' cooking and craft classes.

TOUR DE PORTLAND

Whether you want to see the city on two feet, four feet, two wheels, four wheels, pink wheels, a helicopter, or a jet boat, there's a guided tour just for you.

BY AIR

Konect Aviation Helicopter Tours
VARIOUS LOCATIONS
503-376-0190
www.konect-aviation.com/helicopter-scenic-flights
$$$ ALL AGES

Per reality television, helicopter flights are the best way to see the sights with someone you love, so take the kids on the ultimate kind of tour—the aerial kind. Konect tours depart from Downtown Portland, Salem, and McMinnville and fly anywhere from the Coast to the Gorge, with the shortest tours (a quick six-minute buzz around McMinnville's Evergreen Aviation & Space Museum, page 66) starting at $49 per person. Kids are welcome, and toddlers under 2 can sit in your lap for free.

BY LAND

Big Pink Hop-On Hop-Off Trolley
DOWNTOWN
Contact information on page 7
$$-$$$ ALL AGES

Kids under 5 ride free on these narrated trolley tours, which continuously loop the city, stopping at fourteen points of interest ranging from Tom McCall Waterfront Park to the Oregon Zoo.

Cycle Portland Bike Tours
OLD TOWN/CHINATOWN
Contact information on page 57
$-$$$ ALL AGES

Older riders will dig this Old Town bike shop's Essential Portland tour, an easy 7-mile ride around Downtown's historic Chinatown, the waterfront, the park blocks, and the Pearl District (must be 4 feet 10 inches or taller to fit on a bike).

Forktown Food Tours

VARIOUS LOCATIONS

503-234-3663

www.forktownfoodtoursportland.com

$$$ AGES 6–9 AGES 10–14 🚼 🍴 🎁

Eat your way through Portland's most delicious districts with
Forktown's foodies in the know, on these 1.5-mile culinary
walking tours that combine tastings at some of Portland's best
restaurants with well-researched historical insights about the
neighborhood. Tour are geared for adults, and there isn't kid
pricing, but older kids who are crazy about food will have a
great time.

Pedal Bike Tours

OLD TOWN/CHINATOWN

Contact information on page 57

$$$ ALL AGES

This family-friendly Old Town bike shop welcomes kids of all
ages on their tours, and the two that are particularly well suited
to younger riders are the three-hour, 9-mile Historic Downtown
Tour, and the three-hour, 5-mile Food Cart Tour, which entices
with five delicious food-cart pit stops.

Portland Walking Tours

DOWNTOWN

701 SW 6th Ave.

503-774-4522

www.portlandwalkingtours.com

$$$ AGES 3–5 AGES 6–9 AGES 10–14 🍴 🚼

Take the basic Best of Portland tour with this award-winning
walking-tour company, or go off the grid with the Beyond Bizarre
tour, detailing Portland's paranormal side, or the Underground
tour, which descends into the city's infamous Shanghai tunnels.
While the latter two are rated PG and for more mature children,
even little ones will love the Chocolate Decadence, Epicurean
Excursion, and Flavor Street food-cart tours.

Secrets of Portlandia

DOWNTOWN

701 SW 6th Ave.

503-703-4282

www.secretsofportlandia.com

FREE! ALL AGES 🛒 ✗

Oh-so-Portland before you even begin, this wonderfully wacky all-ages walking tour is led daily July–October, rain or shine, for free, by local people-lover Erik Dodson. No reservations or payment required—if you enjoy the two-hour tour, which promises that you'll "laugh your butt off" while learning lots of interesting and obscure Portland factoids, leave a tip when Erik passes his fedora.

BY WATER

Portland Spirit

DOWNTOWN

Contact information on page 4

FREE!–$$$ ALL AGES ✗

Catch one of these relaxed river cruises from the dock near Salmon Street Springs fountain (reservations recommended, book online at book.portlandspirit.com), then take a leisurely round-trip ride along the Willamette. Small fry will love the onboard Sailor Training program, especially when they earn their Captain's Certificate.

Willamette Jetboat Excursions

HOSFORD-ABERNETHY

Contact information on page 4

$$$ ALL AGES

If your junior boaters have a need for speed, this is the tour—the jet boats go up to 50 miles an hour, perform thrilling 360-degree turns and provide splashing aplenty. Kids of all ages are welcome, and those age 3 and under ride free on the one-hour downtown bridge and harbor tour. Tours board at the Oregon Museum of Science and Industry dock (page 66) and since the jet boats are bathroom free, consider using OMSI's facilities beforehand.

TOY STORY

From mini trucker hats to Melissa & Doug puzzles, here are the best places to buy the trappings of the Portland kiddie good life.

Black Wagon

BOISE

3964 N. Mississippi Ave.

503-916-0000

www.blackwagon.com

ALL AGES ⚓ ✕

From mini trucker hats to banana-covered Vans, this NoPo shop is a hip kid's haven, with a perfectly curated cache of unique clothes, shoes, toys, books, and gifts. For restless and easily distracted shoppers, there's a play table in the back.

Child's Play

NORTHWEST

2305 NW Kearney St.

503-224-5586

www.childsplayportland.com

ALL AGES ⚓ ✕

Shopping at this Northwest Portland toy store really *is* child's play, and it's all too easy to leave with that glow-in-the-dark terrarium or Neil Gaiman book you didn't know you needed. The shop also holds fun special events, like Easter egg hunts, Pokémon training, and silhouette making.

Cloud Cap Games

SELLWOOD

1226 SE Lexington St.

503-505-9344

www.cloudcapgames.com

AGES 3-5 AGES 6-9 AGES 10-14 ⚓ ✕

Encourage iPhone-free, face-to-face family interaction with the help of this fantastic Sellwood shop that specializes in board games, card games, and puzzles, all of which you can play before you even leave the shop, per the try-before-you-buy policy. Cloud Cap also hosts tons of fun weekly events, from Friday-afternoon Magic tournaments to Pokémon League.

Finnegan's Toys & Gifts

DOWNTOWN

820 SW Washington St.

503-221-0306

www.finneganstoys.com

ALL AGES ☂ ✗

Open since 1977, this Downtown Portland favorite has amassed a vast inventory of classic books and toys—from Mr. Potato Head, Etch-a-Sketch, and every Lego under the sun, to a wall full of stuffed animals. Street parking can be scarce; use the nearby SmartPark garage and it'll validate an hour, with purchase.

Grasshopper

VERNON

1816 NE Alberta St.

503-335-3131

www.grasshopperstore.com

AGES 0-2 AGES 3-5 AGES 6-9 ☂ ✗

Just walking inside this sweet store induces happiness, so imagine how you'll feel after shopping for awhile. Browse the owner's signature handmade clothing line, Wild Carrots; pick up a play chocolate fondue set; get your budding artist a set of oil pastels or watercolor crayons; and then have everything gift-wrapped for free.

Hello! Good Morning!

IRVINGTON

2419 NE Broadway St.

503-841-5120

ALL AGES ☂ ✗

Curated by a former Laika animator, this shop's as eccentrically cool as you'd imagine, with gallery-level decor and a genuinely unique collection of toys and clothes, like hand-embroidered Greek woolen slippers, Donna Wilson's whimsical wares, old-fashioned candies, and strange and wonderful vintage carvings and collectibles.

Kids at Heart Toys
SUNNYSIDE

3445 SE Hawthorne Blvd.
503-231-2954
www.kidsathearttoys.com

AGES 0-2 AGES 3-5 AGES 6-9 ☂ ✗

Kids will think they've walked into their dreams, thanks to
this Hawthorne toy store's darling window displays, vivid wall
murals, well-stocked shelves of ethically and environmentally
conscious toys, interactive play sets, and life-size plush animals
waiting to be held. Every Wednesday, grandparents get
10 percent off, so spoil away.

Milagros
CONCORDIA

5433 NE 30th Ave.
503-493-4141
www.milagrosboutique.com

AGES 0-2 ☂ ✗

New parents are in very good hands at this doula-owned-and-
run Concordia baby boutique, which stocks everything from
compression socks and Chimparoo baby carriers to teething
necklaces, and hosts weekly meet-ups; new-mom support
groups; and breastfeeding, babywearing, and diapering classes.

Oodles 4 Kids
SELLWOOD

7727 SE 13th Ave.
503-719-7670
www.oodles4kids.com

AGES 0-2 AGES 3-5 AGES 6-9 ☂ ✗

With a relaxed, friendly vibe that's perfectly suited for small-town
Sellwood, Oodles is the just the spot to do a little gift shopping
(they wrap too) before continuing down the street to your tea-
and-macaroon date at Jade Bistro & Patisserie (page 212).

Piccolo Mondo Toys

BETHANY
4768 NW Bethany Blvd.
503-617-0250
www.piccolomondotoys.com
ALL AGES 🛆 🍴

PROGRESS RIDGE
12345 SW Horizon Blvd.
503-579-8100

Delighted kiddos will hardly suspect that they're *learning* something at these fun family-owned toy shops, which emphasize playthings that encourage kids to use their imagination and creativity, like Möbi number tiles and magnetic world maps. Check the calendar and Facebook page for special events like book readings and release parties, science labs, and art classes.

Polliwog

KERNS
234 NE 28th Ave.
503-236-3903
www.polliwogportland.com
AGES 0-2 AGES 3-5 AGES 6-9 🛆 🍴

This sunlit Kerns cutie focuses on meaningful toys and clothing made with natural materials and fibers, like Winter Water Factory's certified organic cotton rompers and tees, Charley Harper board books, and soft felted stuffed animals. Plus it's next door to Staccato Gelato (page 232).

Posh Baby

BEAVERTON
12345 SW Horizon Blvd.
503-747-3539
www.poshbaby.com
AGES 0-2 🛆 🍴

PEARL DISTRICT
916 NW 10th Ave.
503-478-7674

This upscale baby boutique has everything necessary to outfit a fashionable nursery, from sleek Monte bassinets and Aden + Anais bamboo Dream blankets to chic Babyletto play sets. It also has an online gift registry; schedule a consultation to set one up.

Smallfry
GRANT PARK
4107 NE Tillamook St.
503-284-1276
www.smallfrypdx.com

ALL AGES 🛗 ✕

Bring your gently used clothes (preemie through age 14),
equipment, gear, toys, and books here for consignment, then
use the proceeds to browse the neatly organized racks for top
brands like Boden, Patagonia, and Janie and Jack.

Spielwerk Toys
BOISE
3808 N. Williams Ave.
503-282-2233
www.spielwerktoys.com

AGES 0-2 AGES 3-5 AGES 6-9 🛗 ✕

Believing that good play is hard werk, this cheery NoPo shop
stocks top-quality toys, many sourced from European and
American makers. It also produces its own line of Portland-made
toys, if you're teaching kids the principles of buying local early
on. On second Thursdays, Spielwerk hosts a free Tot Thursday
hour at nearby Hopworks Bike Bar—a half hour of toddler story
time followed by craft time, with healthy snacks provided.

Thinker Toys
MULTNOMAH VILLAGE
7784 SW Capitol Hwy.
503-245-3936
www.thinkertoysoregon.com

AGES 0-2 AGES 3-5 AGES 6-9 🛗 ✕

Eschewing more mainstream toys for "thinking" ones, like
Melissa & Doug puzzles and Haba play sets, this longtime
Multnomah Village gem encourages hands-on interaction and
is much loved for its playhouse, rewards card program, and fun
events, like First Friday, when the shop's open late and snacks
are served.

YOU'VE BEEN FRAMED

Junior creatives need constant inspiration, so start 'em early with infant art museum meet-ups, plan a First Thursday gallery hop, or encourage them to submit their work to the Art4Life Children's Gallery.

FINE ARTS

Portland Art Museum

Downtown

1219 SW Park Ave.

503-226-2811

www.portlandartmuseum.org

FREE!-$$ ALL AGES 🛒 ↑ ✕

The oldest museum in the Pacific Northwest, this 112,000-square-foot labyrinth displays over forty-two thousand objets d'art and is particularly known for its extensive collection of Native American art, English silver, and graphic art. While kids 17 and under are always free, on the first Thursday of every month, everyone's admission is free after 5 p.m., and those with babies in tow can join the First Thursday Baby Morning art walk and tea. Friday nights after 5 p.m., adult admission drops to $5 and everyone lets their hair down, with a pop-up pizza pub, quirky themed tours, games, and a photo booth.

GALLERIES

First Thursday

Northwest

www.firstthursdayportland.com

Every first Thursday of the month, Portland gets even artsier than usual. Scores of galleries in Old Town/Chinatown, the Pearl District, and Northwest Portland open their doors for the masses to tour, free of charge, and some even serve snacks. It's also Portland Art Museum's monthly free night (5–8 p.m.).

Splendorporium
BROOKLYN
3421 SE 21st Ave.
503-953-2885
www.splendorporium.net
FREE! ALL AGES

Part of the nonprofit arts and culture program Art4Life, this Southeast Portland gallery showcases a wide variety of visual arts and performances every first Friday of the month, as part of the Central Eastside's First Friday art walk (www.facebook .com/1FPDX). Budding artists of all ages can submit their work for consideration; check their Facebook page for details.

ART WALK
If all the kids really want to do is look at their smartphones, fine—have them take the family on an *app*-led art walk, via the free **Public Art PDX** app (www .publicartpdx.com).

ITINERARIES

Whether you're seeking activities for a certain age range, time frame, or season; trying to beat the heat/sleet; or looking for fun freebies, these itineraries will lead the way.

HEY, BABY

AGES 0–4

Portland is known for its supreme walkability, so bundle *le bébé* or toddler into the stroller and set off on this one-day walking tour of Downtown's greatest hits.

Most likely you could use a little caffeine, so jump-start the morning at hip, happy **Heart Coffee Roasters** (537 SW 12th Ave.; 503-224-0036; www.heartroasters.com), then walk down to the aptly named **Mother's Bistro** (page 194), which backs up its kid-friendly moniker with patient servers, a play area, and a kids' menu. If the wait proves prohibitive, grab bacon, eggs, and Mickey Mouse–shaped pancakes at less-crowded **the Original Dinerant** (300 SW 6th Ave.; 503-546-2666; www.originaldinerant .com). And if it's Saturday, a.k.a. **Portland Farmers Market** day (page 84), have an alfresco breakfast at one of the excellent market food stalls.

Afterward catch a midmorning Book Babies, Tiny Tots, or Toddler story-time session (page 38) at Downtown's grand **Central Library** (801 SW 10th Ave.; 503-988-5123; www.multcolib .org/library-location/central). Or ride the **Portland Streetcar** (page 8) to **Powell's City of Books** (page 38) and spend some time in the phenomenal kids' section. (Check the calendar before you go; Powell's hosts its own story time on Saturday mornings.)

Grab lunch at **Hot Lips Pizza** (page 218) or **Laughing Planet Café** (page 203), both located in the historic Ecotrust Building, then cross the street to **Jamison Square** (page 49), where kiddos can climb on the rock fountain, or come summertime, splash around in it. Pop across the street to **Cool Moon Ice Cream** (page 229) for scoops, and if you're in the mood to shop, browse

organic onesies and Jellycat plushies at **Posh Baby** boutique
(page 91), or stock up on slipover dresses and leggings at nearby
Hanna Andersson (327 NW 10th Ave.; 503-321-5275; www
.hannaandersson.com).

Post nap time, continue the day's adventures in **Washington
Park** (page 210), where you have your pick of a peaceful walk
around the spectacular **International Rose Test Garden** (page 32) or
neighboring **Portland Japanese Garden** (page 33), or an afternoon
of hard play at the **Portland Children's Museum** (page 64). If time
allows, the **Oregon Zoo** (page 9) is steps from the museum, with
64 acres of winding trails. You'll want to bring wheels—otherwise,
rent a Safari Stroller at the front entrance, by the gift shop.

For a casual downtown dinner, try fun counter-service pasta
joint **Grassa** (page 214) or neighboring **Lardo** sandwich shop
(page 223), or graze the **Pine Street Market** food hall (126 SW
2nd Ave.; www.pinestreetpdx.com), where nine vendors serve
up everything from fancy hot dogs to superb soft serve, and
the din from the communal dining area will mask any noise
emissions from spirited little ones.

KIDDO ON THE GO

AGES 5–9

The previous itinerary largely applies to this age group as well,
but let's bump things up a notch with more outlying activities, a
submarine tour, and a DIY pancake palace.

Start the day snuggled in a booth at Southeast Portland's
Slappy Cakes (page 196), where you flip your own flapjacks on
magical tabletop griddles. Post belly-busting breakfast, take a
hike around nearby **Mt. Tabor Park** (page 53), which has a full
playground, some of the best views in the city, and a 282-step
staircase that's great for wringing the excess energy out of anyone
who's ingested too much syrup. (*Sure* there are 282 steps in the
summit staircase? Better count!)

Afterward head down to lively Hawthorne Boulevard,
for book browsing at **Powell's Books on Hawthorne** (3723 SE
Hawthorne Blvd.; 800-878-7323; www.powells.com/locations
/powells-books-on-hawthorne), toy shopping at **Kids at Heart
Toys** (page 90), and waffle ice-cream sundae gobbling at

(literal) hole-in-the-wall **Waffle Window** (page 197). Keep going west toward the Willamette River to the **Oregon Museum of Science and Industry** (page 66), and explore the hundreds of exhibits and labs, planetarium, and submarine. No need to leave if all that brain-boosting play works up an appetite—OMSI has a solid on-site café that serves lunch with a side of river views.

Hop on SE McLoughlin Boulevard and zip over to Sellwood, a sweet, small-town-esque suburb that's home to old-fashioned and much-loved **Oaks Park** (page 72). Kids can ride the Big Pink Slide and Frog Hopper, stuff corn dogs and cotton candy, and play the pretty peewee golf course. There's also a vintage roller rink, one of the largest in the country, that holds all-ages open skate sessions most afternoons from 1 to 5 p.m. (double-check the online calendar before you go).

Come dinnertime, nab noodles and sesame balls at **Jade Bistro & Patisserie** (page 212), or cozy up in a well-worn wooden booth at popular **Gino's** (page 213) for an Italian-style family feast. For a special treat, stop at popular dessert den **Papa Haydn** (5829 SE Milwaukie Ave.; 503-232-9440; www.papahaydn.com) on the way back for salted caramel macaroons, homemade mint-chip ice cream, and big ol' slices of triple chocolate buttermilk cake.

TWEENS 'N' TEENS ABOUT TOWN

AGES 10–14

It's hard to impress a t(w)een, but Portland has a sizeable hipster population for a reason—it's a pretty cool city! You know, if you're into art or music or video games or skateboarding or doughnuts. Or whatever.

In this town the early bird gets the doughnut, so maybe that will coax your tween or teen out of bed, because getting to **Voodoo Doughnut** (page 229) before the infamous line forms is no joke. Some argue that **Blue Star Donuts** (page 228) trumps Voodoo, so obviously the responsible thing to do is try them both, then decide for yourself. And not to complicate the doughnut wars, but the **Donut Byte Labs** mini-doughnut cart (page 200) is parked just a block from Voodoo. Then, for a slightly more balanced breakfast after/in lieu of all that fried dough, walk down a block to **Bijou Café** (page 192) for buttermilk fried chicken and buckwheat pancakes with marionberry syrup.

Next, set course for North Portland's hip-and-happening Mississippi Avenue, a five-block stretch of quintessential Portland about a ten-minute drive from Downtown (sans traffic). Browse zines and graphic novels at **Reading Frenzy** (3628 N. Mississippi Ave.; 971-271-8044; www.readingfrenzy.com), find one-of-a-kind indie wares and a regularly rotating upstairs art exhibit at **Land** (3925 N. Mississippi Ave.; 503-451-0689; www.landpdx.com), and peruse the vast inventory of recyclables at **the ReBuilding Center** (3625 N. Mississippi Ave.; 503-331-1877; www.rebuildingcenter .org). For lunch, pig out at **Por Qué No** (page 203), a supercool little taco shack with a perma-line, then cross the street for scoops and sundaes at **Ruby Jewel** (page 231).

Back Downtown, let everyone loose in epic **Powell's City of Books** (page 38) for a nice lengthy afternoon book browse. Afterward walk ten minutes east to Old Town/Chinatown's landmark **Lan Su Chinese Garden** (page 32) for a tour and traditional *gaiwan*-style tea service. Then hone those vintage video-game skills at **Ground Kontrol** arcade (page 59), which boasts nearly one hundred classic arcade games *and* the largest pinball room in the region. If you've got the family skater in tow, walk a couple blocks to **Cal Skate Skateboards** shop (210 NW 6th Ave.; 503-248-0495; www.calsk8.com), which has a vast selection of unique decks and accessories, plus the very coolest apparel and Vans shoes.

If agreeing on what to eat for dinner is proving problematic, no worries—hit the delightfully diverse **Pine Street Market** food hall (page 96), where nine vendors sling everything from mac 'n' cheese dogs to PB&J ice-cream sundaes. Or go for burgers and bottomless fries at boisterous **Killer Burger** (page 199).

After dinner, putt at pirate-themed **Glowing Greens** (page 16), a black-light-lit, glow-in-the-dark mini golf course marooned in a basement near the **Regal Fox Tower Stadium 10** movie theater (846 SW Park Ave.; 844-462-7342; www.regmovies .com/theatres/theatre-folder/regal-fox-tower-stadium-10-135)—in case anyone's keen to see the latest Marvel movie.

BEAT THE HEAT

KEEP YOUR COOL ON A SWELTERING SUMMER DAY

Portland gets so much press for its precipitation, sometimes it's easy to forget that the dog days of summer can be long and fierce. When temperatures soar, tempers fray, and the Popsicle supply runs low, retreat to these refreshing oases.

Start the day with icy drinks and icy air at one of the city's air-conditioned coffeehouses—depending on where you are in the city, try **Woodlawn Coffee and Pastry** (NE, page 191), **Posie's Café** (N, page 206), **St. Honoré Boulangerie** (NW & SE, page 207), **Jim & Patty's Coffee** (NE and NW, page 205), or **Ford Food + Drink** (2505 SE 11th Ave.; 503-236-3023; www.fordfoodanddrink.com).

Every Portland library is air-conditioned, so check the **Multnomah County Library** (page 38) story-time calendar, and make a beeline for the nearest branch. **Powell's City of Books** (page 38) in the Pearl District has A/C too, plus it's a half mile from one of the best fountains in town, **Jamison Square** (page 49).

Speaking of water features, Portland has dozens—Downtown's **Salmon Street Springs** (page 49), historic **Sellwood Outdoor Pool** (page 50), and Southwest Portland's lazy-river-looped **Wilson Outdoor Pool** (page 51) are among the best.

Hot pizza for lunch might seem counterintuitive, but at **Life of Pie** pizzeria (page 219), not only is the A/C strong, but from 11 a.m. to 6 p.m., they offer full-size happy hour *margherita* pizzas for $5 *and* share the block with **What's the Scoop?** ice-cream shop (page 232).

When the sun's at its peak, and you need to take cover—go bowling (page 13), catch a matinee (page 20), or if you'd rather stay underwater, try the indoor water park at **Mt. Scott Community Center** (page 62). If twirling around on a giant block of ice sounds particularly appealing, try the **Lloyd Center Ice Rink** (page 72) or the **Winterhawks Skating Center** (page 74), which hosts a public skate several afternoons a week in the summer. The **Oaks Park Roller Rink** (page 73) also has open skate in the afternoon, and it's near the aforementioned Sellwood Outdoor Pool, so plan those activities back to back.

Since everyone's already hot and sticky, who would object to a drippy ice-cream cone? **Ruby Jewel** (page 231), **Fifty Licks** (page 230), and **Cloud City Ice Cream** (page 229) all beckon with fully stocked ice-cream cases, while fro-yo enthusiasts will love **Eb & Bean**'s (page 230) organic toppings bar.

If your air-conditioned car is calling your name, pack the kids and a picnic and set out for the not-so-far shores of **Sauvie Island** (page 47), with a side of berry picking (page 116). Or just throw in the (beach) towel altogether and make for the breezy beaches of the **Oregon Coast.**

RAINY-DAY ROUTE

BEST BETS FOR STAYING BUSY & DRY

Sing the "Rain, Rain, Go Away" nursery rhyme as often as you like, Portland just doesn't listen. So if the pitter-patter of little drops on the window coupled with the pitter-patter of little feet racing around the house is driving everyone bonkers, let's get out and do some rainy-day adventuring!

A proper rainy-day breakfast should be somewhere cozy, so dig into a basket of warm mini scones at old-school **Zell's Café** (page 197), stuff yourself at bustling neighborhood favorite **Jam on Hawthorne** (page 194), or grab grub at good ol' **Gravy** (page 194).

Settle in for story time at the local library (page 38), get lost in a favorite bookshop (page 37), or dabble in the arts and crafts at **100th Monkey Studio** (page 25) or **the Craft Factory** (page 26). If today's the perfect day to start that scrapbook, stock up on supplies at **Collage** (page 26) and start snipping and pasting.

OMSI (page 66) and the **Portland Art Museum** (page 93) are always high and dry, and after checking out the latest PAM exhibit, see if you can find the **Behind the Museum Café** (hint: it's behind the museum), then see if you can find the *matcha* parfait (because ice cream's still delicious on a rainy day!). Then hop the **MAX** train (page 5) to the **Oregon Zoo** (page 9) to see what the animals think of the rain, and while in the neighborhood, pay a visit to the nearby **Portland Children's Museum** (page 64).

For lunch, something hot and melty sounds good, so how about thick, creamy mac 'n' cheese at **Cheese & Crack Snack**

Shop, **Herb's Mac and Cheese**, or **Chkchk** (see Mac 'n' Cheese, Please! on page 216)? And for dessert, the warm, decadent drinking chocolate at **Cacao** chocolate shop (page 224 or **Moonstruck Chocolate Café** (page 225) will hit the spot.

A rainy-day matinee is always in order, so check the listings at **McMenamins Kennedy School** theater (page 22), the **Academy Theater** (page 20), or the **Avalon Theatre** (page 21), where you can hit the **Wunderland** nickel arcade afterward. For a thrill with your chill, take the **Portland Aerial Tram** (page 8) on a blustery day and try to count all the raindrops on the window (one million and *one*...) as you glide to and from Oregon Health & Science University's Pill Hill.

If a little action's needed, prove your Ping-Pong supremacy at **Pips & Bounce** (page 18), take a spin around the **Oaks Park Roller Rink** (page 73), or continue your quest to bowl a perfect game (page 13). Climb the walls at a rock gym (page 18), channel your inner Katniss or Gale at **Trackers PDX**'s open archery hours (page 12), disco down on the interactive dance floor at **Playdate PDX** (page 62), or see how high you can fly at **G6 Airpark** (page 60). And if all this indoor activity is making you feel too, well, *dry*, hit the toasty indoor pool and water park at **Mt. Scott Community Center** (page 62).

THE GREAT OUTDOORS

EXPLORING THE CITY'S NATURAL WONDERS

When the sun shines, and sometimes even when it doesn't, Portlanders can't resist getting out and about for fresh air, fun, and that ever-elusive vitamin D.

After a hearty breakfast alfresco, perhaps on the patio at bustling **Screen Door** (page 196), or at a sidewalk table at lovely **Lauretta Jean's** (page 186), break out the bikes (for rentals, see page 57) and make a leisurely loop around the **Eastbank Esplanade** (page 58) and **Tom McCall Waterfront Park** (page 54). Keep riding past OMSI and catch the **Springwater Corridor** (page 56), which winds along the Willamette River past **Oaks Bottom Wildlife Refuge** (page 70).

While gorge-ous hikes abound in the Columbia River Gorge, along the Oregon Coast, and around Mt. Hood, there's no need to leave the city to get lost in nature—take a trillium-hunting hike at **Tryon Creek State Park** (page 70), join one of the city-sponsored **Ladybug Nature Walks** for wee ones (page 69), or toddle around the lush **Leach Botanical Garden** (page 70) on the weekly Honeybee Hike.

Since the best kind of outdoor lunch is a picnic lunch, stop into a **New Seasons Market** (page 210) for sandwiches, deli salads, and snacks. For a picnic in the posies, spread a blanket in the **Peninsula Park** (page 53) rose garden; for a picnic with a playground, try **Mt. Tabor Park** (page 53); and for a picnic with a view, hike or drive to **Pittock Mansion** (page 77) and feast like royalty on the majestic back lawns. Since you're in the neighborhood, take a walk around the **Hoyt Arboretum** (page 68) or explore the trails of **Forest Park** (page 68).

Make like Huck Finn and get out on the river at **Alder Creek Kayak, Canoe, Raft & SUP** (page 48), which rents all sorts of vessels for navigating the area's rivers (if you're a newbie, go to its Tualatin location—no experience necessary).

For dinner, hit the east side and continue the alfresco theme with big burgers and sloppy sandwiches at a **Lardo** picnic table (page 223), or *arepas* on **Teote**'s hidden back patio (page 214). Or join the restaurant-cruising crowds on Division Street with a food-cart crawl at open-air **Tidbit Food Farm and Garden** (page 201), *Thali* meals and mango lassis on the **Bollywood Theater** (page 213) patio, and strawberry sorbet at **Pinolo Gelato** (page 230).

Nothing caps a long day outdoors quite like s'mores, but since you're sans campfire, go to **Pie Spot** (page 233), get the s'more pie hole, and eat it outside by the fire pit.

FREE DAY

AN ENTIRE ITINERARY OF FREE TO-DOS

Full-price family adventures can really add up, so if you're trying to give your wallet a breather, or just want to make a game out of seeing how many free things you can find to do around Portland, here's your no-budget blueprint!

Everyone knows the **Multnomah County Libraries** (page 38) are our most wonderful resource for free reads, but the libraries host free events too; check calendars online. And while **Powell's Books** locations are book*stores*, they let patrons browse to their heart's content.

Exploring nature is one of the most invigorating and budget-friendly activities in town–check out **Forest Park**'s maze of trails (page 68), navigate the **Hoyt Arboretum** (page 68), or admire the blooms at the **International Rose Test Garden** (page 32). All Portland parks are free, so pack a picnic lunch, blanket, and badminton set, and discover a new neighborhood park.

The **Oregon Rail Heritage Center** (page 6) is always free– Thursday through Sunday from 1 to 5 p.m., browse the exhibits and railroad memorabilia and admire the lovingly restored vintage engines on display. Or sit in a fire-truck simulator and slide down a fire pole at the **Historic Belmont Firehouse**'s (page 80) free weekly Open House Wednesdays and monthly Safety Saturdays.

On **First Thursdays** (page 93), mix and mingle with fellow art lovers at a very nice price: free. Browse numerous Old Town/Chinatown and Pearl District galleries gratis (some even have snacks), and visit the **Portland Art Museum** (page 93); entry is free from 5 to 8 p.m. To art hop any day of the week, download Travel Portland's **Public Art Guide** (www.travelportland.com), which details where to find over one hundred public sculptures, statues, paintings, and murals. You can also download the free **Public Art PDX** app on your smartphone (www.publicartpdx .com). Alberta Street's funky, artsy **Last Thursday** (www .lastthursdayonalberta.com) is always free too.

The **Portland Children's Museum** (page 64) is free on first Fridays from 4 to 8 p.m. With proof of residency, admission to **the Oregon Historical Society** (page 81) is always free to Multnomah County residents. And while not *totally* free, several otherwise spendy attractions give patrons a big break on designated days–

103 PART 1: OUT & ABOUT

OMSI (page 66) is $2 on first Sundays; the **Oregon Zoo** (page 9) is $4 on second Tuesdays.

On Saturdays, the PSU **Portland Farmers Market** (page 84) is free to browse, and you can do some free sampling too—check out Gathering Together Farm for melon and tomato slices, Freddy Guys for Oregon's finest filberts, and Baird Family Orchards for bites of the sweetest peaches this side of Georgia. There are many other markets around town too; see To Market, to Market for more info (page 82).

Also free on Saturdays is the **Portland Saturday Market** (page 78), but don't let the name fool you: it runs on Sundays too. Admire the work of hundreds of artists and craftspeople, watch live entertainment, and perhaps splurge on an elephant ear or two.

Summer's one of the best seasons for free activities—**Movies in the Park** (page 24) and **Concerts in the Park** (page 46) are both free, the city sets up a free rock-climbing wall at various parks, and free swim times are offered at several public pools (www.portlandoregon.gov/parks). **Pioneer Courthouse Square** is a mecca for free fun, from the Monday-morning farmers' market to Friday-night **Flicks on the Bricks** (page 24). There's also a free **Secrets of Portlandia** guided tour of Downtown (page 87) that meets in front of the **Pioneer Courthouse** (page 76) every day at 11 a.m.—no reservations necessary. And speaking of the courthouse, it permits free self-guided tours weekdays from 9 a.m. to 4 p.m., all year long.

For free playtime and perhaps a new neighborhood hangout, sign up to tour the **Southside Swap & Play** (page 65) or **Woodlawn Swap 'n Play** (page 65) to learn about what membership entails, then stay, play, and mingle afterward.

The **Pinball Outreach Project** (4605 NE Fremont St., Suite 104; www.pinballoutreach.org) offers free pinball to kids 13 and under most days of the week, and at the **Interactive Museum of Gaming and Puzzlery** (page 59) in Beaverton, the fee to play for the day is waived with the donation of a new or gently used board game.

If all this free stuff has you pretty worked up, chill out at the National Sanctuary of our Sorrowful Mother, a.k.a. **the Grotto** (page 31)—visiting the lower garden, Grotto, and chapel is free every day.

WINTER WONDERLAND

STEP-BY-STEP GUIDE TO WINTER FUN

It's the most wonderful time of the year . . . as long as the kids don't get cabin fever, especially during winter break, when you've got two whole weeks of unfettered family time to fill with festivity. Whether watching the Christmas ships glide down the Willamette, counting the seconds until the Pioneer Courthouse Square tree lights up, or eating scones and clotted cream with your pinkies up in the Hotel deLuxe's opulent Old-Hollywood-style dining room, 'tis the season for making merry memories!

Don't risk your favorite holiday event selling out; book tickets early for festive favorites like the **Oregon Ballet Theatre**'s (222 SW Clay St.; 503-222-5538; www.obt.org) performance of *The Nutcracker*, and the Singing Christmas Tree show at Keller Auditorium (222 SW Clay St.; 503-248-4335; www.singing christmastree.org). Beforehand, while dolled up in your fa-la-la-la finest, sip Earl Grey and nibble tea sandwiches at **Hotel deLuxe**'s holiday tea service (729 SW 15th Ave.; 503-219-2094; www.hoteldeluxeportland.com). Or get cozy by the fireplace in the **Heathman Hotel**'s historic Tea Court (1001 SW Broadway St.; 503-790-7752; portland.heathmanhotel.com), which serves a gorgeous Russian-style holiday tea services.

Plenty of free performances pop up around town this time of year; don't miss the triumphant trumpeting of **Tuba Christmas** (www.tubachristmas.com), a gathering of nearly three hundred volunteer tuba players who perform a free public concert of tuba-fied Christmas carols in Pioneer Courthouse Square. The square is also the site of Portland's majestic Christmas tree, and the annual lighting is held each year on Black Friday evening, with musical guests and live performances (www.thesquarepdx.org).

For tree-decorating ideas, tour the **Providence Festival of Trees** (www.oregon.providence.org/our-services/p/providence -festival-of-trees-portland), a winter wonderland where the whole family can admire the uniquely decorated themed Christmas trees, enjoy live entertainment, get pictures taken with Santa, decorate cookies, make holiday crafts, and visit the teddy-bear hospital.

Starting in early December, the **Christmas Ships** fleet (www.christmasships.org) cruises both the Willamette and Columbia rivers wrapped in creative light displays to the delight of the crowds clustered along the riverbanks. And kiddos will never forget their trip on the Oregon Rail Heritage Foundation's **Holiday Express** (page 6)—a forty-five-minute ride along the Willamette River in a train car decorated to the North Pole nines. Nor will they be able to contain their delight over the smaller scale but equally enthralling model train layout at the **Columbia Gorge Model Railroad Club**'s annual open house (www.columbiagorgemodelrailroadclub.com), held every weekend in November.

Some people really go Griswold come Christmas, so it's only polite to admire their efforts—the merriest stretch of street in Portland is **Peacock Lane** (www.peacocklane.org), but the folks in Alameda Ridge, Eastmoreland, and Arbor Lodge put on quite a show too.

Since snow rarely comes to Portland, go to the snow! It's only an hour or so to **Mt. Hood** (page 247), and after a day of sledding, skiing, and snowboarding, nothing's cozier than hot cocoa or caramel apple cider by the fireplace at **Timberline Lodge** (27500 E. Timberline Rd.; 503-272-3410; www.timberlinelodge .com). Or make the trip to Hood River and take a ride on Mount Hood Railroad's **Polar Express** (page 6).

Light shows set the city aglow—make the trip out to **Portland International Raceway** for its annual **Winter Wonderland** extravaganza (1940 N. Victory Blvd.; 503-823-2117 www.winterwonderlandportland.com), or walk the twinkle-lit forest of **the Grotto** (page 31), then listen in the chapel to the city's best youth choirs.

Washington Park doesn't skimp on the merry making— starting the day after Christmas, the grand **Pittock Mansion** (page 77) opens for its annual holiday festival, where poinsettias line the sweeping marble staircase, live choirs perform in the breathtakingly beautiful front parlor, and each room is decorated to the nines by a local designer. Just up the road is one of the city's most popular holiday traditions—Oregon Zoo's annual **ZooLights** (page 9). Once winter break begins, it's a madhouse, so consider going the week beforehand, or be prepared for long lines.

Shop 'til you drop for homemade artwork, crafts, and holiday sweets and treats at **Crafty Wonderland** (www .craftywonderland.com), and if you waited 'til you could see the whites of Christmas morning's eyes to buy gifts, haul the whole family to the **Portland Saturday Market's Festival of the Last Minute**, held during Christmas Eve week.

Sure, you can technically hit the ice any time of year at the **Lloyd Center Ice Rink** (page 72), but there's something so festive about going at Christmastime. Plus the rink is decked out for the holidays and plays all your favorite carols as you skate. Or to watch someone else do the skating, get tickets to a **Winterhawks** hockey game (page 41).

Don't forget about the farmers' markets (see page 82) just because it's winter—the Portland State market is open year-round, as are the Hollywood and Hillsdale markets, and St. Johns' market runs through December, so you can stock up on dark leafy greens for nourishing winter soups, gourds for roasting, and perhaps some fresh mistletoe.

And just when you think all the sparkle's left the season, the **Portland Winter Light Festival** (www.pdxwlf.com) plugs in the first week of February—hosted by OMSI, this magnificent display of installations by local light artists and designers really wows the crowd, especially the Silent Disco.

CHRISTMAS TREE FARMS 411

When it comes time to get the family Christmas tree, you can do things the easy way (tree from nearby drugstore parking lot), or you can do things the hard way (trudge through forest, chop tree, wrestle tree onto car). Or you can compromise—visit one of these sublime-smelling country tree farms, buy a freshly precut tree, then relax around the fire pit with hot chocolate.

Christmas Trees West
FOREST GROVE
45619 NW David Hill Rd.
503-939-5511
www.christmastreeswest.com

U-cut and precut trees, fresh wreaths, tractor rides to the trees, free hot chocolate and candy canes around the wood stove, holiday baubles to browse in the Tree Top Cottage gift shop.

Helvetia Christmas Tree Farm
HILLSBORO
12814 NW Bishop Rd.
503-647-5858
www.helvetia-christmas-tree-farm.com

U-cut and precut trees, gift shop, Santa Claus photo ops, warm drinks, marshmallows roasting on an open fire.

SPRING HAS SPRUNG

SPRINGTIME FROLICKING IN THE CITY

When the winter rainfall finally starts to relent, interrupted by pockets of bright and much welcome sunshine, Portland does its spring thing—cherry trees and daffodil bulbs burst into bloom, birds and squirrels run rampant, and farmers' markets fill with bundles of bright rhubarb, tender young asparagus,

Pollard Ranch
NORTHWEST
13225 NW Skyline Blvd.
971-238-9799
www.pollard-ranch.com

U-cut and precut trees, fresh wreaths, garland, free hot cocoa, dogs welcome, warming fires, preorder online for delivery or will-call pickup at the farm.

Redland Landing U-Cut Christmas Tree Farm
OREGON CITY
19400 S. Redland Rd.
503-462-3636
www.redlandlanding.com

U-cut and precut trees, fresh wreaths, free hot chocolate, free hayrides, dogs welcome, treats and ornaments for sale, Tree of Light lighting daily at 4 p.m.

Sunny Day Tree Farm
SHERWOOD
25100 SW Neill Rd.
503-628-1017
www.sunnydaytreefarm.com

U-cut and precut trees, fresh wreaths, cedar garland, tree barn, occasional Saturday Santa visits, free trees for those in need.

and green garlic. It's the season of spring break, Easter Feaster, dragon boats, and *all* the gardens.

Come March, the double row of waterfront cherry trees start to bloom, and it's a sight to behold. This is an excellent time to take a bike ride (for rentals, see page 57)—start at the north end of Downtown's **Tom McCall Waterfront Park** (page 54), then cross the Steel Bridge and loop along the **Eastbank Esplanade** (page 58).

Now that you're in the mood for blossoms, might as well hit all the parks—the **Lan Su Chinese Garden** (page 32) is splendid in the spring, the **Portland Japanese Garden** (page 33) is emerging from hibernation, and just up the way, the **Hoyt Arboretum** (page 68) is aflutter with flowers. Watch the **International Rose Test Garden** (page 32) carefully—the roses will be blooming soon, as they will be in North Portland's **Peninsula Park** (page 53), home of Portland's original rose garden. Make the trip to Eastmoreland's **Crystal Springs Rhododendron Garden** (page 31), especially in April and May, when the rhododendrons and azaleas are at their peak. And at **Tryon Creek State Park** (page 70) in Southwest Portland, go hunting for the elusive trillium flower, which blooms March through May only.

The **Wooden Shoe Tulip Fest** (page 279) in Woodburn, about a forty-five-minute drive from Downtown Portland, is a spring must. This family-owned farm runs a tight ship, and the grassy play area (complete with bounce houses, a mini zip line, and wooden shoe cobbler in action) is pristinely clean and organized. Go early, before the fields fill up, for the best photo ops.

The family soccer fans will be ready for the **Timbers** (page 42) and **Thorns** (page 42) seasons to start, so grab tickets to a game and break out the green-and-gold gear.

Kick off May with a fiesta, as the annual **Cinco de Mayo** festival (www.cincodemayo.org) hits Tom McCall Waterfront Park with lots of good food (churros!), live entertainment, and carnival rides.

The Saturday **Portland Farmers Market** at Portland State University (page 84) runs all year, but many of the smaller markets close in the winter, and come May and June, everyone gets up and going again (see To Market, to Market, page 82), with piles of rosy radishes, bundles of dark green kale, and wild-foraged mushrooms galore.

And of course, as we slip into June, everyone gears up for the weeklong annual **Portland Rose Festival** (www.rosefestival .org), a citywide party—watch the dragon-boat races, ride the Ferris wheel, and most importantly, get there early for prime Starlight Parade-watching real estate.

GOT EGGS?

This lineup of Easter events reads like a kid's dreams come to life—6-foot-tall chocolate bunnies, glow-in-the-dark and underwater egg hunts, and a helicopter dropping twenty thousand candy-filled eggs from the sky.

Alberta Street Egg Hunts

VERNON

503-954-2354

www.albertamainst.org

Easter story time and crafts at Green Bean Books (page 37), morning egg hunt for kids 8 and under, and glow-in-the-dark evening hunt for kids 9 and up. Free; registration required.

Alpenrose Dairy Easter Egg Hunt

SOUTHWEST

6149 SW Shattuck Rd.

503-244-1133

www.alpenrose.com

Popular annual morning egg hunts for kids 3–5 and 6–8. Easter Bunny on site, lots of candy and prizes, including seven 6-foot-tall bunnies and a family trip. Free.

Code Orange Easter Egg Drop

BRENTWOOD

SE 60th Ave. and SE Duke St.

www.hopecitychurch.cc

Real helicopter drops twenty thousand eggs into Brentwood Park, plus face painting, balloons, Easter bunny photo op, carnival games, and an obstacle course; ages 1–11, preregistration required and fills up quickly.

Lake Oswego Hop at the Hunt

LAKE OSWEGO

2725 SW Iron Mountain Blvd.

503-636-0674

www.lakeoswegohunt.com

continued

Morning egg hunt for 12 and under, with fifteen thousand treasure eggs, pony rides, bunnies, an egg challenge, fire truck, and police cruiser. Free.

Maddy's Blue Lake Adventure All-Abilities Egg Hunt
FAIRVIEW
21160 NE Blue Lake Rd.
503-760-6325
www.oregonmetro.gov

Open egg area and adventure course for kids with disabilities and their friends and families. All ages; free.

Mt. Scott Community Center EGGstraordinary Egg Hunt and Breakfast
MT. SCOTT
5530 SE 72nd Ave.
503-823-3183
www.portlandoregon.gov/parks/60409

Continental breakfast, spring-themed arts and crafts, ten thousand toy- and candy-filled eggs scattered throughout the park. All ages; $3 for breakfast or egg hunt or $5 for both.

Oregon Zoo Rabbit Romp
WASHINGTON PARK
4001 SW Canyon Rd.
503-226-1561
www.oregonzoo.org/events/rabbit-romp

Candy egg hunts between 9 a.m. and 3 p.m., bunny crafts, games, Easter bunny photo op. Ages 3–10; free with zoo admission. Separate hunt for toddlers age 2 and under.

Pearl District Hippity Hop Bunny Hop
PEARL DISTRICT
503-227-8519
www.explorethepearl.com

Store-to-store egg hunt, arts and crafts, raffle prizes, live music, and Easter bunny photo ops. All ages; free.

Pix Patisserie Egg Hunt and Easter Tea
KERNS
2225 E. Burnside St.
971-271-7166
www.pixpatisserie.com

Good for older kids; doors open at 2 p.m. sharp; fifty eggs are hidden around the restaurant with prizes inside. Reservations-only Easter tea at 2, 3, and 4 p.m.; $30 per person.

Underwater Egg Hunt at Conestoga Recreation and Aquatic Center
BEAVERTON
9985 SW 125th Ave.
503-629-6313
www.thprd.org/events

Underwater swimming-pool egg hunt, coloring contest, bunny bingo, photo booth, indoor play park, cupcake walk, bounce house, arts and crafts. All ages; $7.

SUMMER FUN

THE PERFECT SUMMER DAY IN PORTLAND

Mention summer to Portlanders and watch their expressions soften, their eyes mist over, their smiles grow wistful—summer in the Pacific Northwest is as good as it gets, and you've got to make hay (or waves, or chalk drawings, or wheelies . . .) while the sun shines. You've also got to get the kids out of the house before everyone goes nuts. So tuck this guide in your pocket, slather on the sunscreen, and tally ho!

When school lets out and the weather heats up, everyone's got one thing on their minds—the pool. Fortunately Portland's public pool system is awesome, and while most every neighborhood has one within easy reach, two of the best are the old-fashioned **Sellwood Outdoor Pool** (page 50) and Southwest Portland's wet 'n' wild **Wilson Outdoor Pool** (page 51). Or go play in an interactive fountain—Portland's got nearly a dozen (page 48), like the ever-popular Downtown **Salmon Street Springs** (page 49) and the Pearl District's **Jamison Square** fountain (page 49).

For a heart-racing river ride, take a **Willamette Jetboat Excursion** (page 4), which roars up and down the river at speeds up to 50 miles an hour, as guides impart fun facts about Portland. If you prefer making smaller waves, rent a kayak or canoe from **Alder Creek Kayak, Canoe, Raft & SUP** (page 48), which has locations on the Willamette, Columbia, and Tualatin Rivers.

There's no better eating than in summertime, so hit the farmers markets for peak produce and strawberry shortcake (page 82), go berry picking on a family farm (page 116), or create your own scoop-shop crawl (page 229). Don't forget the summer foreign-food festivals either—stuff yourselves with chicken tikka masala and mango lassis at **India Festival** (www.icaportland.org), pizza and spaghetti at **Festa Italiana** (page 279), and pierogis and gingerbread cake at the **Portland Polish Festival** (page 280). And kids under 12 are free at the popular annual **Bite of Oregon** (page 279), held in Tom McCall Waterfront Park in mid-August.

From May to September, explore new neighborhoods and meet new friends as you ride the monthly **Sunday Parkways** routes (page 58), and be sure to register for August's **Providence Bridge Pedal** (page 58), your one yearly opportunity to ride a bike across up to eleven of the city's bridges and even on (gasp) the *freeway*. To find new and interesting family-friendly bike routes across the city (and state), consult the **Ride Oregon** website (page 56), or take a guided city tour from **Pedal Bike Tours** (page 57), like the one that visits five different food carts.

As temperatures soar, let nature provide the air-conditioning—take a hike in well-shaded **Mt. Tabor Park** (page 53), **Forest Park** (page 68), or **Tryon Creek State Park** (page 70), join the city-sponsored **Ladybug Nature Walks** (page 69) for wee ones, or head into the Columbia Gorge for a hike to **Multnomah Falls** (page 237).

One of the best summer perks is moving movie night outdoors, so mark the calendar for **Movies in the Park** (page 24) and **Flicks on the Bricks** (page 24), a family movie series that projects movies onto a screen at Pioneer Courthouse Square.

Or make the hour-long trip to Newberg and catch a movie at historic **99W Drive-In** (page 23).

Pioneer Courthouse Square also hosts the summertime Noon Tunes concert series every Tuesday from 12 to 1 p.m.—either BYO picnic lunch or patronize the nearby food carts, then tap and clap along with local performers. Or, come evening, gather a pile of old blankets and pillows and settle in for free **Concerts in the Park** (page 46). On Thursday nights, get a picnic group together and drive out to scenic **Kruger's Farm** (page 117) on Sauvie Island for its summer concert series. For live entertainment with an athletic bent, take in a **Portland Pickles** baseball game (page 39) at Walker Stadium.

For everyday amusement-park fun, **Oaks Park** (page 72) is a local favorite, but the last week of August, the **Oregon State Fair** (2330 17th St. NE, Salem; www.oregonstatefair.org) arrives, so pack up the whole gang and make the trek to Salem for carnival rides, a petting zoo, live music, and, of course, deep-fried cheesecake.

Summer brings out the neighborhood street fairs in full force, so mark your calendar for the **Mississippi** (page 279), **Division/Clinton** (www.divisionclinton.com/the-division-clinton -street-fair), and **Lents** (www.facebook.com/lentsstreetfair) street fairs in July; the **Alberta** (page 279), **Fremont**, and **Hawthorne** (www.hawthornepdx.com/event/hawthorne-street-fair) street fairs in August (plus Multnomah Days in Multnomah Village); and the **Belmont Street Fair** (www.belmontdistrict.org/belmont -street-fair) in September. Kids will love the rambunctious mix of arts-and-crafts booths, live music, food carts, face painting, and general revelry.

Cherries and berries are at their sweet peak this time of year, so take a day trip to the **Hood River Fruit Loop** (page 244), which is dotted with u-pick farms, farm stands, and fun stops like **Cascade Alpacas of Oregon** (4207 Sylvester Dr.; 541-354-3542; www.cascadealpacas.com). In July, **Hood River Lavender Farms** (www.lavenderfarms.net) hosts its charming annual Lavender Daze celebration—graze the food booths or pack a picnic and eat in the orchard, shop the arts-and-crafts vendors, and snip your own lavender. From the Fruit Loop, it's about a forty-five-minute drive to lovely **Lost Lake** for a refreshing dip, or head southwest on scenic State Route 35 to cool off at **Mirror Lake** or **Trillium Lake**, then go wild at **Mt. Hood Adventure Park** at **Skibowl** (page 247).

FINGER-LICKING BERRY PICKING

Trolling the berry patch with sticky fingers and strawberry-stained faces is a summer rite of passage, so here are some of the berry best u-pick places in town.

Baggenstos Farm
SHERWOOD
15801 SW Roy Rogers Rd.
503-590-4301
www.baggenstosfarms.com

U-pick strawberries, raspberries, blueberries, blackberries, and marionberries; boxes for sale or BYO; call ahead and plan a farm field trip with berry picking, pygmy-goat petting, and a hayride.

Bella Organic
SAUVIE ISLAND
16205 NW Gillihan Rd.
503-621-9545
www.bellaorganic.com

Certified organic u-pick strawberries, blueberries, marionberries, raspberries, and blackberries; buckets available or BYO containers; picnic tables available.

Columbia Farms U-Pick
SAUVIE ISLAND
21024 NW Gillihan Rd.
503-621-3909
www.columbiafarmsu-pick.com

Sustainably farmed u-pick strawberries, raspberries, blueberries, blackberries, marionberries, boysenberries, and black and red currants; boxes for sale or BYO containers; picnic tables available.

Hoffman Farms

BEAVERTON

22242 SW Scholls Ferry Rd.

503-628-0772

www.hoffmanfarmsstore.com

U-pick raspberries, strawberries, tayberries, and blueberries; farm store with homemade pie for sale; picnicking area; playground.

Kruger's Farm

SAUVIE ISLAND

17100 NW Sauvie Island Rd.

503-621-3489

www.krugersfarm.com/upick-harvest

U-pick strawberries, raspberries, blueberries, blackberries, marionberries, boysenberries; farm store; picnic area; birthday parties include picnic-table party area, private tractor-driven hayride to the fields, and a pint per child to take home.

Lee Farms

TUALATIN

21975 SW 65th Ave.

503-638-1869

www.leefarmsoregon.com

U-pick strawberries; country store with produce, preserves, and gifts; bakery with pies, doughnuts, cookies, pastries, breads, and fudge; Father's Day Strawberry Festival; hosts parties.

Lolich's Family Farm

BEAVERTON

18407 SW Scholls Ferry Rd.

503-476-6662

Eight varieties of u-pick blueberries; BYO containers; farm store with produce, preserves, and pie; playground; hosts picnic parties.

continued

Smith Berry Barn
HILLSBORO
24500 SW Scholls Ferry Rd.
503-628-2172
www.smithberrybarn.com

No-spray u-pick red raspberries, golden raspberries, marionberries, blackberries, boysenberries, loganberries, and tayberries; garden market and greenhouse; gourmet gift shop.

Tom's Berry Patch
FOREST GROVE
43775 NW Greenville Rd.
503-327-3717
www.facebook.com/tomsberrypatch

U-pick strawberries, raspberries, blueberries, marionberries, and blackberries; BYO containers; vegetable and berry CSAs.

ALL IN THE FALL

FALL IN LOVE WITH THE CITY

Everyone has a favorite Portland season, and while spring and summer score high, fall really takes the (pumpkin spice) cake. The leaves turn brilliant shades of red and gold, the weather is calm and mild, and there's a hint of the holidays in the air. Of course, if you're a kid, fall means you're headed back to school, which might taint your impressions of the season, but rest assured, there's still tons of fun to be had!

Hiking-wise, fall is the best season to get out and explore the city's trails; the suffocating heat of summer is gone, and the trees are putting on a grand show of color. Besides the usual suspects—**Pittock Mansion** (page 77), the **Portland Japanese Garden** (page 33), and **Hoyt Arboretum** (page 68)—some of the hottest leaf-spotting locations are the **South Park Blocks** (SW Park Ave. from SW Salmon St. to SW Jackson St.) in Downtown Portland, St. Johns' **Cathedral Park** (N. Edison St. and

N. Pittsburg Ave.), **Mt. Tabor Park** (page 53), **Lone Fir Cemetery** (page 75), and **Elk Rock Garden** (page 31).

The trees aren't the only interesting fall colors; the **Trail Blazers** (page 40) kick off their season in October, so don your red, black, and silver spirit wear and cheer on the home team. It's also a perfect time of year to catch a **Portland State Vikings** football game (page 40), or one of the final **Timbers** (page 42) or **Thorns** matches (page 42), at Providence Park.

In early September, the Alphabet District goes on high bird alert during **Swift Watch** (page 10), when all the Vaux's swifts in the area congregate at Chapman Elementary School before their long flight south for the winter. Spread a blanket on the hillside, and watch the kids play until the big bird moment—at dusk, the swifts begin to swarm overhead, until finally, one makes a break for the school chimney to roost for the night, and the rest of the flock follows, forming a spellbinding black bird swirl that rivets its appreciative audience. Pack a picnic for the show, or grab dinner nearby on charming NW 23rd Avenue—slurp spaghetti at **Grassa** (page 214), sup on salmon rolls at **Bamboo Sushi** (page 211), or devour cheese pasties and chicken potpies at **Pacific Pie Company** (page 189).

The first weekend of October, get your *opa!* on at the annual **Portland Greek Festival** (www.portlandgreekfestival.com), held at the Holy Trinity Greek Orthodox Cathedral. There's a children's corner with face painting and games, and the older kids will appreciate the Greek folk dancing and spit-roasted lambs. Everyone will love the bountiful homemade food offerings, especially the addictive *loukamades*, golden deep-fried dough balls doused in honey.

The annual mid-October **Hood River Valley Harvest Fest** (www.hoodriver.org/harvest-fest) is a great excuse for a fall drive into the Gorge, which is indeed pretty gorge-ous this time of year. Set along the Hood River Waterfront, the old-fashioned festival features fresh produce from the Hood River Valley, over one hundred arts-and-crafts vendors, a food court, and a kids' zone with face painting, live music, games, contests, and treats.

Every October since 2003, the city of Tualatin has been delighting visitors with its wonderfully eccentric **West Coast Giant Pumpkin Regatta** (www.tualatinoregon.gov/pumpkinregatta), which draws around twenty thousand spectators from all over the country. Kids will love watching the teams of costumed competitors clumsily row gigantic hollowed-out pumpkins across Tualatin Lake. There are also harvest-themed food and craft booths, a pie-eating contest, and the Regatta Run.

As for opportunities to show off your costume, Halloween activities abound—there's the **Halloween Spooktacular** skate at the **Oaks Park Roller Rink**, Sellwood's all-ages **Monster March** parade (www.sellwoodwestmoreland.com), and **Howloween** trick-or-treating at the **Oregon Zoo** (page 9) for kids ages 3–11. The **Streets of Tanasbourne** mall (19350 NW Emma Way; 503-533-0561; www.streetsoftanasbourne.com) in Hillsboro also hosts a trick-or-treat event for kiddos 12 and under; Multnomah Village's small businesses (page 151) put on **Halloween in the Village**; and kids can candy-hop along Belmont Street between 33rd and 47th as part of the Belmont Area Business Association's **Trinkets and Treats** event (www.belmontdistrict.org).

Some of the bigger Halloween haunted houses are a bit gory for younger—and even not so younger—kids, but for frightful fun the whole family can enjoy, drive up to St. Helens (about forty-five minutes) for **the Spirit of Halloweentown** (www.facebook.com/Halloweentown.or). Parts of the movie *Halloweentown* were filmed in this quaint town, and it's parlayed its film credit into a monthlong October festival that includes a widely attended pumpkin lighting, a haunted hot-rod parade, haunted tours, a costume contest, and lots of general spookiness about town. This is also a prime time of year to take **Portland Walking Tours' Beyond Bizarre** ghost-hunting tour (page 86), a spooky look at Portland's underground tunnels, complete with scary and sometimes scandalous stories (rated PG).

The city libraries schedule special Halloween story times and events, the Portland parks and recreation department has a full calendar of kid-friendly community events like Peninsula Park Community Center's **Monster Mash**, and the **Portland Children's Museum** (page 64) hosts Eek Week the last week of October. Check the **Portland Farmers Market** (page 84) calendar for **Great Pumpkin** events at the weekly markets too.

THE GREAT PUMPKIN PATCH

Have a quintessential autumn outing at these local family farms, where you can pick the perfect pumpkin, take a hayride, get lost in the corn maze, fire a pumpkin cannon, climb the hay pyramid, sip hot apple cider, and go to the Nut House.

Baggenstos Farm
SHERWOOD
15801 SW Roy Rogers Rd.
503-590-4301
www.baggenstosfarms.com

This pumpkin-patch experience comes fully loaded with tons of free fun, from hayrides and pumpkin bowling, to duck races and fall-themed cutouts for photo ops. The corn maze is open daily, but on Friday and Saturday nights you're encouraged to bring a flashlight and brave it in the dark.

Bauman's Farm
GERVAIS
12989 Howell Prairie Rd.
503-792-3524
www.baumanfarms.com

Open daily in October, Bauman's really goes off on the weekends, when the $5 Harvest Festival fee includes the hayride, animal barn, cider sampling, corn tunnels, Frontier Fort, and playground. Then send all the kids to the Nut House, a giant bin of hazelnuts for jumping around in—that is, the Chuck E. Cheese ball pit gone country.

Bushue's Family Farm
BORING
9880 SE Revenue Rd.
503-663-6709
www.bushuefarming.com

Tuesdays through Sundays in October, entry to this bucolic Boring (not *that* kind of boring!) family farm is free, so you can

continued

pick your pumpkin; then, for a fee, take a hayride, play in the Adventure Park or Lil' Punkin's Playground, ride a pig train, or make a dirt baby.

Fir Point Farms
AURORA
14601 Arndt Rd.
503-678-2455
www.firpointfarms.com

Besides the pumpkins, obviously, one of the main attractions at this Aurora farm is the vittles—feast on homemade cinnamon rolls, pie, and apple-cider doughnuts. The farm's open Tuesdays through Sundays in October, but activities ramp up on weekends; for a fee, navigate the corn maze, play in the covered Kids Zone, and pet the farm animals.

Heiser Farms
DAYTON
21425 SE Grand Island Loop
503-868-7512
www.heiserfarms.com

The admission, hayrides, petting zoo, and hay pyramid are all free at this Dayton farm, while extras like the corn maze, fire-engine ride, and firing a pumpkin cannon will set you back a few dollars. There's also a simple menu of kid-friendly snacks like hot dogs, nachos, apple dippers, and kettle corn.

Lakeview Farms
NORTH PLAINS
32055 NW North Ave.
503-647-2336
www.thelakeviewfarms.com

At this charming North Plains family farm, open daily from late September to Halloween, you choose your mode of transportation to the pumpkin patch—train or boat (included with $4 admission ticket). For an extra fee, get lost in the 7-mile corn maze, take a pony ride, and sip hot apple cider.

Roloff Farms

23985 NW Grossen Dr.
503-647-2917
www.therolofffamily.com

Made famous on the TLC reality show *Little People Big World*,
this busy Hillsboro farm is open weekends during October, with
free admission to the pumpkin patch. For a fee, take the wagon
tour, race through the corn maze, see a tiger, and play pumpkin
mini golf, then sample pumpkin salsa and caramel corn in the
gift barn.

The Pumpkin Patch on Sauvie Island

SAUVIE ISLAND

16511 NW Gillihan Rd.
503-621-3874
www.thepumpkinpatch.com

The big red barn marks the spot at this wildly popular Sauvie
Island pumpkin patch, open from Labor Day weekend to
November 1. Poke around the fields for your perfect pumpkin,
take a free hayride, or climb the hay pyramid and gobble berry
cobbler at the Patio Café. For an extra fee, navigate the colossal
corn maze. Come October, Sauvie Island is pumpkin-patch central,
so expect traffic.

ONE DAY IN PORTLAND

THE CITY'S GREATEST HITS FOR KIDS

One of Portland's most endearing qualities is its coziness, both philosophically and geographically–sans traffic, you can cross the entire city in about twenty minutes. So if you've got only a day for sightseeing, fear not: you'll get a very well-rounded experience . . . whether the family is fast walking or just toddling along.

Start in the center of it all, lovely Downtown Portland. Yes, you've probably heard that no trip to Portland is complete without a box of strange and wonderful **Voodoo Doughnut** (page 229), but if your timeline won't accommodate the long wait, go to **Blue Star Donuts** (page 228) instead. Then walk down the block and tuck into a hearty breakfast of *tasso* hash and Auntie Paula's French toast at **Tasty n Alder** (page 196). (If you need coffee to help pass the wait, cross the street to **Heart Coffee Roasters**, page 95.)

> **TRIP TIP**
> If it happens to be Saturday, catch the **Portland Streetcar** (page 8) to Portland State University to experience the delicious hustle-bustle of the **Portland Farmers Market** (page 84)–also a good spot to grab an alfresco breakfast or lunch from one of the many excellent food stalls.

From Downtown, take the **MAX** train (page 5) into **Washington Park** (page 210), a gorgeous 160-acre patch of greenery adjacent to majestic **Forest Park** (page 68). Seeing everything in the park would take the entire day, so tailor your itinerary to who you've got in tow–if with baby, take a gentle stroll in the **International Rose Test Garden** (page 32) or the **Portland Japanese Garden** (page 33); if you've got a rambunctious toddler or preschooler, head for the **Portland Children's Museum** (page 64); and if you've got older kids or a mixed bunch, everyone loves the **Oregon Zoo** (page 9). Daily from June through Labor Day, and weekends in May, September, and October, the park runs a free shuttle service between all major attractions—to see stops and track the shuttle in real time, check www.explorewashingtonpark.org/getting-here.

For lunch, hit the food carts that Portland's so famous for. The most popular downtown "pod," or collective, of carts is at SW 10th Avenue and SW Alder Street—a few favorites include chicken and rice champion **Nong's Khao Man Gai** (page 212), the deliciously nostalgic **Grilled Cheese Grill** (page 200), and **the Frying Scotsman** (www.thefryingscotsmanpdx.com), popular purveyor of fish and chips and deep-fried Mars bars. The Pearl District **Whole Foods Market** (page 211) is also nearby if you want to pick up picnic provisions and eat lunch in Director Park, which has dozens of tables and benches, an oversize chess set, and a wading fountain.

After lunch walk down to **Pioneer Courthouse Square** (page 77), a.k.a. "Portland's Living Room," and check out the famous Milepost sign, bronze statuary, and seemingly endless sets of steps. Then hop the MAX Orange Line train to the **Oregon Museum of Science and Industry** (page 66), enjoying the grand river and city views as you glide over **Tilikum Crossing**, the first major bridge in the country to accommodate public transportation, cyclists, and pedestrians, but no cars. After exploring all OMSI has to offer, walk or ride the Orange Line back downtown. If time allows, hop off at the **South Waterfront** stop, and hop on the **Portland Aerial Tram** (page 8), which loops up to the Oregon Health & Science University campus, a.k.a. Pill Hill, and back. Afterward catch either the **MAX** (page 5) or **Portland Streetcar** (page 8) to return downtown.

For dinner, nosh on noodles at casual downtown pasta joint **Grassa** (page 214), or line up at neighboring **Lardo** (page 223) for big ol' sandwiches and dirty fries. For dessert, cross the street to **Ruby Jewel** (page 231) for ice cream, or head up the block and around the corner to **Cacao**'s West End shop (page 224) for the divine drinking-chocolate flight. Cross West Burnside Street and curl up with a pre-bedtime story in the aisles of famous **Powell's City of Books** (page 38), the largest independent bookstore in the world.

If it's summertime, consult the city's **Concerts in the Park** (page 46), **Movies in the Park** (page 24), and **Flicks on the Bricks** (page 24) calendars to see if there's any open-air evening cinema to be found nearby. Or end the day with a movie at the **Regal Fox Tower Stadium 10** theater (page 98), or nine holes of mini golf at pirate-themed **Glowing Greens** (page 16). There may also be a kids' theater or music production that night; check the **Oregon Children's Theatre** (page 29) and **Portland Youth Philharmonic** (page 46) calendars.

FORTY-EIGHT HOURS IN PORTLAND

EXPANDED GUIDE TO SEEING THE SIGHTS

For waterfall watching and beachcombing, consider spending your second day in Portland exploring the spectacularly scenic **Columbia River Gorge** and **Hood River Fruit Loop** (see the day trip guides on pages 236 and 244), or the **Oregon Coast** (see the **Cannon Beach/Seaside** guide on page 250). But if you're sticking around town, let's eat moon cakes in the Tower of Cosmic Reflections, take a riverfront bike ride, and have a food-cart feast, followed by cones and coconut cream pie.

Fuel up for your day of fun in Portland's hip-and-happening Pearl District, with banana chocolate walnut croissants at stylish **Nuvrei** (page 187), vanilla-cashew-cream-drizzled coconut waffles and Bunny Juice at health-conscious **Prasad** (page 188), or hearty, no-frills breakfast fare at friendly old-fashioned **Fuller's Coffee Shop** (136 NW 9th Ave.; 503-222-5608), where the counter stools convert to booster seats for little ones, who also get to order the off-menu bear-shaped pancake.

After breakfast walk a few blocks to the oasis-esque **Lan Su Chinese Garden** (page 32), where you can wander around at your own pace or join one of the several daily forty-five-minute docent-led tours, then enjoy tea and moon cakes in the two-story teahouse, a.k.a. the Tower of Cosmic Reflections. If it's Saturday or Sunday, continue down to the **Portland Saturday Market** (page 78)—even if your brood isn't interested in browsing the 250-plus arts-and-crafts booths, they'll be enthralled by the live performers, toe-tapping musical acts, and freshly fried elephant ears.

Rent wheels at nearby **Pedal Bike Tours** (page 57), then bike along the sparkling Willamette River through **Tom McCall Waterfront Park** (page 54), cross the Steel or Hawthorne Bridge (depending on which direction you go—each bridge has easy bike access), and loop back via the **Eastbank Esplanade** (page 58), a mostly flat 2-mile ride with a few metal ramps that little ones might need to walk their bikes up. After returning your bikes, walk to nearby **Pine Street Market** food hall (page 96), where kids will have a tough time choosing between ramen, hot dogs, burgers, and pizza for lunch . . . but most everyone will agree on **Wiz Bang Bar** soft serve (503-384-2150; www .saltandstraw.com/wizbangbar) for dessert.

Or, if you'd prefer a longer bike ride, instead of making the loop when you reach the east end of the Hawthorne Bridge, continue south under the bridge and pass OMSI, following the signs to link up with the **Springwater Corridor** (page 56), a flat, scenic, car-free, multiuse pathway that winds along the river. Three miles south, you'll come to old-fashioned **Oaks Park** (page 72)—lock up the bikes and hit the rides, roller rink, and mini golf course. Oaks Park maintains a large and lovely grassy picnic area, so consider bringing a picnic lunch. From here, you're not far from the historic **Sellwood Outdoor Pool** (page 50) and adjoining **Sellwood Park** (page 54), if anyone's keen on a swim or swing session. And if the family's up for exploring old-fashioned downtown **Sellwood** (page 165), continue along the bike trail to SE Spokane Street, then turn east and ride or walk (it's quite a hill) a half mile to SE 13th Street's bustling retail row. (Trip tip: if you don't want to make the trek to Oaks Park and Sellwood via bike, it's a fifteen-minute drive from Downtown.)

For dinner, make your way to Southeast Portland's bustling Division Street. If the weather's nice, opt for the outdoor **Tidbit Food Farm and Garden** food-cart pod (page 201); with nearly twenty carts catering to every whim, it's one of the few spots that nobody can legitimately complain about (except the fresh-air averse). If dining alfresco isn't in the cards, nosh on *vada pav* and mango lassis at **Bollywood Theater** (page 213), or dig into tacos, nachos, and black bean bowls at **Stella Taco** (page 204). For dessert, queue up for cones at **Salt & Straw** (page 231) or organic coconut cream caramel fro-yo at **Eb & Bean** (page 230), walk up to **Pinolo Gelato** (page 230) for extraordinary seasonal gelatos and sorbets, or get pie à la mode at lovely little **Lauretta Jean's** (page 186). Quick reminder: if it's summer, check the **Concerts in the Park** (page 46) and **Movies in the Park** (page 24) calendars.

PART 2:

NEIGHBORHOOD GUIDES

Just like kids, each of Portland's neighborhoods has a *distinct* personality of its own. To get a true sense of just how unique, creative, and, yes, weird this city is, make it a priority to poke around as many of its nooks and crannies as possible, whether you're a full-timer or a weekender.

Use these guides to find kid-friendly fun, from the sleepy streets of small-town **St. Johns** (page 155) and the posh park-dotted confines of the **Pearl District** (page 159) to the far-flung tech-meets-rural reaches of **Hillsboro** (page 179). Each guide offers insider insights into the vibe, recommended restaurants, parks and playgrounds, museums, movie theaters, shop stops, and best walking trails within each hood, as well as the nitty-gritty details, like parking and public transportation.

As you tackle each trip you'll expand your Portland horizons a little further, touring Downtown's Shanghai tunnels then eating pepperoni pies with a ghost at **Old Town Pizza** (page 220), riding your bikes along the **Springwater Corridor** (page 56) to play mini golf at **Oaks Park** (page 72), hiking a **Forest Park** trail (page 68) to the spooky stone Witch's Castle, singing and stomping along with a **Red Yarn** show (page 46) at the **Woodlawn Swap 'n Play** (page 65), making a pillow-and-blankets fort for a summertime **Concerts in the Park** performance (page 46), or trekking into the Beaverton suburbs to set sail at **Pirate Park** (page 177).

Your mission on each expedition is to try something new, chat with the locals, and learn something you didn't already know about this fun, funky, forested city. So pick a neighborhood and go!

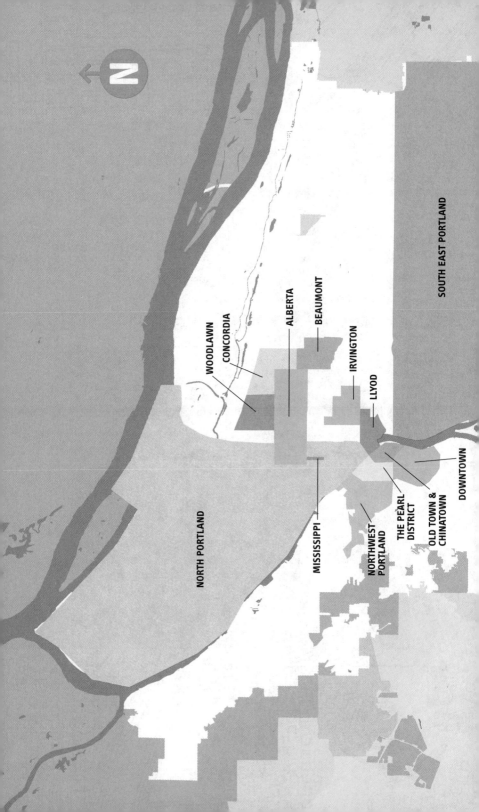

N

WOODLAWN
CONCORDIA

ALBERTA

BEAUMONT

IRVINGTON

LLYOD

NORTH PORTLAND

MISSISSIPPI

NORTHWEST
PORTLAND

THE PEARL
DISTRICT

OLD TOWN &
CHINATOWN

DOWNTOWN

SOUTH EAST PORTLAND

PORTLAND NEIGHBORHOODS

OREGON CITY

MILWAUKIE

SELLWOOD-
MORELAND

MULTNOMAH
VILLAGE

NEIGHBORHOODS

DOWNTOWN, OLD TOWN & CHINATOWN

THE MOOD

Portland's buzzy, brick-lined epicenter is home to historical sights and tourist to-dos galore, gateway to the myriad natural wonders of Washington Park, crammed with more delicious food carts than you can shake a fish stick at, *and* boasts the highest concentration of (tax-free!) shopping in the land.

PARK IT RIGHT THERE

Street parking isn't too hard to come by, but if you don't want to worry about the meter running dry, opt for one of the city's easily accessible and affordable **SmartPark** garages (www .portlandoregon.gov/transportation/35272), three of which have electric-vehicle (EV) charging stations. If taking the **MAX** train (page 5) or **TriMet** bus (page 5), both merge at Pioneer Courthouse Square, while the **Portland Streetcar** (page 8) runs a few blocks west, along 10th and 11th Avenues.

STROLLER ALONG

Balancing its urban hustle-bustle with quiet side streets and pretty parks, Downtown Portland is a wealth of scenic walks. In the city core find both the stately **South Park Blocks**, a graceful green swath of grass and gardens spanning the twelve blocks between Shemanski Park and Portland State University; and **Tom McCall Waterfront Park** (page 54), which runs parallel to the Willamette River and has a wide, flat footpath that's perfect for strollers, bikes, roller skates, and good old walking shoes.

Make your way up to **Washington Park** (page 210), where you can blaze a trail through the blooms at the **International Rose Test Garden** (page 32), meander around the meditative **Portland Japanese Garden** (page 33), or hike through **Hoyt Arboretum** (page 68). You'll also rack up a surprising number

of steps exploring the lushly landscaped trails of the 64-acre **Oregon Zoo** (page 9).

SHOP HOP

If there's shopping to be done, Portland's your city—there are tons of fun boutiques and pop-ups, *and* everything you buy is tax-free. Downtown is home to most major chains like Gap and J.Crew, most housed in **Pioneer Place** mall (public restrooms are located near the food court), but for a more unique shopping experience, hit up local favorite **Finnegan's Toys & Gifts** (page 89), pick up a sweet treat at **Quin** (page 226) in secretish retail arcade **Union Way**, or impress the family skateboarder with Old Town/Chinatown's **Cal Skate Skateboards** shop (page 98).

SNACK BREAK

One of Downtown's most delightful commodities is its doughnuts—start at famous **Voodoo Doughnut** (page 229) while everyone's still patient enough to wait in line, then walk a block to the **Donut Byte Labs** food cart (page 200), and finally, get a box of big brioche bombs at **Blue Star Donuts** (page 228).

For breakfast, **Mother's Bistro** (page 194) is the grande dame of first meal (and has a kids' play area), while old-school **Bijou Café** (page 192) charms with blue-checked tablecloths and Pearl Bakery French toast. For older kids who can withstand a wait, **Tasty n Alder** (page 196) is one of the best brunch spots in town.

Come lunch, your best—and most fun—bet is to cruise the food carts that congregate at SW 10th Avenue and SW Alder Street; but if the weather isn't alfresco-dining-friendly, duck into **Lardo** (page 223) for tuna melts and corn-dog bites with a side of dirty fries, sweet little **Addy's Sandwich Bar** (page 222) for simple Parisian-style baguette sandwiches and fresh salads, **East Side Deli** (page 223) for inexpensive, enormous deli sandwiches, or **Brunch Box** (page 198) for belly-busting burgers.

Sweets and treats-wise, **Saint Cupcake** (page 227) will elicit cries of cupcake joy, **Ruby Jewel** (page 231) will hit the scoop spot, and pretty pink **Petunia's Pies & Pastries'** gluten-free and vegan creations (page 189) are both drool inducing *and* inclusive.

For dinner, if the family's feeling Italiano, get bowls of spaghetti 'n' meatballs at relaxed, counter-service-only **Grassa** (page 214), or see if anyone can spot the resident ghost at **Old Town Pizza** (page 220). For reasonably priced *mezze* and kebabs, there's **DarSalam** (page 215), or for big, messy hamburgers and bottomless fries, **Killer Burger**'s your jam (*and* your peanut butter, if you get the Peanut-Butter-Pickle-Bacon burger; page 199).

SIPS TIPS

When in Portland, drink lots of coffee and hot chocolate, of course. Parents can caffeinate at light and lovely **Heart Coffee Roasters** (page 95) or iconic **Stumptown Roasters** (1026 SW Stark St.; 855-711-3385; www.stumptowncoffee.com) in the Ace Hotel, which also makes a mean hot chocolate, as does **Moonstruck Chocolate Café** (page 225). Or try **Cacao** chocolate shop's divine drinking chocolate (page 224)—which they're happy to pour over a scoop of Salt & Straw's olive-oil ice cream to create a deliciously decadent hot chocolate float.

PARKS & REC

Tom McCall Waterfront Park (page 54) offers both a popular riverfront bike-and-walking path and a vast expanse of tree-lined grass where little ones can get their laps in. The **South Park Blocks** make for a beautiful walk from the downtown core to Portland State University, which has a playground on the south end. A block up from Pioneer Courthouse Square, Director Park's public tables and toddler-friendly fountain make it a good option for a lunch break (grab sandwiches and salads at nearby **Flying Elephants at Fox Tower**). And of course, you can always hop the MAX train to wondrous **Washington Park** (page 210), home to the International Rose Test Garden, Portland Japanese Garden, Hoyt Arboretum, Oregon Zoo, and one of the city's largest playgrounds.

HIDDEN GEMS

Find **Mill Ends Park** (page 76), which at 452 square inches is the smallest park in the world. It's located right in the middle of busy SW Naito Parkway, so dole out dire traffic warnings before attempting a visit.

Walk up the stunning staircase of the **Central Library** (page 95), one of Downtown's architectural gems. Visit the Beverly Cleary Children's Library and check the calendar—if the timing's right, you can attend one of the weekly story times or sign up for a tour of the library's otherwise hidden eco-roof.

Every Saturday year-round, Portland State University hosts the phenomenal **Portland Farmers Market** (page 84). And during the summer there's also a Monday market in **Pioneer Courthouse Square** (page 77) and a Wednesday market in Shemanski Park at the base of the South Park Blocks.

Downtown is full of public fountains for dipping and dunking, and they're well worth the pilgrimage on searing summer days. For a splashy scavenger hunt, touch every jet in the **Bill Naito Legacy Fountain** (page 48), run through the middle of the **Salmon Street Springs** (page 49), stand under a waterfall at the Keller Fountain, and skip across the **Teachers Fountain**'s wading pool (page 50) in Director Park.

SLEEP ON IT

The whole family will appreciate **Hotel Monaco**'s quirky Alice-in-Wonderland-esque decor and fun details (506 SW Washington St.; 503-222-0001; www.monaco-portland.com), like welcome gifts, kid-size bathrobes, complimentary bicycles, and companion goldfish delivered to the room upon request. Parents will particularly love the central downtown location, free Wi-Fi, spacious suite layout, and nightly wine hour.

Sleep peacefully in your two-room suite, get up for the free breakfast and perhaps a dip in the indoor pool, then step outside the **Embassy Suites Portland** (319 SW Pine St.; 503-279-9000; www.embassysuites3.hilton.com/en/hotels/oregon/embassy-suites-by-hilton-portland-downtown-pdxpses/index.html) and straight into the middle of the downtown action—you're blocks from the waterfront, **Lan Su Chinese Garden** (page 32), **Pioneer Courthouse Square** (page 77), and the MAX train to **Washington Park** (page 210).

Not only can you see **OMSI** (page 66) from **RiverPlace Hotel**'s Willamette-River-facing rooms (1510 SW Harbor Way; 503-228-3233; www.riverplacehotel.com), you can ride there too, thanks to the free loaner bikes. It's a slightly longer walk to the downtown core and public transportation than other options, but in return you get unparalleled river views, easy access to the waterfront's gorgeous green spaces, and complimentary chocolate chip cookies.

LLOYD, IRVINGTON, BEAUMONT, ALBERTA, WOODLAWN & CONCORDIA

THE MOOD

Beyond the nondescript urban hustle of the Lloyd district, Northeast Portland's stately manors and cozy bungalows surround the restaurant- and retail-rich Irvington, Beaumont, Alberta, Woodlawn, and Concordia neighborhoods.

PARK IT RIGHT THERE

Street parking is free in the residential neighborhoods, metered in the zones surrounding the Oregon Convention Center, Moda Center, and Lloyd Center (rates and hours vary, so check carefully; some meter as late as 10 p.m.). Close-in Northeast is serviced by the **Portland Streetcar** (page 8) and **MAX** train (page 5), and **TriMet** buses (page 5) run through all neighborhoods.

STROLLER ALONG

While there are several enclaves of interest in Northeast Portland, the quadrant's most walkable and engaging main drag is fun, funky Alberta Street, so if thin on time, make this your main destination.

SHOP HOP & SNACK BREAK

While not quite as walkable as other neighborhoods, the rapidly developing Lloyd Center area has a lot going on—Lloyd Center mall, first-run movie theaters, easy proximity to the Oregon Convention Center and Moda Center, and plenty of public transportation to whisk you downtown in minutes. Pick up a biscuit sandwich breakfast at **Pine State Biscuits'** NE Schuyler Street walkup window (page 195), people watch in

Holladay Park (which sports a summer splash pad and Tuesday farmers' market, page 83), satisfy sweet teeth at **Creo Chocolate** (122 NE Broadway St.; 503-477-8927; www .creochocolate.com), and go for a twirl at the **Lloyd Center Ice Rink** (page 72).

If eschewing the big-box retail of Lloyd Center mall in favor of nearby Irvington's locally owned boutiques and eateries, start on busy NE Broadway Street at **Hello! Good Morning!** (page 89), a genuinely unique children's boutique curated by a former Laika animator. Walk a block west to festive **Taco Pedaler** (2225 NE Broadway St.; 503-946-1173; www.tacopedalerpdx.com) for tacos, burritos, and 'dillas, then cross the street for Spanish-style *xurros* and drinking chocolate at bright and friendly **180** (page 227). Pick up the newest Maggie Stiefvater novel at **Broadway Books** (1714 NE Broadway St.; 503-284-1726; www.broadwaybooks.net), then make a tough decision—freshly baked cake doughnuts and sugar cookies at old-timey **Helen Bernhard Bakery** (page 185), or organic, handmade frozen yogurt with artisan toppings at darling **Eb & Bean** (page 230)? Answer: both, of course.

When in beautiful Beaumont, where the regal bluff-top mansions of NE Wistaria Drive meet sweet little Klickitat Street (yes, Beverly Cleary buffs, *that* Klickitat Street; and a few blocks over, you can actually walk by Beverly's childhood home as part of the library's Walking with Ramona tour, page 75), don't miss **Pip's Original Doughnuts** (page 228), worth a pilgrimage alone for the hot made-to-order mini doughnuts and hand-blended chai. Afterward take a restful walk through **Rose City Cemetery** or check out the **Pinball Outreach Project** (page 104).

Moving north, enter the Alberta Arts District, home to the epic **Alberta Street Fair** (page 279), oft-controversial Last Thursday, and plenty of family-friendly eats and treats. Start with a classic grilled cheese (with or without crusts) at the **Grilled Cheese Grill** food cart (page 200), where the "dining room" is a converted school bus. Afterward take a peek at the neighboring **Caravan Tiny House Hotel** (page 142), a fascinating collection of rentable miniature homes. One block up, satisfy your sweet teeth at darling **Candy Babel** (page 225), then continue on to classic **Green Bean Books** (page 37), where you just might catch story time. Older kids will love the supercool **Community Cycling Center** (1700 NE Alberta St.; 503-287-8786;

www.communitycyclingcenter.org) a block east, and you'll love the **Barista** coffee shop (1725 NE Alberta St.; www.baristapdx .com) across the street, which has outdoor tables that make stroller parking a cinch. On the next block, browse the beautifully curated collection of books, games, and handmade frocks at **Grasshopper** boutique (page 89), then keep going for a lunch break at **Little Big Burger** (page 199), **Bollywood Theater** (page 213), or **Pine State Biscuits** (page 195), followed by a salted caramel cupcake cone at **Salt & Straw** (page 231). If anyone in the group is gluten sensitive, nearby **Back to Eden Bakery** (page 188) is ready with gluten-free chocolate root-beer doughnuts and PB&J whoopie pies. And if dinner's in demand, choose from tacos and nachos at **La Bonita** (page 203), *mezze* platters on the patio at **DarSalam** (page 215), or vegetarian fare (and a dollar kids' menu) at **Vita Café** (page 217), with a waffle-sundae chaser at **Waffle Window** (page 197), naturally. If you can still waddle at this point, mosey a half mile or so to **McMenamins Kennedy School** (page 22) for a cheap family flick in its marvelous movie theater.

For a sense of life in the charming, off-the-beaten path Woodlawn hood, breakfast with the locals at **Woodlawn Coffee and Pastry** (page 191), then head a block east to **Woodlawn Park** (www.portlandoregon.gov/parks/finder/index.cfm?action =viewpark&propertyid=865). Admire the picnic basket collection at sweet **P's & Q's** market (page 210)—for a deposit, they'll let you borrow one so you can schlep your picnic to the park in style. A short ways up NE Dekum Street, **Tamale Boy** (page 204) is a guaranteed lunch (or dinner) hit; sit on the patio if the weather's agreeable. Then scoot next door to **Bassotto Gelateria** (1760 NE Dekum St.; 503-209-2399; www.bassottopdx.com) for scoops of marionberry cream gelato and watermelon sorbet.

En route to the Concordia hood, stop along NE Killingsworth Street for wood-fired whole-grain pastries at **Seastar Bakery** and **Handsome Pizza**'s (page 190) shared space, followed by bubble tea at neighboring **Tea Bar** (1615 NE Killingsworth St.; 503-477-4676; www.teabarpdx.com), then let the kids loose in nearby **Alberta Park** (NE 22nd Ave. and NE Killingsworth St.). Continuing on to Concordia's cozy Fox Crossing neighborhood at NE 30th Avenue and NE Killingsworth, you'll find a handful of sweet vintage shops and boutiques like doula-owned **Milagros** (page 90), **Extracto** coffeehouse (2921 NE Killingsworth St.;

503-281-1764; www.extractocoffee.com), and upscale but family-friendly Asian-influenced **Yakuza** (5411 NE 30th Ave.; 503-450-0893; www.yakuzalounge.com).

If the clan's clamoring for pasta and pizza, go to **Pizza Jerk** (page 220), which is fun to shout over and over again and has a kids' play area too. After dinner get shakes and sundaes at old-timey **Rose's Ice Cream** (5011 NE 42nd Ave.; 503-256-3333; www.rosesicecream.com). And once again, from this point you're but a popcorn tub's toss away from **McMenamins Kennedy School**'s movie theater (page 22).

PARKS & REC

If roaming around Irvington or Beaumont, you're mere minutes from **Grant Park**, where the restless can run wild, and literary sorts can stand on the hallowed ground of the **Beverly Cleary Sculpture Garden** (page 75), which doubles as a splash pad come summertime. When in Woodlawn, run a few laps around **Woodlawn Park** (opposite page), which also hosts summertime Movies in the Park (page 24) and Concerts in the Park (page 46). And wherever you are in Northeast (or the city, really) it's worth making the trip (bring a picnic!) to regal **Peninsula Park** (page 53), home to Portland's first rose garden, a sizeable playground, and an old-fashioned community center and pool.

HIDDEN GEMS

If in the hood on a summer Thursday, check out the **Cully Farmers Market** (page 83), held in the Rose's Ice Cream parking lot. Afterward have a nice family meal at **Pizza Jerk** (page 220) or **Red Sauce Pizza** (page 221), then pick up sweet treats at nearby **Miss Zumstein Bakery & Coffee Shop** (page 187).

ON THE SIDE

From Northeast, you're minutes from the **Oregon Food Bank**'s warehouse (page 36), where volunteers are welcome; check the website and sign the whole family up for a shift.

SLEEP ON IT

The Lloyd District has several solid affordable lodging options, from the dependable **DoubleTree** (1000 NE Multnomah St.;

503-281-6111; www.doubletreeportland.com) across the street from the Lloyd Center mall and movie theater, to the newer and more stylish **Hotel Eastlund** (1021 NE Grand Ave.; 503-235-2100; www.hoteleastlund.com), a beautifully appointed boutique hotel with an in-house bakery/café.

To live like a local, try the **Kuza Garden Cottage** (www .airbnb.com/rooms/362775) in Concordia, a serene retreat tucked into the gorgeous Japanese-style garden behind kid-friendly Yakuza restaurant.

Fans of HGTV's *Tiny House, Big Living* will love the Alberta district's one-of-a-kind **Caravan Tiny House Hotel** (5009 NE 11th Ave.; 503-288-5225; www.tinyhousehotel.com)—an eclectic roundup of playhouse-size homes that sleep up to four (very cozily).

MILWAUKIE & OREGON CITY

THE MOOD

These sleepy Portland communities are sparse on action and rich in state history. Visit for a small-town experience and a glimpse of Oregon's storied past, plus a fun, floury detour to Bob's Red Mill's world headquarters.

PARK IT RIGHT THERE

Street parking is free, albeit timed in busier commercial areas. The Portland Streetcar doesn't reach this far, but if you're headed to Milwaukie, the Orange Line **MAX** train (page 5) from Downtown Portland stops in Downtown Milwaukie. The area is also served by **TriMet** buses (page 5).

STROLLER ALONG

Do a little window shopping in Milwaukie's old-fashioned downtown core, then cross SE McLoughlin Boulevard to the **Milwaukie Riverfront Park** (SE Monroe St. and SE McLoughlin Blvd.), a lovely 8.5-acre green space that fronts the Willamette River. Within the park, you'll find the Trolley Trail, a scenic 6-mile walking and biking path following the retired streetcar line that ran between Milwaukie and the nearby community of Gladstone from 1893 through 1968.

In Oregon City, the Oregon Territory's first capital, walk around the quaint downtown, taking care to spot historic landmarks like the **McLoughlin House** (713 Center St.; 503-656-5151; www.mcloughlinhouse.org), then visit the city's famous vertical street, a.k.a. the **Oregon City Municipal Elevator** (6th St. and High St.; www.orcity.org/publicworks/municipal-elevator), built in the early 1900s to ferry settlers up the sheer cliff from town to their homes.

SHOP HOP

In Downtown Milwaukie, pop into Parisian-inspired candy shop **Enchante** (10883 SE Main St.; 503-654-4846; www.enchantechocolatier.com), for old-fashioned sweets and the addictive cheese popcorn, then browse the thousands (possibly millions) of vintage treasures at **Main Street Collectors Mall & Soda Fountain** (10909 SE Main St.; 503-659-7632; www.mainstreetcollectorsmallandsodafountain.com), and take a shake break at the old-timey soda-fountain counter. And good luck prying the family comics, collectibles, and graphic-novel enthusiast out of **Things From Another World** (10977 SE Main St.; 503-652-2752; www.tfaw.com), owned and operated by Dark Horse Comics, which is headquartered across the street.

The family model builder or collector will be fascinated with Oregon City's **Coyote Hobby** (1128 Main St.; 503-656-2172; www.coyotehobby.com), which sells everything from essentials like batteries and glue, to model airplanes and Proto-N drones. A couple blocks down Main Street, kids can get ideas for their Christmas list at friendly **First City Cycles** bike shop (916 Main St.; 503-344-4901; www.firstcitycycles.com), which is also the driving (er, biking) force behind the **First City Central Marketplace & Bistro** (1757 Washington St.; www.facebook.com/firstcitycentral) inside the historic Oregon City Amtrak station.

SNACK BREAK

In Milwaukie, sit alongside the locals at no-nonsense **Gramma's Corner Restaurant** (10880 SE McLoughlin Blvd.; 503-654-7110; www.grammascorner.net) for the hearty Gramma's Full Breakfast, plus a classic kids' menu. Come lunch or dinner, **Cha Cha Cha** (page 202) dishes up fresh, tasty Mexican meals at its cute corner taqueria, while **Ohana Hawaiian Café** (10608 SE Main St.; 503-305-8170; www.ohanahawaiiancafe.com) provides a mini island getaway via plates of kalua pork and cups of soft, snowy shave ice. Every Sunday from May through October, check out the **Milwaukie Farmers Market** (page 84), which sets up near city hall and hosts over seventy-five vendors, live music, and cooking demonstrations.

Milwaukie is also home to **Bob's Red Mill**'s world headquarters (page 168). Take the free seventy-five-minute factory tours (weekdays at 10 a.m.), then drive a mile to the **Whole Grain Store, Restaurant & Bakery** (page 168), where the family can tuck into buttermilk Belgian waffles, buckwheat flapjacks, and ten-grain French toast, before going nuts in the five-hundred-plus bulk bins.

In Oregon City, get wood-fired pies at **Mi Famiglia** (701 Main St.; 503-594-0601; www.mi-famiglia.com), Norwegian meatballs and raspberry lemon lefse at **Ingrid's Scandinavian** (209 7th St.; 971-570-5659), and no-frills pub grub at **McMenamins Oregon City** (102 9th St.; 503-655-8032; www.mcmenamins.com/342 -mcmenamins-oregon-city-home). For fun retro vibes, big burgers, and creamy soft serve, crowd into a picnic table at **Mike's Drive-In** (905 7th St.; 503-656-5588; www.mikesdrivein.com).

PARKS & REC
A mile from Downtown Milwaukie, **Spring Park Natural Area** (www.ncprd.com/parks/spring-park) encompasses nearly 7 acres of wildlife-filled woodlands, with shady walking trails, a playground, and picnic tables. It also connects to **Elk Rock Island**, a volcanic cinder cone, via a jagged rocky land bridge that's exposed only in summer when the slough waters dry up. While you're there, try to spot a resident bald eagle or osprey.

PLAY DATE
Check the calendar at Milwaukie's **Ledding Library** (10660 SE 21st Ave.; 503-786-7580; www.milwaukieoregon.gov/library)—it hosts regular story times, kids' book group meetings for readers 7 and up, Saturday-afternoon craft sessions, and Tuesday-night drop-in arts and crafts for preschoolers.

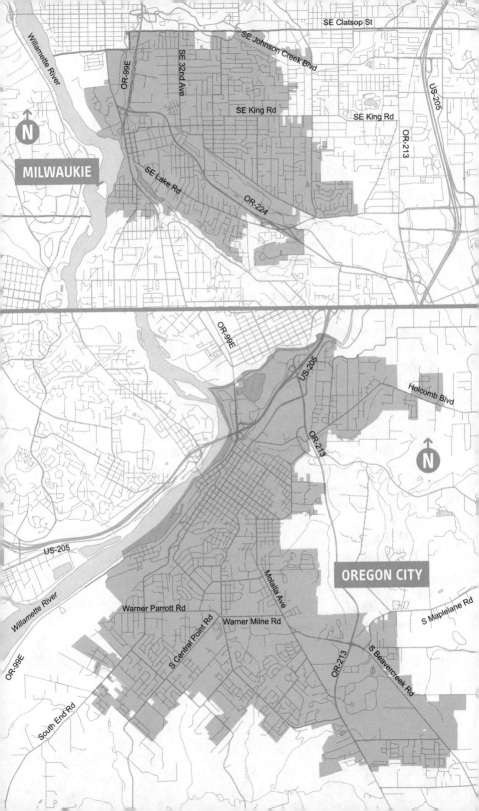

Milwaukie's home to not one but two vintage bowling alleys, so show off your strike skills—**Kellogg Bowl** (page 13) charms with twenty-four old-fashioned wooden lanes and a retro feel, and **Milwaukie Bowl**'s Saturday-morning junior leagues (page 14) welcome players as wee as 3, a.k.a. the Bumper Thumpers.

HIDDEN GEMS

A nineteenth-century farmhouse turned community museum, the **Milwaukie History Museum** (3737 SE Adams St.; www .milwaukiehistoricalsociety.com) houses a unique collection of photographs, paintings, and other antiques offering insight into the city's earliest days. It's open to the public on Saturday afternoons, and admission is free.

Sure to hold the interest of even the most history-averse youngin, Oregon City's **End of the Oregon Trail Interpretive Center** (1726 Washington St.; 503-657-9336; www .historicoregoncity.org) features interactive exhibits, the *Bound for Oregon* film, authentically dressed staff demonstrating long-lost skills like butter churning, and period crafts for the kids, such as rag-doll making and candle dipping. If the weather's fair, head outside into the heritage garden, stroll the interpretive trail, or play pioneer lawn games on Abernethy Green.

Oregon City favorite **Wenzel Farm** (19754 S. Ridge Rd.; 503-631-2047; www.fantasytrail.com) goes all out for the holidays, tricking out its Fantasy Trail with a seriously spooky Halloween setup and turning it into a twinkle-lit wonderland for Christmas.

ON THE SIDE

From Downtown Milwaukie, it's a fifteen-minute drive to **Oaks Park** in Sellwood (page 72).

SLEEP ON IT

There are a few affordable chains along 99, but it's only a fifteen-minute drive to Downtown (page 132).

MISSISSIPPI

THE MOOD

This once notorious NoPo neighborhood is now a full-fledged hipster haunt, with the big shiny condo buildings; packed restaurants; and trendy bars, breweries, and boutiques to match.

PARK IT RIGHT HERE

Street parking on the main drag is free but timed, so if you're staying awhile, park on a residential side street. If taking public transportation, **TriMet**'s number 4 bus line (page 5) makes several stops along Mississippi Avenue.

STROLLER ALONG

It's easy to see everything of interest in this historic hood even if you don't have much time, because it's all merrily mashed into a six-block stretch, which takes about thirty minutes to traverse on foot if you're just window shopping, and a few hours if you're stopping to eat and browse.

SHOP HOP

Start by poking around **the ReBuilding Center** (page 98), an immense warehouse crammed with an array of recycled building materials that would make any devoted DIYer dizzy. Admire the faux forest front entrance, then see who can spot the most pink toilets.

Across the street lies bright, sassy **Reading Frenzy** (page 98), a longtime source of one-of-a-kind books, zines, and other indie media that literarily inclined teens and tweens will love (even if they maintain an impassive facade). Take any comic-book and graphic-novel enthusiasts to the well-stocked **Bridge City Comics** (3725 N. Mississippi Ave.; 503-282-5484; www.bridgecitycomics.com), which shares the block with **Ruby Jewel** (page 231).

Walk through the beautiful gardens of **Pistils Nursery** (3811 N. Mississippi Ave.; 503-288-4889; www.pistilsnursery.com), and see if the resident chickens are strutting around. Considering the cramped and delicate inventory, it's probably

not advisable to march the whole brood through **Sunlan Lighting** (3901 N. Mississippi Ave.; 503-281-0453; www.sunlanlighting. com), but definitely check out the shop's famously eccentric window displays.

Those who appreciated Reading Frenzy will also dig impeccably curated **Land** (page 98), which sells indie books, crafts, and gifts, and has an art gallery tucked upstairs. Across the street, teens and tweens will dig the eclectic variety of new and vintage trinkets and books at **Flutter** (3948 N. Mississippi Ave.; 503-288-1649; www.flutterpdx.com), and parents and little ones alike will love nearby **Black Wagon** (page 88), for both the unique toys and clothes and the interactive play table.

Word of warning: the family naturalist will want *everything* in weird and wonderful **Paxton Gate** (4204 N. Mississippi Ave.; 503-719-4508; www.paxtongate.com), a mecca of taxidermy, science equipment, impaled insects, stones, and bones.

SNACK BREAK

Line up with the locals at beloved all-day breakfast joint **Gravy** (page 194) for heaping portions of corned beef hash, biscuits 'n' gravy, and its famous oatmeal brûlée. For an older crowd, both **Radar** (3951 N. Mississippi Ave.; 503-841-6948; www.radarpdx .com) and **Interurban** (4057 N. Mississippi Ave.; 503-284-6669; www.interurbanpdx.com) serve a sophisticated weekend brunch; if it's a nice day, take advantage of Interurban's hidden back patio.

For lunch, queue up at wildly popular **Por Qué No** taqueria (page 203); order a big cheesy pie at **Mississippi Pizza Pub** (page 220); browse the **Mississippi Marketplace** food-cart pod (4233 N. Mississippi Ave.; 503-358-7873; www.missmarketplace.com); get burgers, fries, and floats at **Little Big Burger** (page 199); or nosh on noodles at **Monsoon Thai** (4236 N. Mississippi Ave.; 503-280-7087; www.monsoonthaipdx.com).

For a delectable dessert, try the blueberry basil doughnut at **Blue Star Donuts** (page 228), lemon lavender ice-cream sandwich at **Ruby Jewel** (page 231), or banana Nutella crepe at **Flapjak** creperie (page 226).

Come dinnertime, head for **Lovely's Fifty Fifty** (page 219), where sisters Sarah and Jane Minnick not only make some of the best pizzas around (including a kids' cheese pizza you'll want for yourself), but they also churn some of the best ice cream too. Or try **Ecliptic Brewing** (825 N. Cook St.; 503-265-8002; www .eclipticbrewing.com), an impressive 14,000-square-foot former auto-body shop turned brewery and brewpub, with downtown views from the pet-friendly patio, and a solid kids' menu.

SIP TIPS

Coffee drinkers, get your Stumptown fix at friendly **Fresh Pot** (4001 N. Mississippi Ave.; 503-284-8928; www.thefreshpot.com); tea drinkers, pop into **Townshend's Tea** (3917 N. Mississippi Ave.; 503-477-9646; www.townshendstea.com) for a cuppa loose leaf, bubble tea, or kombucha on tap.

PARKS & REC

A half mile from Mississippi Avenue, 11-acre **Overlook Park** (1599 N. Fremont St.) perches on the North Portland bluffs, with beautiful views of Downtown, Forest Park, and the West Hills. It offers a playground, grassy areas for running free, gentle slopes for rolling down, and up in the northwest corner, a small hidden bluff with the best vantage point for sunset watching.

PLAY DATE

Mark your July calendar for the **Mississippi Street Fair** (page 279), one of the city's most robustly attended summer shindigs, with countless food and craft vendors, all-day live music with one stage devoted just to kids' tunes, fun competitions, and a dunk tank.

HIDDEN GEMS

Veer off onto North Beech Street and see if you can find the **Little Pink House** and **Little Green House**, twin tiny houses that serve as both cheery neighborhood beacons and Airbnb rentals.

ON THE SIDE

A half mile east of Mississippi Avenue lies the rapidly gentrifying North Williams Avenue commuter corridor, rife with new condos, restaurants, bars, boutiques, and a busy

New Seasons Market (page 210). While it is not necessarily a destination neighborhood, there are a few spots worth a visit.

For one of the best brunches in town, queue up at **Tasty n Sons** (page 196), with a *cortado* from neighboring **Ristretto Roasters** (3808 N. Williams Ave.; 503-288-8667; www.rrpdx .com) to tide you over until your table is ready. Come lunchtime, **Life of Pie** pizzeria (page 219) offers one of the best deals in town—$5 *margherita* pies during its daily happy hour, from 11 a.m. to 6 p.m. Next door, **What's the Scoop?** (page 232) uses a supercool nitrogen-based freezing technique to ensure its ice cream's creamy consistency.

Support the local economy at **Spielwerk Toys** (page 92), which sells its own Portland-made line of toys; on second Thursdays, it also hosts a free Tot Thursday story and craft hour at nearby Hopworks Bike Bar. Down the block, **TreeHouse Children's Boutique** (3954 N. Williams Ave.; 503-928-5987; www .misstreehouse.com) charms with unique toys and clothes. Stylish **Poa Café** (page 45) also hosts regular music and story times, and it has a play area for parents who want to have their avocado toast and eat it too, while watching their little ones frolic.

SLEEP ON IT

There aren't any hotels in this neck of the urban woods, but you're quite close to Downtown (page 132) and Northwest Portland (page 159).

MULTNOMAH VILLAGE

THE MOOD

A fifteen-minute-or-so drive from Downtown Portland, step back in time as you stroll this cozy Southwest Portland community's teensy but bustling main drag, which has the requisite bookshop, toy shop, and candy shop lineup that will make any kid's heart go pitter-patter.

PARK IT RIGHT THERE

Street parking is free, albeit timed in busier commercial areas. The Portland Streetcar and MAX trains don't reach this far, but **TriMet** buses (page 5) do.

STROLLER ALONG

Lush **Gabriel Park** (SW 45th Ave. and SW Vermont St.; www .portlandoregon.gov/parks/finder/index.cfm?action=viewpark &propertyid=136)—home to the **Southwest Community Center** (www.portlandoregon.gov/parks/60161)—makes for a relaxing walk. You can also wind through the quiet surrounding residential neighborhoods to Downtown Multnomah Village via SW Canby Street.

SHOP HOP

Downtown Multnomah Village is a kids' paradise—within steps, you'll find colorful and creative **Thinker Toys** toy store (page 92), **Annie Bloom's Books** (page 37), and adorably old-fashioned **Hattie's Sweet Shop** (page 225), which sells all manner of candies and big scoops of Umpqua ice cream. On First Friday, all the village shops stay open later than usual and feature specials, entertainment, and snacks.

SNACK BREAK

With its quaint awning-shaded storefront and massive cinnamon rolls, **Fat City Café** (7820 SW Capitol Hwy.; 503-245-5457) charms with a classic American-style breakfast, while **Down to Earth Café** (7828 SW 35th Ave.; 503-452-0196; www.downtoearthcafe .com) serves organic smoothies, juices, and from-scratch eats. Hit up bustling **Grand Central Bakery** (page 185) for picnic fare if headed to Gabriel Park; for dinner, wood-fired pizzas and farmers'-market salads hit the spot at terrific **Tastebud** (page 222), or join the crowd chowing down on pub grub at kid *and* dog-friendly **Lucky Lab Public House** (7675 SW Capitol Hwy.; 503-244-2537; www.luckylab.com).

PARKS & REC

Gabriel Park (above) has something for everyone—90 acres of wildlife-dotted forest, grassy hills, paved walking trails, and ball

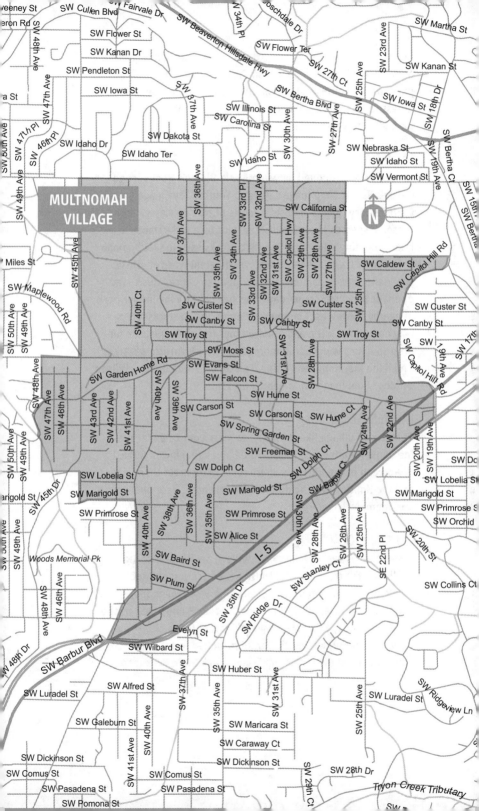

fields, plus a skate park, playground, community garden, picnic areas, and off-leash dog park. In the northwest corner of the park sits the **Southwest Community Center**, which has a pool, fitness room, basketball and volleyball courts, and an indoor park for kids ages 9 months to 5 years.

PLAY DATE

Conveniently positioned between **Annie Bloom's Books** (page 37), **Hattie's Sweet Shop** (page 225), and **Thinker Toys** (page 92), **the Craft Factory** (page 26) hosts all sorts of crafting classes, from seasonal specials like embellishing your own lucky clover, to Friday morning's Toddler Time. Two blocks east, the **Multnomah Arts Center** (page 27) encourages all different types of artistic experiences, from painting and sculpting to dance, music, and dramatic play. If the rainy-day blues have hit, try the **indoor park** at nearby **Southwest Community Center**, which stocks lots of play equipment, cars, and assorted toys (check the website for drop-in times; www.portlandoregon.gov/parks/article/432317). And if the thermometer's rising, splash, dive, and dunk at **Wilson Outdoor Pool** (page 51) in nearby Hillsdale.

HIDDEN GEMS

Multnomah Village likes to party, so mark your calendar for the annual **Multnomah Days** parade and street fair in August, **Halloween in the Village**'s afternoon trick-or-treat shenanigans, and the **Holiday Gala** held the first weekend in December (www .multnomahvillage.org).

ON THE SIDE

About 2 miles east of Multnomah Village on SW Capitol Highway, you'll find the community of Hillsdale, where you can gobble maple twists and lemon tarts at **Baker & Spice** (page 184), paddle around wet 'n' wild **Wilson Outdoor Pool** (page 51), and shop the Sunday **Hillsdale Farmers' Market** (page 84). For a shady hike through a mystical trillium-dotted forest, the village is about a ten-minute drive from **Tryon Creek State Park** (page 70).

SLEEP ON IT

Since you're only about ten minutes from Downtown, use the recommendations in the Downtown neighborhood guide (page 132).

NORTH PORTLAND

THE MOOD

The working-class neighborhoods of old-fashioned North Portland are a melting pot of young couples, families, and longtime residents who love the quiet streets, still-affordable housing, and cozy downtown cores of up-and-coming Kenton and St. Johns, where the mom-and-pop shops and cafés seem frozen in time.

PARK IT RIGHT THERE

Street parking is free, albeit timed in busier commercial areas. The Portland Streetcar doesn't reach this far, but if you're headed to Kenton, the **MAX** Yellow Line (page 5) from downtown stops on Interstate Avenue a short walk from North Denver Avenue. The area is also served by **TriMet** buses (page 5).

STROLLER ALONG

North Portland's elegant, bluff-skimming **University Park** neighborhood is a lovely place for a peaceful walk; start at the **University of Portland** (5000 N. Willamette Blvd.) and continue along North Willamette Boulevard, or weave through the residential neighborhoods.

SHOP HOP

In old-fashioned St. Johns, regale kids with tales of life before laptops and smartphones at **Blue Moon Camera and Machine** (8417 N. Lombard St.; 503-978-0333; www.bluemooncamera .com), then poke around the vintage shops, pick up tacos and piñatas at **Tienda y Taqueria Santa Cruz** (8630 N. Lombard St.; 503-289-2005; www.tiendasantacruz.com), and treasure hunt

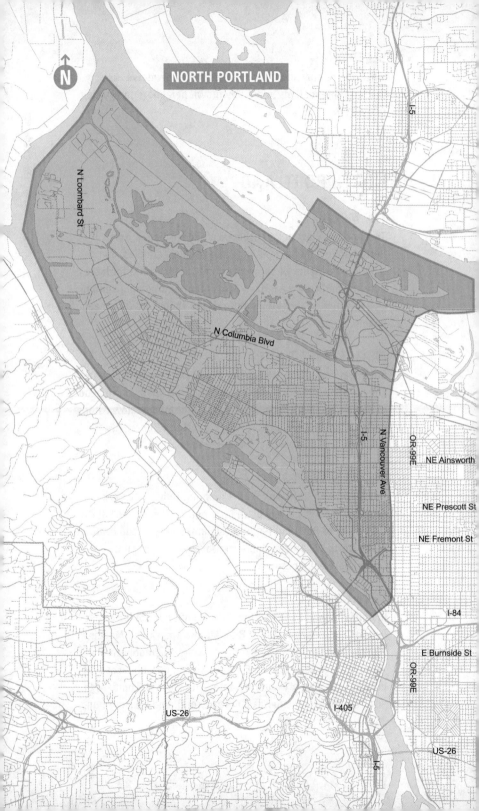

NORTH PORTLAND

N Loombard St

N Columbia Blvd

I-5

I-5

N Vancouver Ave

OR-99E

NE Ainsworth

NE Prescott St

NE Fremont St

I-84

E Burnside St

OR-99E

US-26

I-405

I-5

US-26

then slurp chocolate malts at **Pattie's Home Plate Café** (8501 N. Lombard St.; 503-285-5507)–part soda fountain, part thrift shop, part old-timey drugstore. And down at historic (but air-conditioned!) **McMenamins St. Johns Theater** (page 22), catch a first-run family flick for only $5 before 6 p.m., or check the listings at main-street favorite **St. Johns Twin Cinemas** (8704 N. Lombard St.; 503-286-1768; www.stjohnscinema.com), where kids are welcome up until 8 p.m.

Cute Downtown Kenton might be only a few blocks long, but make a morning of it with story time at the Kenton branch of the Multnomah County Library, and some selfie-taking with the **Paul Bunyan statue** that's adjacent to **Disjecta Contemporary Art Center** (8371 N. Interstate Ave.; 503-286-9449; www.disjecta.org), where you can visit the rotating gallery exhibit on weekends. Also worth a stop–**Bamboo Craftsman Company** (2104 N. Willis Blvd.; 503-285-5339; www.bamboocraftsman.com), where you can marvel at the bamboo structures that dot its garden, like the fantastical Bamboo Tower.

SNACK BREAK

When in St. Johns, start the morning with waffles and yogurt squeezers at mellow, play-area-endowed **Anna Bannanas** café (8716 N. Lombard St.; 503-286-2030), or fork in the Frisbee-size black-currant-and-hazelnut pancakes at **John Street Café** (8338 N. Lombard St.; 503-247-1066; www.johnstreetcafe.com). Lunch on cheap, tasty tacos and tostadas at **Taqueria Santa Cruz**, which feels like a secret thanks to its hidden location in the back of piñata-strung Tienda y Taqueria Santa Cruz (page 155). For healthy, local, and organic fare, **Proper Eats** (8638 N. Lombard St.; 503-445-2007; www.propereats.org) has kids' veggie bowls and quesadillas, plus a grocery section should you need snacks for a picnic at nearby **Cathedral Park** (page 118). If pizza's what's for dinner, try supercute **Signal Station Pizza** (8302 N. Lombard St.; 503-286-2257; www.signalstationpizza.com), set inside a former filling station. For sweet treats, don't miss the shakes and malts at **Pattie's Home Plate Café** (above) or the homemade doughnuts at neighborhood icon **Tulip Pastry Shop** (8322 N. Lombard St.; 503-286-3444; www.tulippastryshop.com). If you're in town on Saturday, visit the vibrant **St. Johns Farmers'**

Market (page 84), and be sure to stop at **Sweetheart** bakery's booth (www.sweetheartstjohns.com) for breathtakingly beautiful cakes, tarts, and other sweet treats. And if you're in town on a weekday, visit the **Moonstruck Chocolate Café** (page 225)–up until 2:30 p.m., you can catch a glimpse of the chocolate factory in action through the café's viewing window.

If touring Kenton, start the day with soul food and Southern 'tude at nonprofit **Po'Shines Café** (8139 N. Denver Ave.; 503-978-9000; www.poshines.com) run by the neighboring church. Or stuff in scrambles and sour-cream coffee cake at **Cup & Saucer Café** (8237 N. Denver Ave.; 503-247-6011; www.cupandsaucercafe.com), which has vegan and gluten-free options. For homemade pastries and granola, try pretty **Posie's Café** (page 206), well-known for its sizeable play area. When the lunch bell rings, bright, beautiful **Swift & Union** (8103 N. Denver Ave.; 503-206-4281; www.swiftandunion.com) dishes up a great kids' burger, grilled cheese, and fish fry. And if the group's pulling for pepperoni pies and meatballs, lively **Pizza Fino** (8225 N. Denver Ave.; 503-286-2100; www.finopdx.com) is open nightly. Or pick up a mess of house-smoked ribs at **Cason's Fine Meats** (8238 N. Denver Ave.; 503-285-4533), for the carnivores in your clan. For an afternoon pick-me-up, get a cup of Coava coffee and a *stroopwafel*–caramel or Nutella sandwiched between two thin waffle-esque wafers–at **Prince Coffee** (2030 N. Willis Blvd.; www.princecoffeepdx.com), tucked inside an upholstery shop just down the block from Paul Bunyan.

PARKS & REC

St. Johns' alfresco pride and joy is **Cathedral Park** (page 118), a gently sloping swath of lush green grass stretching from the railroad tracks to the Willamette River, directly underneath the grandly Gothic **St. Johns Bridge** (page 79). Bring your lunch and stay awhile, especially in fall, when the grassy grounds explode into color.

If you've got a disc-golf guru in the family, NoPo's nearly 90-acre **Pier Park** (N. Lombard St. and N. Bruce Ave.; www.portlandoregon.gov/parks/finder/index.cfm?propertyid=513&action=viewpark) is worth the pilgrimage–its Douglas-fir-shaded eighteen-hole course is considered one of the best and most challenging in the Pacific Northwest. And for those who don't have disc golf in their athletic repertoire, there's also a playground, skate park, soccer field, swimming pool, and splash pad.

PLAY DATE

Known for both its pastries *and* playroom, **Posie's Café** (page 206) in downtown Kenton is just the place for a *matcha* latte and avocado toast for Mom, and a hot chocolate and homemade cookie for *le bébé*.

HIDDEN GEMS

In mid-May, the popular annual **St. Johns Bizarre** (www .stjohnsbizarre.com) kicks off the city's summer street-fair season in style, with live music, food, arts-and-crafts booths, and kids' activities.

ON THE SIDE

From St. Johns it's about a ten-minute drive to **Sauvie Island** (page 47), land of riverfront beaches, berry and pumpkin patches, and farm-animal sightings galore.

SLEEP ON IT

If staying in St. Johns, bunk down at the Colony (7525 N. Richmond Ave.; 503-206-7051; www.thecolonystjohns.com), a rustic-chic event space that rents out its two apartments and stylishly refurbished 20-foot-long, 150-square-foot vintage travel trailer with adjacent private bathroom and shower.

NORTHWEST PORTLAND & THE PEARL DISTRICT

THE MOOD

Stretching from the fashionable Pearl District to the posh, mansion-lined West Hills, the city's northwest quadrant teems with trendy boutiques and hip restaurants, with lots of interesting history in between.

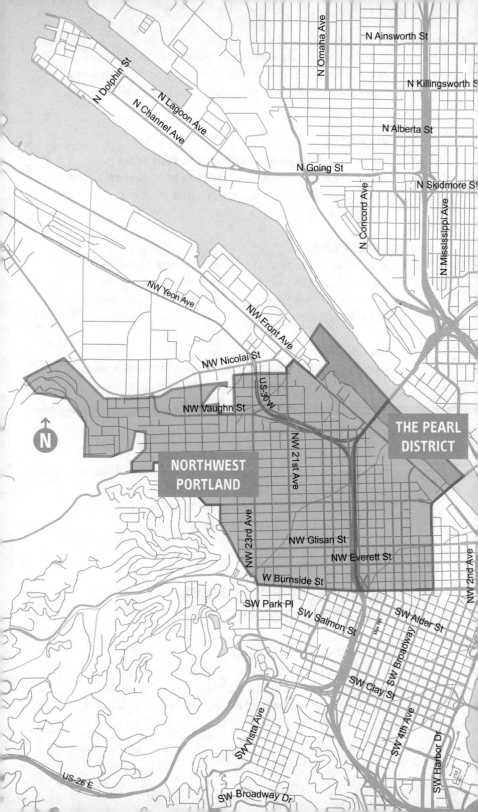

PARK IT RIGHT THERE

Street parking in the Pearl District is metered, while in the densely residential Alphabet District, parking spots are few and far between and either timed or metered (unless you venture up into the quiet residential neighborhoods west of NW 23rd Ave.). The **Portland Streetcar** (page 8) loops through the heart of the Pearl District and goes all the way to NW 23rd.

STROLLER ALONG

Orienting yourself in Northwest is easy—the streets are both in numerical order *and* alphabetized from Burnside to Vaughn, hence the hood's Alphabet District nickname. No matter which direction you head, this is one of the city's prime walking neighborhoods, especially as you pass from the hip, high-rise-dotted Pearl District into stately, historic-building-lined Northwest.

Intrepid walkers and stair climbers will relish the Chutes-and-Ladders-like landscape leading up into the West Hills, while those who like a little less incline can stick around the sweet little commercial core at NW Thurman Street and 24th Avenue—a hidden but happening hood that includes the Northwest library branch, **St. Honoré Boulangerie** (page 207), **Food Front Cooperative Grocery** (page 208), and a handful of boutiques. And if you are seeking a cool hike on a hot day, find the MacLeay Park entrance to **Forest Park** (page 68) and take a well-shaded stroll along the creek.

SHOP HOP

In the Pearl, find upscale baby gear and garb at **Posh Baby** (page 91); stop into local favorite **Hanna Andersson** (page 96) for slipover dresses and leggings; and shop unique toys, clothing, and baubles at **Moulé** (1225 NW Everett St.; 503-227-8530; www.moulestores.com).

Along NW 23rd, little ones will love **Child's Play** toy shop (page 88), while older kids will appreciate the fun vintage finds at **3 Monkeys** (811 NW 23rd Ave.; 503-222-5160) and the through-the-roof quirk factor at the **FreakyButTrue Peculiarium and Museum** (page 164), part shop, part superfreaky museum.

SNACK BREAK

In the Pearl, if a big breakfast is what you seek, there are several solid options, including longtime local charmer **Byways Cafe** (page 193), and fast and friendly **Daily Café in the Pearl** (page 193). If you are craving something simple and sweet, peruse the case of croissants, scones, and macaroons at **Nuvrei** (page 187), or stop into **Pearl Bakery** (page 190) for chocolate panini and orange-flecked *gibassier*, plus a peek at the flour-dusted inner workings of an artisan bakery.

If you need to stock up on groceries, snacks, or picnic provisions, try **Whole Foods Market** (page 211), which offers free parking, or eclectic **World Foods** (830 NW Everett St.; 503-802-0755; www.worldfoodsportland.com), a sure hit with the junior foodie who's fascinated by exotic ingredients and cuisines.

Come lunchtime, let the group choose their lunch adventure in the Ecotrust Building, which houses both **Hot Lips Pizza** (page 218) and **Laughing Planet Café** (page 203). Eat in, or if the weather's nice, cross the street and eat in **Jamison Square** (page 49), then get cones at **Cool Moon Ice Cream** (page 229).

As the offices empty and the watering holes fill up, dinnertime in the Pearl is a more adult-oriented affair, but area breweries are quite kid-friendly—try **BridgePort Brew Pub** (1313 NW Marshall St.; 503-241-3612; www.bridgeportbrew.com), or **Deschutes Brewery Public House** (210 NW 11th Ave.; 503-296-4906; www.deschutesbrewery.com).

For a hearty Portland-style breakfast in Northwest Portland, slip into a booth at **Besaw's** (page 192), or start the day with pastries at cozy **Ken's Artisan Bakery** (page 185), baguette with jam at **St. Honoré Boulangerie** (page 207), or Pig Newtons and mochas at **Jim & Patty's Coffee** (page 205).

Come midday, there's something for everyone at big, busy **Elephants Delicatessen** (page 223), or lunch Down Under with sausage rolls and sweet and savory pies at **Pacific Pie Company** (page 189). For gooey grilled cheese with tomato soup and a kids' play area, head for **Breken Kitchen** (page 222). Then line up at **Salt & Straw** (page 231) for triple scoops, or let the family chocolate fiends loose in **Moonstruck Chocolate Café** (page 225).

For dinner, get grass-fed buffalo burgers and nitrate-free hot dogs at **Dick's Kitchen** (page 198), go the tuna roll route at

Bamboo Sushi (page 211), or slurp noodles at Grassa (page 214), all centrally located along NW 23rd Avenue.

SIPS TIPS

In the Pearl, **World Cup Coffee** inside **Powell's City of Books** (page 38) lets you sip lattes while sifting through a stack of books, while **Daily Café in the Pearl**'s (page 193) liveliness level is perfect for kids. In Northwest try **St. Honoré Boulangerie** (page 207), or locals' hangout **the Clearing Café** (2772 NW Thurman St.; 503-841-6240; www.theclearingcafe.com), a great coffee, bagel, and Berrylicious smoothie stop en route to Forest Park.

PARKS & REC

For being one of the city's densest urban neighborhoods, the Pearl District has excellent parks—**Jamison Square** (page 49) delights with its famous fountain, **Tanner Springs Park** (NW 10th Ave. and Marshall St.) offers peaceful people-watching on the grassy steps, and **the Fields Park** (page 53) has a playground, off-leash dog park, and big grassy expanse for frolicking and picnicking.

Up in Northwest, there's a cute playground at pet-friendly **Couch Park** (NW 19th Ave. and NW Glisan St.); huge lawns and a popular playground at **Wallace Park** (1600 NW 25th Ave.) adjoining Chapman Elementary School; and, of course, the granddaddy of all Portland green spaces, **Forest Park** (page 68).

PLAY DATE

If the natives are restless, head to **Playdate PDX** (page 62), an indoor play space and café, or drop in to an art session at **Portland Child Art Studio** (page 27). See if a show's playing at **NW Children's Theater** (page 29)—while a production is sometimes more serious in nature and best for older kids, most are silly enough to entertain little ones. Speaking of silly, check the **ComedySportz Improv 4 Kids** (page 28) calendar for the family jokers. And for an interactive afternoon with your junior foodie, sign up for **Forktown Food Tours'** delicious *and* educational food-fueled romp (page 86) through the Alphabet District.

HIDDEN GEMS

One of Northwest Portland's most fun (and sweat-inducing) secrets is its stairs—the long, steep staircases that dot the West Hills, Chutes and Ladders style. Finding them yourself can take a while, so pack a copy of Laura O. Foster's *The Portland Stairs Book*, which highlights the best routes.

Be it jokes, magic tricks, candy, bug-topped sundaes, or a graphic alien dissection exhibit, there's plenty to see and gasp about at in the unabashedly odd **FreakyButTrue Peculiarium and Museum** (2234 NW Thurman St.; 503-227-3164; www.peculiarium .com). There's a small entrance fee to the museum, but dogs and those wearing a "decent costume" get in for free. As some of the exhibits are of a rather gruesome nature, it's best for older kids, especially those who are into aliens, zombies, and eating bugs; to get a taste of what's in store, peruse the website, which offers helpful testimonials from "surviving customers."

And in September, Northwest Portland's Chapman Elementary School hosts the famous **Swift Watch** (page 10), when everyone congregates on the hillside to watch the Vaux's swifts dive into the school chimney turned migratory roost.

ON THE SIDE

From the Pearl District and Northwest, it's about a fifteen-minute drive to **Sauvie Island** (page 47) for river stomping, berry or pumpkin picking, or lighthouse hunting.

SLEEP ON IT

Tucked into a peaceful corner of the Pearl District (well, if you don't count the train tracks a block away), this mellow yellow **Residence Inn** (1150 NW 9th Ave.; 503-220-1339; www.marriott .com/hotels/travel/pdxpd-residence-inn-portland-downtown -pearl-district) is a sleek but comfortable pick, with spacious, modern rooms (that include sofa beds), free daily breakfast, and an indoor pool.

A perennial favorite that kids will *never* forget, thanks in part to the big jars of candy scattered about, Northwest Portland's fun, zany **Inn at Northrup Station** (2025 NW Northrup St.; 503-224-0543; www.northrupstation.com) boasts big, brightly decorated rooms with kitchenettes and balconies, free on-site parking, and a streetcar stop right outside the front door.

SELLWOOD-MORELAND

THE MOOD

Just a ten-minute drive from Downtown Portland, Sellwood has the nostalgic feel of a small town, with the mom-and-pop shops, antique malls, old-fashioned amusement park, and turn-of-the-century community pool house to match.

PARK IT RIGHT THERE

Street parking is free, albeit timed in busier commercial areas. The Portland Streetcar doesn't reach this far, but **TriMet** buses (page 5) do. If going by bike, take the car-free **Springwater Corridor** trail (page 56) all the way from the Inner Southeast waterfront near OMSI to the base of SE Spokane Street, then head east up the hill.

STROLLER ALONG

Family-friendly Sellwood's peaceful residential streets make for serene strolling, but if you'd like a little action, there are two main commercial areas—the intersection of SE Milwaukie Avenue and SE Bybee Boulevard, and the stretch of SE 13th Avenue between SE Malden Street and SE Tacoma Street. On SE Milwaukie Avenue, you'll find the city's nitty-gritty—grocery stores, a hardware store, coffee shops, the historic Moreland Theater, and antique malls with a gimlet-eyed staff. For a less trafficky, more boutiquey experience, keep going to SE 13th Avenue.

SHOP HOP

Right around SE Malden Street, the quaint bungalows of SE 13th Avenue give way to a retail-rich stretch, where you'll find gems like **Oodles 4 Kids** (page 90), **Cloud Cap Games** (page 88), and the Sellwood branch of arts-and-crafts temple **Collage** (page 26). Older kids will get a kick out of **Sock Dreams'** zany collection of foot warmers (8005 SE 13th Ave.; 503-232-3330; www.sockdreams.com), and if anyone in the family needs to add to their fleece collection, there's a **Columbia Sportswear Outlet** (1323 SE Tacoma St.; 503-238-0118; www.columbia.com). Even if you don't have canning and cheese-making aspirations, it's worth a trip into **Portland Homestead Supply Co.** (8012 SE 13th Ave.; 503-233-8691; www.homesteadsupplyco.com) just to visit the resident goats and chickens.

SNACK BREAK

For your morning meal get hearty breakfast sandwiches at neighborhood hangout **Grand Central Bakery** (page 185), or go the biscuits 'n' gravy route at **Bertie Lou's Café** (8051 SE 17th Ave.; 503-239-1177), where kids can try their hand at a wall-worthy napkin-art masterpiece. For a simple spread of steamers, hot chocolate, bagels, and cinnamon buns, there's jovial **Blue Kangaroo Coffee Roasters** (7901 SE 13th Ave.; 503-756-0224; www.bluekangaroocoffee.com). Come lunch- and dinnertime, it seems like the whole town's nabbing noodles and sesame balls at **Jade Bistro & Patisserie** (page 212), or divide and conquer at the fun food-cart pod at SE Lexington Street and SE 13th Avenue, next to the Sellwood Antique Mall. If celebrating, cozy up in a well-worn wooden booth at popular **Gino's** (page 213), where kids are greeted with a smile and a snack plate.

PARKS & REC

Pretty **Sellwood Park** (page 54) is laced with wide, flat walking trails and picnic tables, plus it's home to the historic **Sellwood Outdoor Pool** (page 50), a pool so cool it attracts kids from all over the city, so expect cramped quarters on hot afternoons.

Just south of the park, SE Spokane Street points toward the Willamette River, where you'll find the **Springwater Corridor**, a car-free, multiuse pathway that grazes the **Sellwood Riverfront Park** (SE Spokane St. and SE Oaks Park Way; www.portlandoregon.gov/parks/finder/index.cfm?&propertyid=668 &action=viewpark), **Oaks Park** (page 72), and **Oaks Bottom Wildlife Refuge** (page 70), before feeding into the **Eastbank Esplanade** (page 58) near **OMSI** (page 66). Flat and scenic, with unparalleled river views, it's lovely whether you're on bike, trike, skates, or foot.

A half mile east of Downtown Sellwood sits **Westmoreland Park** (page 52), a beautifully developed 42-acre park with a little bit of everything—baseball diamonds, tennis courts, picnic tables, streams and ponds, and an all-natural teaching playground where kids can get busy with boulders, blocks, sticks, stumps, sand, and, in the summertime, water pumps.

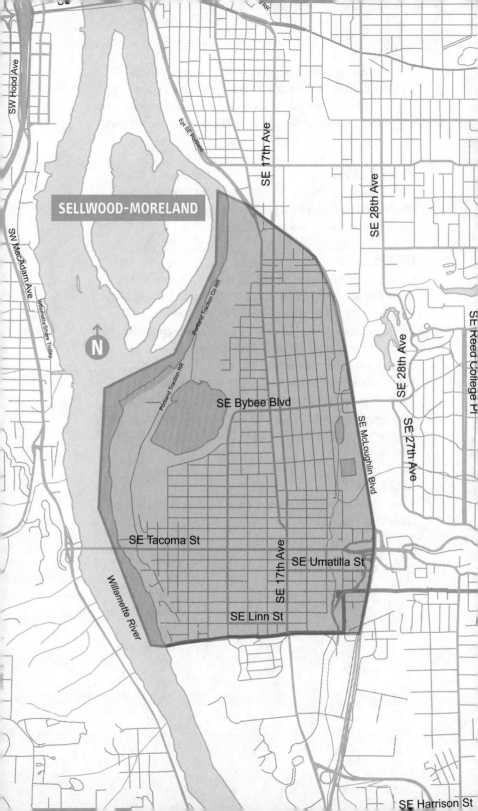

SELLWOOD-MORELAND

N

SW Hood Ave

SW MacAdam Ave

Willamette Shore Trolley

End SE Portland RR

Portland Traction Co RR

Portland Traction RR

SE 17th Ave

SE 28th Ave

SE 28th Ave

SE 27th Ave

SE Reed College Pl

SE McLoughlin Blvd

SE Bybee Blvd

SE Tacoma St

SE 17th Ave

SE Umatilla St

SE Linn St

Willamette River

SE Harrison St

PLAY DATE

Sellwood happens to be home to one of the city's most prime playdate destinations, **Oaks Park** (page 72), where kids of all ages can spend hours riding coasters, playing carnie games, and eating cotton candy. If the weather's iffy, take cover in the park's roller rink.

HIDDEN GEMS

From Sellwood it's a five-minute drive to the **Crystal Springs Rhododendron Garden** (page 31), a magical land of bridges, secret hiding places, and ravenous ducks.

ON THE SIDE

From Sellwood drive ten minutes to the world headquarters of **Bob's Red Mill** (13521 SE Pheasant Ct., Milwaukie; 503-654-3215; www.bobsredmill.com/tour-our-world-headquarters.html), which grinds its whole-grain flours using quartz millstones sourced from century-old mills. Take the free seventy-five-minute factory tour (weekdays at 10 a.m.), then drive a mile to the **Whole Grain Store, Restaurant & Bakery** (5000 SE International Way; 503-607-6455; www.bobsredmill.com), where you can scarf stacks of buckwheat pancakes and Golden Spurtle–winning steel-cut oatmeal, then shop the five-hundred-plus bulk bins.

SLEEP ON IT

There aren't any hotels in Sellwood, but you're quite close to Downtown (page 132).

SOUTHEAST PORTLAND

THE MOOD

For being so close to Downtown, the quiet bungalow- and cherry-tree-lined streets of Southeast Portland feel a world away. With the exception of the busy industrial inner waterfront, most neighborhoods are heavily residential, with petite pockets of shops and restaurants perfect for quick and easy exploring.

PARK IT RIGHT THERE

Street parking is free, albeit timed in busier commercial areas. The Inner Southeast is serviced by the **Portland Streetcar** (page 8), which makes regular stops along Grand Avenue and Martin Luther King Jr. Boulevard, and **TriMet** buses (page 5) run through all neighborhoods.

STROLLER ALONG

Southeast Portland's residential neighborhoods are prime walking territory, with peaceful, beautifully landscaped streets, and fetching architecture. One of the loveliest routes runs through **Ladd's Addition**, a historic neighborhood sandwiched between SE Hawthorne Boulevard and SE Division Street, and SE 12th Avenue and SE 20th Avenue. Designed in the image of L'Enfant Plan of Washington, DC, the neighborhood's diagonal streets form a web around the park-like central traffic circle, and there are four diamond-shaped rose gardens tucked within. Start on the outskirts at **Farina Bakery** (page 184) for tea and macaroons or darling **Oui Presse** coffee shop (1740 SE Hawthorne Blvd.; 503-384-2160; www.oui-presse.com) for cappuccinos and pistachio cake, then get lost in the Ladd's alleyways, stopping to smell the roses along the way.

SHOP HOP & SNACK BREAK

While Inner Southeast Portland is still very much a working industrial neighborhood, this gritty stretch of waterfront is full of eating and shopping treasures. Older kids can spend hours combing through the multiple floors of treasure/junk at **City Liquidators** (823 SE 3rd Ave.; 503-230-7716; www.cityliquidators.com), while those with bohemian sensibilities will never want

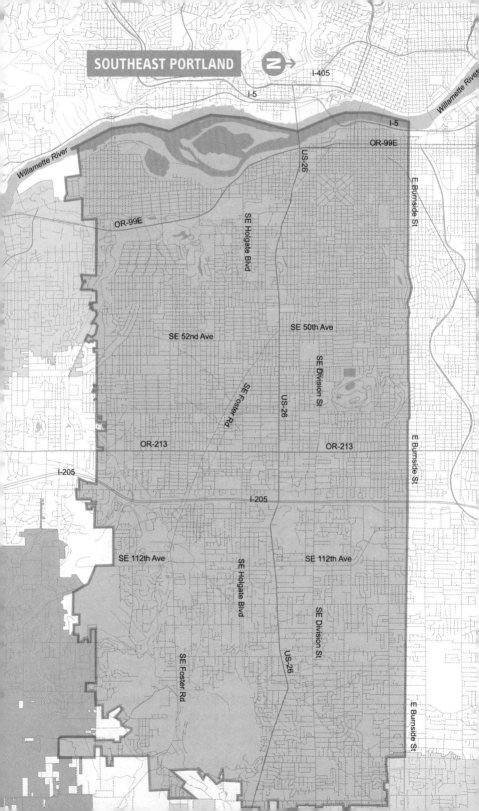

SOUTHEAST PORTLAND

Willamette River

Willamette River

I-405

I-5

I-5

I-5

OR-99E

OR-99E

US-26

E Burnside St

SE Holgate Blvd

SE 50th Ave

SE 52nd Ave

SE Division St

SE Foster Rd

US-26

OR-213

OR-213

I-205

I-205

E Burnside St

SE 112th Ave

SE 112th Ave

SE Holgate Blvd

SE Division St

SE Foster Rd

US-26

E Burnside St

to leave **Cargo** (81 SE Yamhill St.; 503-209-8349; www.cargoinc
.com). If Halloween or a family party is nigh, pick up party
favors and costumes at **the Lippman Company** (50 SE Yamhill
St.; 503-239-7007; www.lippmancompany.com). Come lunchtime
hit bustling **Boke Bowl** (page 212), for the kids' ramen *and*
house-made Twinkies; for dinner, eccentric **Le Bistro Montage**
(page 217) offers nine types of mac 'n' cheese, and just this once,
try *not* to clean your plate, because leftovers are woven into
elaborate foil animal sculptures.

Follow busy Burnside Street east to Kerns, for a stroll
along popular retail and restaurant row 28th Avenue. Browse
exquisite **Artemesia** (110 SE 28th Ave.; 503-232-8224; www
.collagewithnature.com), purveyor of everything needed to build
a terrific terrarium, and let teen trendsetters put together one-
of-a-kind looks at **Wanderlust** vintage boutique (2804 SE Ankeny
St.; 206-898-4308; www.shopwanderlustvintage.com). A few
blocks north, pop into bright and cheery **Polliwog** (page 91) for
board books and baby clothes.

Eating well is not a problem around here—overeating
might be though (*if* you consider that a problem). For a classic
breakfast in a charming diner setting, slide into a booth or picnic
table at **City State Diner** (page 193), or pick up hot chocolate and
homemade cardamom buns at **Crema Coffee + Bakery** (2728 SE
Ankeny St.; 503-234-0206; www.cremabakery.com). Come lunch,
don't forget to Instagram your gorgeous cheese tray, mac 'n'
cheese, and espresso-dusted soft serve at **Cheese & Crack Snack
Shop** (page 216) before you eat it. Or set sail for **the Ocean**
(NE Glisan St. and NE 24th Ave.), a collection of microrestaurants
slinging everything from tacos to burgers to spaghetti and
meatballs. Top your meal off with a peanut-butter-chocolate
pie hole from darling **Pie Spot** (page 233), where on Fridays
at 4 p.m., you can catch the weekly **Story Time with Olive &
Dingo** (page 39). Come dinnertime, line up early to claim a
table at popular **Ken's Artisan Pizza** (page 219), or if you've got
sophisticated eaters, let the chopsticks fly at sleek **Bamboo Sushi**
(page 211). For dessert, head straight for **Staccato Gelato** (page
232) or **Fifty Licks** (page 230).

While mostly a commuter corridor for the surrounding
residential neighborhoods, particular pockets of SE Belmont are

worth investigating. Heading east from Downtown, past **Grand Central Bowl** (page 13) and **Colonel Summers Park** (SE Salmon St. and SE 20th Ave.), you'll come to the hood's cute two-block commercial core, which for our purposes starts at **Saint Cupcake** (page 227) and ends at the **Avalon Theatre and Wunderland** arcade (page 21). If it's lunch- or dinnertime, kids can choose from burgers and sweet potato fries at **Dick's Kitchen** (page 198), Mexican food with a healthy bent at **Laughing Planet Café** (page 203), or straightforward slices at **Straight From New York Pizza** (3330 SE Belmont St.; 971-279-5970; www.sfnypizza.com). For dessert, take your beret off and stay awhile at ooh-la-la little **Suzette Creperie** (3342 SE Belmont St.; 503-546-0892; www .suzettepdx.com).

The Southeast's most vibrant retail row is quirky SE Hawthorne Boulevard, which has preserved much of its funky '70s-era charm. Sidewalks are narrow and get crowded, so sideline the stroller if possible, and keep a close eye on little ones. Before you go, check showtimes at **McMenamins Bagdad Theater** (page 22), easily one of the coolest places in the city to see a family flick.

Kids will love the cozy eastern annex of **Powell's Books on Hawthorne** (page 96), which has a large children's book section, and its nearby sister shop, **Powell's Books for Home and Garden**, which has a large children's *toy* section. Older kids will get a kick out of the silly cards and gag gifts at **Presents of Mind** (3633 SE Hawthorne Blvd.; 503-230-7740; www.presentsofmind.tv), while wee ones will want to spend some time taking the merchandise for a test run in **Kids at Heart Toys** (page 90). Vintage-hunting tweens and teens can roam the racks at **Buffalo Exchange** (1420 SE 37th Ave.; 503-234-1302; www.buffaloexchange.com), **Red Light Clothing Exchange** (3590 SE Hawthorne Blvd.; 503-963-8888; www.redlightclothingexchange.com), and the small, boutiquey **Goodwill** (3557 SE Hawthorne Blvd.; 503-231-3095; www.goodwill.org).

You can go a few ways for morning meal here—health hounds, join the line for blueberry smoothies and banana walnut pancakes at organic, gluten-free **Harlow** (page 188); those who want a standard bacon 'n' eggs breakfast can queue up at popular **Cup & Saucer Café** (3566 SE Hawthorne Blvd.;

503-236-6001; www.cupandsaucercafe.com) or **Bread and Ink Café** (3610 SE Hawthorne Blvd.; 503-239-4756; www .breadandinkcafe.com). If your family's wild about waffles, turn the corner to find (literal) hole-in-the-wall **Waffle Window** (page 197). Holey food lovers, don't miss **Blue Star Donuts** (page 228), and if your sweet tooth skews more sweet 'n' swirly, embrace **the Maple Parlor**'s "Sundaes for everyone" motto (3538 SE Hawthorne Blvd.; 503-206-4757; www.themapleparlor .com). For tacos and *agua frescas*, try perennially popular **Por Qué No** (page 203) or brake for bike-tire-size pies at equally adored **Apizza Scholls** (page 218). For dessert, **Ruby Jewel** (page 231) is a few doors down—for the best deal and most variety, get the ice-cream-cone-shaped scoop sampler.

Giving Hawthorne a run for its money as the most popular Southeast dining and shopping destination is previously sleepy Division Street, where an influx of development has created a curious mix of modern and old-school Portland. Most of the retail on Division Street is adult oriented, but older culinarily inclined kids will enjoy a poke around cozy **Mirador Kitchen & Home** (2106 SE Division St.; 503-231-5175; www .miradorkitchenandhome.com), exquisite **Little Otsu** stationery shop (3225 SE Division St.; 503-236-8673; www.littleotsu.com), arts-and-crafts supply mecca **Collage** (page 26), and **Carter & Rose** (page 24), a cool homewares and ceramics shop that hosts summer art camps and kid-friendly "open clay" studio time. Thrifters and collectors can root through the affordable treasures at **Village Merchants** (4035 SE Division St.; 503-234-6343; www.villagemerchants.net), which happens to share its parking lot with one of the city's best taco trucks, **Taqueria Lindo Michoacan**.

Breakfast-wise you'll do very well in the Division hood. For big ol' biscuit sandwiches, join the **Pine State Biscuits** queue (page 195), or line up at **Little T Baker** (page 187) for bacon-and-egg croissant sandwiches and pear Danishes. Snack on house-made pastries and granola at **Roman Candle Baking Co.** (page 190), or cross the street for biscuits 'n' gravy at homey **Lauretta Jean's** (page 186). A couple of blocks off Division, on SE Clinton Street, find beloved **Café Broder SE** (page 192), legendary for its skillets of soft, doughy just-baked *aebleskiver*, a.k.a. Danish pancake balls, served with lemon curd and lingonberry jam for dipping. For lunch and dinner if the weather is fair, hit the open-air **Tidbit Food Farm and Garden** (page 201) food-cart pod; with nearly twenty carts peddling everything from mac 'n' cheese–heaped hot dogs to banana-and-Nutella-stuffed waffle sandwiches, there's something for everyone. If the weather is foul, order huge pepperoni pies at affable **Scottie's Pizza Parlor** (page 221); nosh on *vada pav* and mango lassis at **Bollywood Theater** (page 213); or dig into tacos, nachos, and black bean bowls at **Stella Taco** (page 204). For dessert, queue up for cones at **Salt & Straw** (page 231) or **Fifty Licks** (page 230), organic fro-yo at **Eb & Bean** (page 230), or extraordinary gelatos and sorbets at **Pinolo Gelato** (page 230).

PARKS & REC

Fortify with cardamom coffee crumble cake and fried egg sandwiches at hidden neighborhood gem **Coquine** (6839 SE Belmont St.; 503-384-2483; www.coquinepdx.com), then cross the street and walk a few blocks to **Mt. Tabor Park** (page 53). Or follow cherry-tree-lined SE Salmon Street from **Colonel Summers Park** (page 172) up to the public playground at **Sunnyside Elementary School** (3421 SE Salmon St.), then walk over to SE Belmont Street for a frosting-topped treat at **Saint Cupcake** (page 227). And for one of the prettiest park walks in Portland, make the **Laurelhurst Park** (page 55) loop, hit the playground, then continue down to NE 28th Avenue for scoops at **Staccato Gelato** (page 232).

PLAY DATE

On a rainy day, cart older kids to the **Avalon Theatre** (page 21), a second-run movie theater that plays all family flicks (nothing over PG-13) for a few dollars a show, and has a **Wunderland** arcade, with over one hundred nickel games. For younger kids there's the **Southside Swap & Play** (page 65) in laid-back Woodstock, with 3,000 square feet of indoor play space. It's members only, but you can sign up for a group tour, then stay and play and mingle afterward.

HIDDEN GEMS

For a totally unique dessert experience, check out **Rimsky-Korsakoffee House** (707 SE 12th Ave.; 503-232-2640; cash only), Portland's most venerable dessert house (literally, it's in a historic house), which mesmerizes guests with spinning tables, live piano music, ooey-gooey desserts, and a delightfully creepy bathroom.

ON THE SIDE

From the heart of SE Division, it's a quick ten-minute drive south to the often-overlooked **Crystal Springs Rhododendron Garden** (page 31), a magical land of bridges, secret hiding places, and a densely inhabited duck pond.

SLEEP ON IT

There aren't any kid-suitable hotels in this neck of the urban woods, but you're just minutes from Downtown (page 132).

SUBURBS

BEAVERTON

THE MOOD
Named for the beaver-dam-dotted swamplands that have long been paved over, and famous for housing Nike's international headquarters, Beaverton boasts a small old-fashioned downtown, beautiful parks, and one of the biggest and best farmers' markets around.

PARK IT RIGHT THERE
Most street parking is free, albeit timed in busier commercial areas. The Portland Streetcar doesn't reach this far, but **TriMet** buses (page 5) do, and the **MAX** Red Line (page 5) connects the Portland airport and Downtown with the Beaverton Transit Center, where commuters can transfer to the Blue Line to continue on to Hillsboro.

STROLLER ALONG
If a nature walk is calling your name, explore **Tualatin Hills Nature Park** (15655 SW Millikan Way; www.thprd.org/parks-and-trails/detail/tualatin-hills-nature-park), **Cooper Mountain Nature Park** (18895 SW Kemmer Rd.; www.thprd.org/parks-and-trails/detail/cooper-mountain-nature-park), or the **Fanno Creek Greenway Trail** (www.thprd.org). Otherwise, there's a small but pretty city park outside the downtown library, and on Saturdays, the **Beaverton Farmers Market** (page 83) is prime walking and people-watching territory—if the weather's warm, splash around in the fountain after shopping, then walk over to **Beaverton Bakery** (12375 SW Broadway; 503-646-7136; www.beavertonbakery.com) for red velvet cupcakes and butter crispies.

SHOP HOP

At **Progress Ridge TownSquare** (14805 SW Barrows Rd.), find locally owned favorites **Piccolo Mondo Toys** (page 91) and **Posh Baby** (page 91), and before heading into the Cedar Hills area, check the events calendar at **Powell's Books at Cedar Hills Crossing** (3415 SW Cedar Hills Blvd.; 800-878-7323; www.powells.com/locations/powells-books-at-cedar-hills-crossing) to see if any of your favorite children's book authors are doing a reading that day. To shop the usual chain-store suspects, head to neighboring suburb Tigard's popular **Washington Square Mall** (9585 SW Washington Square Rd.; www.shopwashingtonsquare.com) and open-air **Bridgeport Village** mall (7455 SW Bridgeport Rd.; www.bridgeport-village.com).

SNACK BREAK

When in Beaverton, take advantage of the fun and affordable proliferation of ethnic eats. Experiment with the exotic foods and colorful candies at **Uwajimaya** market (10500 SW Beaverton-Hillsdale Hwy.; 503-643-4512; www.uwajimaya.com), slurp noodles at **Taste of Sichuan** (16261 NW Cornell Rd.; 503-629-7001; www.tasteofsichuan.com) or **Duh Kuh Bee** (12590 SW 1st St.; 503-643-5388), or take your Japan-obsessed teen or tween to überauthentic **Yuzu** (4130 SW 117th Ave.; 503-350-1801) for *kara age* and ramen. For *horchata* and bean-and-cheese *pupusas*, try friendly **Sabor Salvadoreño** (3460 SW 185th Ave.; 503-356-2376), or homey **Gloria's Secret Café** (12500 SW Broadway St.; 503-268-2124), which serves formidable tamale and taco plates. And for a quick trip to Scandinavia, brunch at **Broder Söder** (page 192) in the Scandinavian Heritage Foundation's **Nordia House** (www.scanheritage.org), where you can walk around the gorgeous grounds, and if the timing is right, perhaps shop a Nordic rummage sale.

PARKS & REC

If heading west on US Route 26, pull off at exit 65 and make your way to 16-acre Bethany Meadows Park, a.k.a. **Pirate Park** (www.thprd.org), an *arrr*-stremely popular play structure that resembles a pirate ship. For a light hike on easy-to-navigate trails, some paved, visit the 222-acre **Tualatin Hills Nature Park** wildlife preserve (page 176), a wetland and mixed-forest habitat that will captivate your budding botanist or biologist. For forests and prairie lands, try 230-acre **Cooper Mountain Nature Park** (page 176) and if a bike ride's on the books, pedal the peaceful **Fanno Creek Greenway Trail** (page 176).

PLAY DATE
Extreme sports are big in the burbs, where you'll find everything from **Sky High Sports Trampoline Park** (page 61) and **Stoneworks Climbing Gym** (page 19) to **SuperPlay**'s super hybrid (page 14)—a combination bowling alley, laser-tag arena, *and* arcade. Or for a walk on the not-so-wild side, bowl a few frames at **Sunset Lanes** (page 14), play alien-themed black-light mini golf at **Glowing Greens** (page 16), or just mellow out with a movie at **Valley Cinema Pub** (page 23).

HIDDEN GEMS
Board game lovers will boggle over the inventory at the **Interactive Museum of Gaming and Puzzlery** (page 59), which houses one of the largest public collections of board games, puzzles, and collectibles in the world—over five thousand and counting. For a small admission fee (or board game donation in lieu of the fee), anyone in the mood for a round of Scrabble, Jenga, or Alien Autopsy can drop in and play for the day.

ON THE SIDE
If you're road-tripping northwest to **Roloff Farms** (page 123) for fall pumpkin-patch festivities, grab cheeseburgers and onion rings at historic **Helvetia Tavern** (10275 NW Helvetia Rd.; 503-647-5286) en route. If heading southwest to **Smith Berry Barn** (page 118), try **South Store Cafe** (24485 SW Scholls Ferry Rd.; 503-628-1920; www.southstorecafe.com) for fresh-baked pastries and sausage-gravy-slathered buttermilk biscuits.

SLEEP ON IT
If staying in Portland proper isn't possible, the **Hilton Garden Inn** in Beaverton (15520 NW Gateway Ct.; 503-439-1717; www.hilton .com) is clean, comfortable, and centrally located.

HILLSBORO

THE MOOD

Anchored by Intel, this gentle giant of a suburb in Portland's "Silicon Forest" is the fifth-largest city in the state. With a cute downtown core, lots of big-box shopping, nearly two dozen parks, and significant historical sites, Hillsboro has plenty to see and do in Hillsboro, and its proximity to wine country and the coast make it a solid road-trip pit stop.

PARK IT RIGHT THERE

Most street parking is free, albeit timed in busier commercial areas. The Portland Streetcar doesn't reach this far, but **TriMet** (page 5) buses do, and the **MAX** Blue Line (page 5) ends in Downtown Hillsboro.

STROLLER ALONG

Hillsboro is spread out, so match your stroll to your mood. Want to do some window-shopping? Aim for the **Streets of Tanasbourne** mall (page 120), or wheel around the small storefronts and Pleasantville-esque suburban sprawl of **Orenco Station** (www.orencostation.com). Downtown Hillsboro is a sleepily charming throwback; try to time your trip with the Saturday-morning farmers' market. Get off the sidewalks and onto the trails at lovely 60-acre **Rood Bridge Park** (4000 SE Rood Bridge Rd.; www.hillsboro-oregon.gov/index.aspx?page=895), or do a bit of bird-watching at the **Jackson Bottom Wetlands Preserve** (2600 SW Hillsboro Hwy.; www.jacksonbottom.org).

SHOP HOP

The area's main retail draw is the **Streets of Tanasbourne** (page 120), a stylish outdoor mall anchored by Macy's and REI. If shopping local, go downtown, where you'll find mom-and-pop shops like **Let's Play** toy store (263 E. Main St.; 503-640-8301; www.letsplaytoys.com). On Saturday morning, visit the **Hillsboro Farmers' Market** (page 83), where over one hundred vendors fill Main Street with fresh produce, arts and crafts, and live entertainment. Mixed-used "town center" **Orenco Station** is also a popular shop stop; anchored by **New Seasons Market** (page 210), it's also home to **iSpark Toys** (925 NE Orenco Station Loop; 503-207-6570; www.isparktoys.com) and hosts its own Sunday farmers' market in the summer.

SNACK BREAK

Located just off State Route 26 at the Cornelius Pass exit, **McMenamins Cornelius Pass Roadhouse** (4045 NW Cornelius Pass Rd.; 503-640-6174; www.mcmenamins.com/cpr) is a good bet for the whole family, especially if you have little ones who need to run around. Downtown, find solid Mexican food at family-owned **Amelia's** (105 NE 4th Ave.; 503-615-0191; www.ameliasmexicanfood.com) and excellent sushi at **Syun Izakaya** (209 NE Lincoln St.; 503-640-3131; www.syun-izakaya.com). Or if shopping at the Streets of Tanasbourne mall and craving something other than the usual chain fare, stop into popular **Chennai Masala** (2088 NW Stucki Ave.; 503-531-9500; www.chennaimasala.net) for the Indian buffet (there's a kids' menu, which spans *dosas*, fish 'n' chips, and chicken strips). If exploring Orenco Station, twenty-four-hour **Ava Roasteria** (936 NE Orenco Station Loop; 971-713-2136; www.avaroasteria.com) tempts with lavender lattes and pretty pastries, and you'll find solid French fare at **La Provence** (page 186).

PARKS & REC

Less than 2 miles south of Downtown Hillsboro, 725-acre **Jackson Bottom Wetlands Preserve** (page 179) is webbed with short, easy walking trails. Start at the 12,000-square-foot education center and tour the interactive exhibits (including the popular bald eagle nest), shop the nature store, then hit the trails for wildlife spotting. On Wednesdays, January through June, from noon to 1 p.m., enjoy **Lunch with the Birds**, a free, volunteer-led bird-watching lunch outing that skips around to different area parks. And for an easy, shady walk on paved trails, plus a playground, picnic tables, and bathrooms, meander around beautiful **Rood Bridge Park** (page 179), about 4 miles southeast of Jackson Bottom.

PLAY DATE

Kids of all ages will happily hoop it up at **Out of This World Pizza and Play** (6255 NW Century Blvd.; 503-629-8700; www.outofthisworld.net) a huge, high-ceilinged warehouse housing everything from a rocket play structure and inflatable obstacle course to a mini racetrack and arcade games. And from June through September, pick up cheap tickets to see the **Hillsboro Hops** (4460 NW 229th Ave.; 503-640-0887; www.milb.com /index.jsp?sid=t419), the city's minor league baseball team.

HIDDEN GEMS

Quite literally, the gems are hidden at the **Rice Northwest Rock and Mineral Museum** (26385 NW Groveland Dr.; 503-647-2418; www.ricenorthwestmuseum.org), a former home that now displays one of the country's finest collections of rocks, minerals, fossils, meteorites, lapidary art, and gemstones. If your little rock hound has a specimen they'd like ID'd, call or e-mail ahead of time, and the museum curator can help.

If downtown, stop by the **Washington County Museum** (120 E. Main St.; 503-645-5353; www.washingtoncountymuseum .org) in the Hillsboro Civic Center for insights into the region's rich history. On the second Saturday of the month, June through September, admission is free from 10 a.m. to 1 p.m., and there are free kids' hands-on history and art activities.

The **Hillsboro Brookwood Library** (2850 NE Brookwood Pkwy.; 503-615-6500; www.hillsboro-oregon.gov/index .aspx?page=89) is an unexpected oasis—huge and modern (they've even got a 3-D printer), it's beautifully landscaped and looks out over a peaceful pond. The library events calendar always has something fun on offer, from Toddler Time to Storytelling with Jacque.

ON THE SIDE

Come pumpkin-patch time, Hillsboro is convenient to several of the area's most popular destinations, like **Roloff Farms** (page 123) and **Lakeview Farms** (page 122). You'll also pass through the city en route to North Plains' **Pumpkin Ridge Zip Tour** (page 71) and Forest Grove's **Tree to Tree Adventure Park** (page 71), plus it makes a good pit stop en route to the Oregon Coast.

SLEEP ON IT

Live like one of the locals at Orenco Station, except with room service, at **the Orenco Hotel** (1457 NE Orenco Station Pkwy.; 888-503-7094; www.theorenco.com).

PART 3

BEST EATS, SWEETS & SIPS

Eat often and well in this food-obsessed town, where seasoned junior foodies request their favorite sushi joint by name, and farmers' market–savvy small fry can identify their Oregon strawberry of choice by variety (Hoods, of course).

But even if your kiddo's a selective eater, there's tons out there to tempt even the most cautious palate—from **Grassa**'s basic spaghetti and meatballs (page 214), to **Lovely's Fifty Fifty**'s so-good-you'll-want-one-too kid's cheese pizza (page 219), to **Grilled Cheese Grill**'s namesake (page 200), served with or without crusts.

And of course, there's everyone's favorite course: dessert—chomp on freshly made mini doughnuts drizzled with Nutella; get gummy bears and chalk licorice stuck between your teeth; and slurp scoops and swirls at one of the nine ice cream, gelato, and frozen-yogurt shops profiled in **Sweets** (page 224).

So without further ado, here are the city's finest family-friendly restaurants, bakeries, pizzerias, ice-cream parlors, sweet shops, burger joints, coffeehouses, food carts, and even a few first-rate markets—in case you find yourself in a grab-and-go situation.

Rumbly tumblies, get out there and eat!

BAKED GOODS

Fresh-from-the-oven blueberry coffee cake and sticky pecan-caramel Monkey Muffins, muffin-tin doughnuts, and macaroons in every flavor and color of the rainbow, here are the city's most scrumptious bakeries.

Baker & Spice
HILLSDALE
6330 SW Capitol Hwy.
503-244-7573
www.bakerandspicepdx.com
$

From berry bread pudding to buttery croissants, maple twists to mascarpone-filled whoopie pies, nothing at this Hillsdale strip-mall bakery disappoints. Afterward take your little baker next door to its sister cakery for all manner of baking books and supplies, plus thick wedges of fresh-baked cake, for inspiration.

Bakeshop
ROSE CITY PARK
5351 NE Sandy Blvd.
503-946-8884
www.bakeshoppdx.com
$

Whole grain is the name of the game at this darling bakery on busy NE Sandy Boulevard (watch carefully or you'll zoom right by), where everything in the case, from the rhubarb hand pies to the strawberry barley scones, is made using whole-grain flours.

Farina Bakery
HOSFORD-ABERNETHY
1852 SE Hawthorne Blvd.
971-279-5939
www.farinabakery.com
$

Have a banana muffin and blueberry coffee cake breakfast at this homey Ladd's Addition bakery, then walk through the rose gardens in the nearby Ladd's labyrinth. Farina consistently takes top honors in city macaroon-offs, and for good reason; be sure to get a half dozen to go in one of the signature pink boxes.

Grand Central Bakery

BEAUMONT, CEDAR MILL, FREMONT/MISSISSIPPI, HOSFORD-
    ABERNETHY, MULTNOMAH VILLAGE, SELLWOOD, AND WOODSTOCK
www.grandcentralbakery.com
$

Baking the freshest breads and sticky buns and slinging some of the best biscuit sandwiches and tuna melts in the Pacific Northwest since 1972, this family-owned bakery chain is always a reliable pick for sips 'n' pastries or a delicious from-scratch breakfast or lunch.

Helen Bernhard Bakery

IRVINGTON
1717 NE Broadway St.
503-287-1251
www.helenbernhardbakery.com
$

A nostalgia trip for parents and sheer delight for kids, Helen Bernhard's gleaming glass pastry case is packed with old-fashioned goodies like cherry Danishes, lemon bars, and apple fritters. The doughnuts are divine, and a steal at under $10 for a baker's dozen. Sunday is day-old day, which means slim, slightly stale pickings, but there's a silver lining: everything's half off.

Ken's Artisan Bakery

NORTHWEST
338 NW 21st Ave.
503-248-2202
www.kensartisan.com
$

Watch little eyes widen when they spot this Alphabet District bakery's pastry case, lined with jewel-toned tarts, fruit-stuffed macaroons, huge flaky chocolate croissants, and meticulously frosted cakes, then watch them stuff everything in faster than you can say *canelé*, which incidentally is one of the best in town.

La Provence & Petite Provence

BEAVERTON (LA PROVENCE)
15151 SW Barrows Rd.
971-246-8627

HILLSBORO (LA PROVENCE)
937 NE Orenco Station Loop
503-747-3667

LAKE OSWEGO (LA PROVENCE)
16350 Boones Ferry Rd.
503-635-4533
www.provencepdx.com
$-$$

PORTLAND AIRPORT
7000 NE Airport Way
503-493-4460

RICHMOND (PETITE PROVENCE)
4834 SE Division St.
503-233-1121

VERNON (PETITE PROVENCE)
1824 NE Alberta St.
503-284-6564

Bringing a touch of Paris to Portland, this restaurant chain has convenient locations throughout the city, is a reliable spot for a fun family meal, and offers a kids' menu. Its popularity can mean lengthy lines, so go early for weekend brunch.

Lauretta Jean's

DOWNTOWN
600 SW Pine St.
503-224-9236
www.laurettajeans.com
$

RICHMOND
3402 SE Division St.
503-235-3119

From farmers'-market stand to two brick and mortars—one Downtown, one on buzzy Division Street—this popular pie purveyor stocks the shelves with fresh-from-the-oven fruit and cream pies available by the slice (and à la mode, of course), plus seasonal soups, salads, brunch dishes, and its unequaled buttermilk biscuits.

Little T Baker
2600 SE Division St.
503-238-3458
www.littletbaker.com
$

Neighborhood regulars pack the tables, and kids run merrily amok at this busy Division Street bakery beloved for its chocolate-praline croissants, pistachio bear paws, seasonal fruit Danishes, and flawless baguettes. At lunchtime, get your tuna salad sandwiches and chocolate chip cookies to go, and eat in sweet little Piccolo Park, just around the corner on SE 27th Avenue.

Miss Zumstein Bakery & Coffee Shop
CULLY
5027 NE 42nd Ave.
971-279-2746
www.misszumstein.com
$

Warm and welcoming, this Cully community hub is the sort of place you can hang out and enjoy a lavender latte and buttermilk scone by the fireplace while the kiddos enthusiastically take out a few cinnamon buns, muffin-tin doughnuts, and streusel jam bars with gusto, and nobody gives you a second glance.

Nuvrei
PEARL DISTRICT
404 NW 10th Ave.
www.nuvrei.com
$

Nobody takes croissants quite as seriously as this stylish Pearl District bakery, where you'll find no less than nine flavors, including rose, sesame thyme, and chocolate almond. Also exceptional are the fruit scones, flourless chocolate walnut cookies, and macaroons, which are so popular there's a separate Mac Bar downstairs to properly showcase them.

GLUTEN-FREE ZONE

Those who don't eat wheat don't have to miss a beat, thanks to these gluten-free bakeries and cafés.

Back to Eden Bakery

CONCORDIA
2217 NE Alberta St.

HOSFORD-ABERNETHY
2880 SE Division St.

Phone number for both: 503-477-5022
www.backtoedenbakery.com

$

It's ready, set, drool at this darling Alberta Street bakery (and satellite food cart in the Tidbit Food Farm and Garden pod), where the entire menu is vegan and gluten free, from the homemade toffee bars and coconut cream pies to the big ol' banana splits.

Harlow, Prasad & Prasad East

KERNS (PRASAD EAST)
21 NE 12th Ave.
503-231-3606
www.prasadeast.com

RICHMOND (HARLOW)
3632 SE Hawthorne Blvd.
971-255-0138
www.harlowpdx.com

PEARL DISTRICT (PRASAD)
925 NW Davis St.
503-224-3993
www.prasadpdx.com

$

These busy counter-service cafés churn out some of the city's greatest plant-based and gluten-free hits in bright, airy spaces that smell like freshly juiced greens. The kids' menu is both healthy and fun, with ants on a log, strawberry chia pudding, toasted PB&J, and hot chocolate with coconut milk, and at the Hawthorne Boulevard location, adults can choose between smoothies and spirits . . . or maybe both for balance.

New Cascadia Traditional

HOSFORD-ABERNETHY
1700 SE 6th Ave.
503-546-4901
www.newcascadiatraditional.com

$

Nobody does gluten-free breads and baked goods like this Inner Southeast bakery, which also has a stand at the Saturday Portland Farmers Market. Pick up freshly baked loaves of its best-selling Honey Gold sandwich bread, chewy boiled bagels, crisp-crusted pizzas, seasonal salads, and for dessert—gorgeous vegan cupcakes, cookies, brownies, and baked doughnuts.

Petunia's Pies & Pastries

DOWNTOWN

610 SW 12th Ave.

503-841-5961

www.petuniaspiesandpastries.com

$

Pretty in pink, this dreamy downtown dessert den specializes in gluten-free and vegan pastries in a cotton-candy-colored shop. On the sweet side of things, nibble coconut passionberry babycakes, marionberry crumble bars, macaroons, and cowboy cookies, or go savory with flatbreads, soups, salads, and bowls.

Pacific Pie Company

HOSFORD-ABERNETHY

1520 SE 7th Ave.

503-381-6157

www.pacificpie.com

$-$$

NORTHWEST

1668 NW 23rd Ave.

503-894-9482

These cheery, Australian-style potpie shops are an excellent spot for an affordable family meal and to pick up frozen pies to stash in the freezer for those nights when cooking proves impossible. Mature bakers will love the Pie Making 101 class; check the website for upcoming dates or book a private pie-making party.

Pearl Bakery
PEARL DISTRICT
102 NW 9th Ave.
503-827-0910
www.pearlbakery.com

$

A neighborhood original, this elegant European-style bakery tempts with fig-anise panini, cinnamon crowns, raspberry brownies, and the divine candied-orange-peel-flecked *gibassier*. Via the doorway to the commercial kitchen, kids get a glimpse of the bakery's flour-dusted inner workings. Look for its booth at the Portland Farmers Market as well.

Roman Candle Baking Co.
RICHMOND
3377 SE Division St.
971-302-6605
www.romancandlebaking.com

$-$$

This bright, airy Division Street bakery and pizzeria's pastry case is lined with *bomboloni* and tiramisu, while over at the pizza counter, thick slabs of just-baked pizza *bianca* are lined up for easy viewing. The kitchen serves a simple, solid Italian-inspired breakfast, lunch, and dinner menu every day, and since it's part of the Stumptown coffee empire, definitely order a coffee drink.

Seastar Bakery & Handsome Pizza
VERNON
1603 NE Killingsworth St.
503-247-7499
www.seastarbakery.com

$-$$

Here the toast-forward menu is divided into "the basics" and "advanced toasts," the latter piled with everything from cocoa-hazelnut butter and homemade preserves, to sautéed greens. In the pastry case, whole-grain buckwheat scone tarts

and rosemary chocolate chip cookies beckon, and if you don't
happen to have grain on the brain, there are a few items on
the "not bread" list. At 12 p.m. (1 p.m. on weekends), bakery
operations cease and cotenant Handsome Pizza commandeers
the ovens, turning out simple, splendid salads and pies.

Woodlawn Coffee and Pastry
WOODLAWN
808 NE Dekum St.
503-954-2412
www.woodlawncoffee.com
$

Sit on this cozy Woodlawn bakery's pretty patio and sip a well-
made macchiato while fending off demands for please-just-one-
more butterfly-shaped sugar cookie or slice of strawberry cake.
Afterward walk a few blocks up the street to Woodlawn Park
(page 140).

BREAKFAST
The best part of waking up is breakfast, and here are the most
delicious fortresses of first meal (and we do mean fortress,
'cause some are hard to get into . . . go early!).

Batter Griddle & Drinkery
BEAUMONT
4425 NE Fremont St.
971-271-8784
www.batterpdx.com
$$

Sleepy-eyed kiddos will wake up pretty quick when they see this
friendly all-day Beaumont breakfast joint's stacks of bacon and
banana-stuffed pancakes, plates of fried-chicken-topped waffles
dripping with syrup, and the zany dish descriptions (i.e., the
Wakey Wakey, Eggs and Bakey bacon waffle).

Besaw's
NORTHWEST
1545 NW 21st Ave.
503-228-2619
www.besaws.com
$$

A longtime Northwest staple with a devoted following, Besaw's turns out breakfast and lunch classics with creative twists, like cider-braised oatmeal with lemon curd and pecan smoked pastrami sandwiches; kids will love the Liège waffles with choose-your-own dipping sauces. The restaurant is steps from New Seasons Market (page 210); postbrunch, stock up on snacks or picnic fare for later.

Bijou Café
DOWNTOWN
132 SW 3rd Ave.
503-222-3187
www.bijoucafepdx.com
$$

With its blue-and-white gingham tablecloths and efficient staff, this nostalgic little downtown diner gets you fed and on your way in a jiff. You can't go wrong with the griddle cakes or French toast made with Pearl Bakery brioche and served with local marionberry syrup.

Broder Söder, Broder Nord & Café Broder SE
BEAVERTON (BRODER SÖDER)
8800 SW Oleson Rd.
971-373-8762
ELIOT (BRODER NORD)
2240 N. Interstate Ave.
503-282-5555
www.broderpdx.com
$$

HOSFORD-ABERNETHY
(CAFÉ BRODER SE)
2508 SE Clinton St.
503-736-3333

Sprinkled across the city, these popular cafés—Café Broder, Broder Nord, and Broder Söder—have their trademark Scandinavian-style design and bang-up brunch dialed in. If your little diners are keen on *aebleskiver* and Swedish hash, and you're keen on aquavit Bloody Marys, this is your happy place.

Byways Cafe
PEARL DISTRICT
1212 NW Glisan St.
503-221-0011
www.bywayscafe.com
$$

This longtime local charmer has watched the trendy Pearl District grow up around it, but it's stayed largely the same, with checkerboard floors, knickknack-lined walls, and big hearty portions of blue corn pancakes, biscuits 'n' gravy, and burgers. Don't miss the daily homemade coffee cake.

City State Diner
KERNS
128 NE 28th Ave.
503-517-0347
www.citystatediner.com
$$

Old-fashioned ambiance meets no-frills breakfast fare at this fun 28th Avenue diner, where you can cozy up in a booth with an oh-so-Portland spread of pork belly Benedict, hazelnut challah French toast, and the bacon-topped Gravy Train. Kids can order off the Small Plates menu, which includes mini biscuits 'n' gravy, single pancakes, yogurt sundaes, and a classic PB&J.

Daily Café in the Pearl
PEARL DISTRICT
902 NW 13th Ave.
503-242-1916
www.dailyinthepearl.com
$$

A counter-service establishment with a full-service feel, this lively longtime Pearl District favorite is an always-reliable option for a tasty, from-scratch meal, whether you're craving straightforward buttermilk pancakes and steel-cut oatmeal or chive buttermilk biscuits with chorizo gravy.

Gravy
BOISE
3957 N. Mississippi Ave.
503-287-8800
www.eatatgravy.com
$

This all-day Mississippi Avenue breakfast joint dishes up heaping portions of corned beef hash, biscuits 'n' gravy, and its famous oatmeal brûlée. The hot chocolate's excellent, as are the Bloody Marys, you know, if you're into that sort of thing.

Jam on Hawthorne
BUCKMAN
2239 SE Hawthorne Blvd.
503-234-4790
www.jamonhawthorne.com
$

Kid-friendly, vegetarian-friendly, vegan-friendly, gluten-free-friendly; there's something for everyone at this affable Hawthorne hot spot, hence the permanent line. Postwait, dig into the delicious rewards—eggs 'n' crispy hash browns, lemon ricotta Maddie cakes, and Grand Marnier French toast . . . and that's just the kids' menu. Not to mention, little ones will love the play area.

Mother's Bistro
DOWNTOWN
212 SW Stark St.
503-464-1122
www.mothersbistro.com
$$

This venerable downtown restaurant backs up its family-friendly moniker with patient servers, a play area, and a kids' menu with impressive variety—everything from fruit smoothies and banana pancakes to mac 'n' cheese and meatloaf, and for dessert, mini hot-fudge sundaes. Brunch lines can be daunting, so go early.

New Deal Café
ROSE CITY PARK
5250 NE Halsey St.
503-546-1833
www.ndpdx.com

$

Savor a cup of Stumptown and a plate of fresh strawberry pancakes in this convivial Northeast café, while the kids let off some steam in the play area. Breakfast is served all day, ingredients are local and organic, and many menu items are vegan and gluten free.

Off the Waffle
HOSFORD-ABERNETHY
2601 SE Clinton St.
971-258-2730
www.offthewaffle.com

$

Founded by two Liège waffle–loving brothers, this Eugene-based chain occupies a cute Clinton Street corner café, where kids wiggle, wriggle, and ricochet from table to table, visiting their neighborhood friends. Waffles are divided into savory, sweet, and in between, and kids will giggle over the quirky names as they eat their Goat in the Headlights or No Really, Though.

Pine State Biscuits

CONCORDIA	ELIOT	HOSFORD-ABERNETHY
2204 NE Alberta St.	*125 NE Schuyler St.*	*1100 SE Division St.*
503-477-6605	*503-719-5357*	*503-236-3346*

www.pinestatebiscuits.com

$

Be prepared for a line out the door and possibly around the
corner at these beloved biscuit joints, but when the Reggie
Deluxe arrives in all its fried chicken, bacon, and gravy-loaded
glory, you'll forget all about the wait. For strawberry shortcake
alfresco, visit Pine State's booth at the Saturday Portland
Farmers Market at PSU (page 84).

Screen Door
KERNS
2337 E. Burnside St.
503-542-0880
www.screendoorrestaurant.com
$$

When it comes to Portland breakfast spots, this Burnside brunch
boss takes the (pan)cake—a triple stack of buttermilk pancakes
with toasted pecans and chocolate chips, to be exact. The lines
are legendary but well worth it, especially for the epic fried
chicken and sweet potato waffles, which arrive impaled on a
steak knife for dramatic effect.

Slappy Cakes
SUNNYSIDE
4246 SE Belmont St.
503-477-4805
www.slappycakes.com
$$

This Southeast Portland pancake palace is the best possible kind
of DIY—request a booth with a built-in griddle, then watch the
kids go nuts with squeeze bottles of batter and their newfound
freedom of pancake expression (vegan and gluten-free batter
available). There's also a full menu of *other* breakfast classics,
and cocktails for the beleaguered batter-spattered grownups.

Tasty n Alder & Tasty n Sons

BOISE (TASTY N SONS)
3808 N. Williams Ave.
503-621-1400
www.tastynsons.com
$$

DOWNTOWN (TASTY N ALDER)
580 SW 12th Ave.
503-621-9251
www.tastynalder.com

To sidestep the wait at these busy brunch destinations—one on a lively North Portland commuter corridor, the other in the heart of Downtown—arrive a bit before they open. When ordering, you can't go wrong with anything involving biscuits, and Auntie Paula's French toast will have the family fighting over the last smear of rhubarb maple compote.

Tin Shed
KING
1438 NE Alberta St.
503-288-6966
www.tinshedgardencafe.com

$$

They love kids, dogs, groups, and most of all, brunch at this Alberta Street institution, where neighborhood folk queue patiently with mugs of self-serve coffee, waiting for their shot at heaping plates of biscuits 'n' gravy and wild salmon scrambles. Plenty of vegan and gluten-free options abound, and there's a special menu for both the kids and Fido.

Waffle Window
CONCORDIA
2624 NE Alberta St.
503-265-8031
www.wafflewindow.com

$

RICHMOND
3610 SE Hawthorne Blvd.
971-255-0501

Warm Liège waffles come piled with everything from Brie and basil to full-on ice-cream-sundae fixings at these waffle wonderlands. If the weather's nice, aim for the darling flower-framed Hawthorne location, a literal hole-in-the-wall just a block from the McMenamins Bagdad Theater (page 22) and Powell's Books on Hawthorne (page 96).

Zell's Café
BUCKMAN
1300 SE Morrison St.
503-239-0196
www.zellscafe.com

$$

The quintessential neighborhood breakfast joint, this darling corner café wins diners' hearts with its quaint decor, gracious service, *and* the signature baskets of warm mini scones and homemade jam delivered to the table when you sit down, which come in very handy when you're trying to placate ravenous little ones while waiting for the eggs Benedict, bacon waffle, and German pancake with rhubarb compote to arrive.

BURGERS & FRIES

This dynamic duo's a proven kid pleaser, so for some fun in a bun with a side of fries (and hopefully a thick chocolate shake to dip them in), here you go.

Brunch Box
DOWNTOWN
620 SW 9th Ave.
503-287-4377
www.brunchboxpdx.com
$

This downtown food cart turned brick-and-mortar burger joint knows how to cater to the junior diner set—yes, there's a kids' cheeseburger (and four kinds of fries), but they'll probably just want the Cheesasaurus Rex, a dinosaur-shaped grilled cheese that also comes in a PB&J version.

Dick's Kitchen

NORTHWEST	SUNNYSIDE
704 NW 21st Ave.	*3312 SE Belmont St.*
503-206-5916	*503-235-0146*
www.dickskitchen.com	

$

Priding itself on its top-quality ingredients and paleo leanings, Dick's does burgers and fries with a healthy bent—the meat is grass fed, fries are tossed in safflower oil and baked, the kids' menu has mashed yams and turkey sliders, and sweets include

maple-cashew-cream parfaits and milkshakes made with
Coconut Bliss.

Hopworks Urban Brewery
CRESTON
2944 SE Powell Blvd.
503-232-4677
www.hopworksbeer.com
$

Beloved for its award-winning craft beer, sustainably sourced
food, ample bike parking, *and* children's play area, this popular
Powell brewpub also has an awesome kids' menu with
everything from organic baby food and free-range chicken strips
to nitrate-free burgers and a grass-fed Little Brewer's Burger.

Killer Burger
DOWNTOWN
510 SW 3rd Ave.
503-946-8946
HILLSBORO
2130 NW Allie Way
503-268-1757
www.killerburger.com
$

HOLLYWOOD
4644 NE Sandy Blvd.
971-544-7521
SELLWOOD
8728 SE 17th Ave.
503-841-5906

When you're craving a huge, messy burger and bottomless
fries, these loud, boisterous burger bars are your jam (*and* your
peanut butter, if you get the Peanut-Butter-Pickle-Bacon burger).
Even the kids' burger is a bellyful, so order accordingly.

Little Big Burger
BOISE, BUCKMAN, NORTHWEST, PEARL DISTRICT, RICHMOND, SOUTH
    WATERFRONT, AND VERNON
www.littlebigburger.com
$

Decisions come easy at these designer burger shops, seeing
as there are only six items on the menu—hamburgers,
cheeseburgers, veggie burgers, fries, sodas, and floats (well,

HOT WHEELS

Portland is famous for its food carts, all five-hundred-plus of them, so you can't possibly leave town without a meal on wheels, and here are few kid-approved favorites.

Donut Byte Labs

DOWNTOWN
12 SW 4th Ave.
503-801-7321
www.donutbytelabs.com
$

Teeny tiny "donut robot"–made doughnuts topped with everything from plain old powdered sugar to bacon bits, caramel, and peanut-butter-cup crumbles are the draw at this downtown cart, which happens to be a block from famous Voodoo Doughnut, in case you want to compare and contrast.

Grilled Cheese Grill

DOWNTOWN   KING
SW 10th Ave. and SW Alder St.   *1027 NE Alberta St.*
503-206-8959
www.grilledcheesegrill.com
$

Order a classic grilled cheese (with or without crusts) at this guaranteed kid pleaser, then eat it in a converted yellow school bus where the tables are lined with silly school portraits. There's a second downtown location as well, but sans the school bus, so aim for Alberta if possible.

PDX Sliders

SELLWOOD
8064 SE 17th Ave.
971-717-5271
www.pdxsliders.com
$

Juicy, perfectly cooked sliders and fresh-cut fries are the draw at this big, shiny food truck, which moves around town to different events but keeps regular hours at its home base in Sellwood.

Scoop

CULLY

5429 NE 42nd Ave.

www.scooppdx.com

$

Spinning fresh Oregon fruit, locally roasted coffee, and fair-trade chocolate into ice-cream gold, this stout little ice-cream truck has a seasonal spot at the NE 42nd and Killingsworth food-cart pod and also trundles around town to various events, like Sunday Parkways (page 58).

Tidbit Food Farm and Garden

HOSFORD-ABERNETHY

2880 SE Division St.

www.facebook.com/tidbitfoodfarmandgarden

$

While some are lone four-wheeled wolves, most of Portland's food carts congregate in pods, and Division Street's Tidbit Food Farm and Garden is the one to rule them all, with an unbeatable lineup of vendors selling everything from peanut-butter and cinnamon-apple waffles and wood-fired pizza to vegan whoopie pies. Sit in the cozy covered area or huddle around the fire pit.

and beer). Per the chain's unofficial secret menu, add bacon to any burger, pile on as many extra cheeses as you want, and sub lettuce for a bun.

McMenamins Kennedy School
CONCORDIA
Contact information on page 22
$

At this superfun schoolhouse-turned-hotel where the hotel rooms are converted classrooms, families can catch a flick in a former auditorium, and kids can paddle around the soaking pool while their parents socialize at the bar. Once everyone's good and hungry, pile into the Courtyard Restaurant for cheeseburgers, tater tots, and Scooby Snacks.

Slowburger
KERNS
2329 NE Glisan St.
503-477-5779
www.slowburger.net
$

Bookending the Ocean mini-restaurant complex, this cute little annex of hallowed watering hole Slow Bar turns out the same beautiful burgers and golden fries as its sister restaurant, just in a more family-friendly setting and sans the eau de dive bar.

BURRITOS & TACOS
Treat your bundles of joy to a bean-and-cheese-stuffed bundle of joy, tasty taco, tamale platter, or warm, cheesy 'dilla.

Cha Cha Cha
CULLY, GRANT PARK, MILWAUKIE, NORTHWEST, PEARL DISTRICT,
   PORTSMOUTH, SELLWOOD, SOUTH WATERFRONT, AND SUNNYSIDE
www.chachachapdx.com
$

Fast and unfussy, this Mexican chain slings big burritos, enchiladas, tacos, and beans 'n' greens bowls made with local, natural, and sustainable ingredients. For under $5, kids can pick from a handful of classics, from the taco combo and chicken enchiladas to their very own pile of bean-and-cheese nachos.

La Bonita

CONCORDIA
2839 NE Alberta St.
503-281-3662
www.labonitarestaurant.net

OVERLOOK
2710 N. Killingsworth St.
503-278-3050

$

Neighborhood kids and hipster couples sit elbow to elbow in these family-owned Alberta and Killingsworth taquerias, chowing down on huge burritos, towering nacho plates, and ooey-gooey chimichangas. If you come often, ask for a burrito punch card.

Laughing Planet Café

BOISE, CEDAR MILL, DOWNTOWN, GOOSE HOLLOW, HAYHURST, HOLLYWOOD, LAKE OSWEGO, NORTHWEST, PEARL DISTRICT, SUNNYSIDE, AND WOODSTOCK
www.laughingplanetcafe.com

$

Some people love these easygoing cafés for their healthy twist on Mexican classics, some for the resident toy dinos that help pass the wait for your order. There are plenty of locations scattered about town, so you'll always have a Spanky's Bowl or Holy Mole burrito within reach.

Por Qué No

BOISE
3524 N. Mississippi Ave.
503-467-4149
www.porquenotacos.com

SUNNYSIDE
4635 SE Hawthorne Blvd.
503-954-3138

$

Both locations of this fun, festive, trinket-lined taqueria enjoy a cult following, and every day, rain or shine, the line starts to gather before the doors are even open. Kids can nosh on tacos, quesadillas, and rice-and-bean bowls off the menu *para niños*, while parents sip passion fruit–serrano margaritas and spiked *horchata*.

Portland Mercado

MT. SCOTT

7238 SE Foster Rd.

www.portlandmercado.org

$

Both the first Latino public market and prettiest lineup of food carts in town (each is painted a different shade of the rainbow), the Mercado lets you take a mini tour of Mexico and South America without ever leaving town. Sample empanadas, fried plantains, and *pupusas* outside; browse the bright Mexican candies and snacks inside; and finish with sweet, cool, fruity *raspados*.

Stella Taco

CONCORDIA

2940 NE Alberta St.

971-407-3705

www.stellatacopdx.com

$

RICHMOND

3060 SE Division St.

503-206-5446

From green-chile quesadillas, to bowls of warm, gooey *queso*, to the dozen or so Austin-style street tacos, these chill taquerias are a fun pick for lunch or dinner while hanging out on Alberta or Division Street. During the daily happy hour from 3 to 6 p.m., tacos drop to $2, and Mom and Dad get a dollar off margaritas.

Tamale Boy

WOODLAWN

1764 NE Dekum St.

503-206-8022

www.tamaleboy.com

$

Cheap and cheerful, this former food cart turned tamale-and-taco shop charms with big portions at a small price, warm and speedy service, and a roomy patio you'll want to spend all summer sipping tamarind *agua frescas* on.

COFFEE & DRINKS

In a city this persistently drizzly, coffee's more than a beverage—it's a life force. For good coffee form and kid-friendly function, try these bean bars fortified with hot chocolate, cinnamon toast, and play areas.

Bipartisan Cafe

MONTAVILLA

7901 SE Stark St.
503-253-1051
www.bipartisancafe.com

$

This cheery Montavilla café and community hub is just the place to stop for steamers, lattes made with local Water Avenue Coffee, slices of homemade Oregon marionberry pie, and a game of Scrabble.

Jim & Patty's Coffee

BEAVERTON	CULLY	NORTHWEST
4130 SW 117th Ave.	*4951 NE Fremont St.*	*2246 NW Lovejoy St.*
503-530-8379	*503-284-2121*	*503-477-8363*

www.jimandpattys.com

$

These friendly neighborhood hangouts are a sweet spot to settle in with cups of hot chocolate, chunks of sour-cream coffee cake, and the famous savory sausage-and-cheddar chive biscuit roll, a.k.a. Pig Newton.

Papaccino's
WOODSTOCK
4411 SE Woodstock Blvd.
503-771-2825
www.facebook.com/papaccinos
$

Sink into an overstuffed armchair with your mocha and watch the kids romp in the cute play area at this convivial Woodstock coffee shop.

Pied Piper Play Cafe
SELLWOOD
8609 SE 17th Ave.
503-206-8780
www.piedpiperplaycafe.com
$

Sip a chai latte and watch the wee ones run rings around a sizeable play area at this Sellwood café, with its miniature kitchen, bulging toy bins, dollhouse, and jungle gym. (FYI: it's pay to play; $3 per child.)

Poa Café
BOISE
Contact information on page 45
$

A stylish sanctuary offering a hip and health-conscious café experience, Poa's Café offers parents a place to sip on everything from soy lattes and Powerberry smoothies to hot buttered rum, while kids tackle the indoor play area and outdoor sandbox.

Posie's Café
KENTON
8208 N. Denver Ave.
503-289-1319
www.posiescafe.com
$

Known for its house-made pastries *and* its excellent play room, this charming Kenton café is just the spot for hot chocolate, an almond croissant, and avocado toast on a rainy Portland morning.

St. Honoré Boulangerie

LAKE OSWEGO	NORTHWEST	RICHMOND
315 1st St.	*2335 NW Thurman St.*	*3333 SE Division St.*
503-496-5596	*503-445-4342*	*971-279-4433*

www.sainthonorebakery.com

$-$$

Bringing a little ooh-la-la to Division Street, the Alphabet District, and swanky Lake O, these upscale boulangeries are family-friendly havens of café au lait and Normandy apple toast. Kids will go gaga over the pretty pastries and sweets. There's a separate gluten-free menu too.

Taborspace

MT. TABOR

5441 SE Belmont St.
503-238-3904
www.taborspace.org

$

Set inside the stained-glass-window-lit bell tower of Belmont Street's regal Mt. Tabor Presbyterian Church, this donation-based coffee bar serves local Ristretto Roasters coffee, house-made chai, and fresh Bakeshop pastries. Sit by the fireplace in the big, beautiful common room, or if the weather's fair, outside at a sidewalk table.

Warehouse Café

BROOKLYN

3434 SE Milwaukie Ave.
503-206-5766
www.knowthyfood.coop/cafe

$

Inside the Brooklyn hood's Know Thy Food co-op, this good-natured boho café is fully stocked with locally sourced coffee and pastries, and a large "living room," where the pre-K set can play with books, blocks, and bead mazes as long as attention spans permit, or take in one of the regular weekday shows by popular local performers like Tallulah's Daddy and the Pointed Man Band ($5 suggested donation).

MARKETS & TAKEOUT

Whether you're picking up picnic provisions, dining in on deli-case cuisine, or pulling a grab-and-go meal maneuver on your way home from soccer practice, these top city markets are ready and waiting.

Food Front Cooperative Grocery

HILLSDALE
6344 SW Capitol Hwy.
503-546-6559
www.foodfront.coop

NORTHWEST
2375 NW Thurman St.
503-222-5658

With farm-fresh salads and sandwiches and a hot bar lined with broccoli mac 'n' cheese, chicken polenta pie, and pad thai, these vegan- and gluten-free-friendly Northwest Portland and Hillsdale co-ops are particularly well suited to families seeking health-conscious eats.

Green Zebra Grocery

KENTON
3011 N. Lombard St.
503-286-9325
www.greenzebragrocery.com

LLOYD DISTRICT
808 NE Multnomah St.
971-256-3330

Kids will love the zany zebra-striped branding on these cool small-scale "convenience stores"; you'll love their commitment to healthy and delicious sustainably sourced food. The deli case is full of from-scratch salads, soups, and sandwiches, and the shelves are stocked with local snacks to help pad your picnic.

PRETTY PICNICS

Portland wants not for scenic spots to unpack a picnic, but these
particular parks have easy parking, quick car-to-grass access,
bearable public bathrooms, and fun playgrounds (except for
Pittock) in addition to their beautiful backdrops.

Laurelhurst Park

LAURELHURST

Contact information on page 55

Picnickers come from all over the city for this popular park's lush
landscaping, huge grassy areas, and shady nooks and crannies
perfect for beating the heat on hot summer days.

Mt. Tabor Park

MT. TABOR

Contact information on page 53

Eat at a shady picnic table near the playground, then hike
around this dormant Southeast volcano, stopping for a peek at
the drinking-water reservoirs.

Peninsula Park

PIEDMONT

Contact information on page 53

Spread a blanket right in the middle of the spectacular rose
garden, then vanquish any postpicnic stickiness by splashing
around in the fountain.

Pittock Mansion

FOREST PARK

Contact information on page 77

Picnic like a king and queen on the back lawn of this regal
mansion, where the only thing more beautiful than the garden is
the bird's-eye view.

continued

Washington Park
WEST HILLS

400 SW Kingston Ave.
www.explorewashingtonpark.org

Take a stroll around the famous International Rose Test Garden (page 32), then unpack your basket in the grassy amphitheater, or at one of the playground picnic tables if your crew likes to be as close as possible to the slide at all times.

New Seasons Market
ARBOR LODGE, CEDAR HILLS, CONCORDIA, ELIOT, GRANT PARK, HAPPY VALLEY, HILLSBORO, HOSFORD-ABERNETHY, LAKE OSWEGO, NORTHWEST, PROGRESS RIDGE, RALEIGH HILLS, RICHMOND, SELLWOOD, TUALATIN, UNIVERSITY PARK, AND WOODSTOCK
www.newseasonsmarket.com

The first retail grocer in the country to earn B-Corp status, this sustainably minded Portland grocery chain is an excellent spot for one-stop shopping regardless of what's on your list—from organic, local goods to guilty sugar-cereal pleasures. The deli case is superbly stocked, and every store has a big, clean dine-in area, plus orderly bathrooms with changing tables.

P's & Q's
WOODLAWN

1301 NE Dekum St.
503-894-8979
www.psandqsmarket.com

A quintessential neighborhood market, P's & Q's is part café, part deli, and part grocery, so you can order breakfast sandwiches, BLTs, and salads from the deli case; grab drinks from the cooler; pick out chips and cookies; and then borrow

one of its picnic baskets to ferry everything to lovely Woodlawn
Park (page 140) down the street.

Whole Foods Market
BRIDGEPORT, HILLSBORO, HOLLYWOOD, KERNS, PEARL DISTRICT,
   SABIN, AND TIGARD
www.wholefoodsmarket.com

This well-known national chain has several stores in the
Portland area, so you're always in reach of organic, all-natural
grocery options within fifteen minutes or so. Whole Foods also
contracts locally with Instacart, so if you don't have time to shop
and want groceries delivered to your hotel or Airbnb, download
the app, fill your cart, and set your delivery time.

NOODLES & RICE
If all your petite gourmand wants to do at mealtime is noodle
around or thinks rice is nice . . . and that's about it, no problem;
these ethnically diverse dining destinations dish up everything
from plain buttered noodles to *nigiri*.

ASIAN

Bamboo Sushi
DOWNTOWN
404 SW 12th Ave.
503-444-7455
KERNS
310 SE 28th Ave.
503-232-5255
www.bamboosushi.com
$$$

KING
1409 NE Alberta St.
503-889-0336
NORTHWEST
836 NW 23rd Ave.
971-229-1925

Although these sleek, sustainability-obsessed sushi restaurants
give off more of a date-night than family-supper vibe, the
gracious staff is very accommodating to kids, who will happily
scarf their hand roll or steamed bun before moving on to the
coconut panna cotta.

Boke Bowl

BUCKMAN

1028 SE Water Ave.

NORTHWEST

1200 NW 18th Ave.

Phone number for both: 503-719-5698

www.bokebowl.com

$$

Slurp up a storm at these bustling ramen joints, where kids can get a Bambino ramen bowl, sink their teeth into rice tots and PB&J steamed buns, and gobble the ever-popular house-made Boke Twinkies; plus they'll *love* the animal-themed training chopsticks.

Jade Bistro & Patisserie

SELLWOOD

7912 SE 13th Ave.

503-477-8985

www.jadeportland.com

$$

A nice neighborhood crowd fills this airy teahouse to the gills daily, and nobody bats an eye when you bring the whole family along for fresh salad rolls, chicken rice soup, and stir-fried noodles. For dessert, the sweet rice and mango and the fried sesame balls with caramel sauce are a must.

Nong's Khao Man Gai

BUCKMAN

609 SE Ankeny St.

503-740-2907

DOWNTOWN

SW 10th Ave. and SW
Alder St.

971-255-3480

PSU

411 SW College St.

503-432-3286

www.khaomangai.com

$

This wildly popular mini chicken-and-rice empire started as a downtown food cart before expanding to a second cart near Portland State, then a cozy Southeast brick and mortar where you can sip Thai iced teas at a sidewalk picnic table, while your little ones devour the namesake dish, before digging into coconut-milk soft serve.

INDIAN

Bollywood Theater

RICHMOND
3010 SE Division St.
503-477-6699
www.bollywoodtheaterpdx.com
$

VERNON
2039 NE Alberta St.
971-200-4711

Fun and festive, these counter-service Indian restaurants are a feast for all the senses, with authentic decor and art coupled with fresh, delicious Indian street eats like the mild dal and coconut curry over saffron rice, satisfyingly soft and squishy fried potato dumplings on a roll, and refreshing mango lassis.

ITALIAN

24th & Meatballs

KERNS
2341 NE Glisan St.
503-282-2557
www.24thandmeatballs.com
$

Older kids will get the giggles when reading this meatball joint's cheeky slogans and dish descriptions, but little ones will be too busy stuffing in meatball sliders and creamy cheesy polenta to get in on the joke. The restaurant is part of the Ocean microrestaurant complex, so if meatballs aren't the general consensus, it's okay—tacos, burgers, and kale *dosas* are steps away.

Gino's

SELLWOOD
8051 SE 13th Ave.
503-233-4613
www.ginossellwood.com
$$

A longtime city favorite, this cozy old-fashioned Italian joint in small-town Sellwood really packs them in, as families fill the high-backed wooden booths and dig into big plates of ravioli, rigatoni, and ragu. Parents will appreciate the warm service, especially the premeal snack plate offered to wee ones upon being seated.

Grassa

DOWNTOWN
1205 SW Washington St.
503-241-1133
www.grassapdx.com
$

NORTHWEST
1506 NW 23rd Ave.
971-386-2196

No need to break the bank taking the whole family out for a nice Italian meal—these relaxed pasta joints by the folks behind popular Lardo sandwich shops (page 223) serve up exceptional homemade noodles at a very nice price. Little ones can opt for the kid-size mac 'n' cheese or spaghetti and meatballs, a.k.a. the Luke, and even the pickiest eaters will slurp up their order of noodles with butter—especially when tiramisu is on the line.

LATIN AMERICAN

Teote

HOSFORD-ABERNETHY
1615 SE 12th Ave.
971-888-5281
www.teotepdx.com
$

With its bright, bold Latin decor and flavors, this Inner Southeast *areperia* makes for a fun family meal, and its devotion to gluten-free cuisine make it a particularly solid pick if food allergies are in play. Kids can opt for the bean-and-rice-stuffed Niños Bowl, or simple bean-and-cheese *arepas*; and for dessert they'll love the cocoa and cinnamon-sugar dessert *arepas* with *dulce de leche*. The patio is second to none, so make this a fair-weather favorite.

MIDDLE EASTERN

DarSalam

CONCORDIA
DOWNTOWN

2921 NE Alberta St.
320 SW Alder St.

503-206-6148
503-444-7813

www.darsalamportland.com

$$

Color, spice, and culture blend at this family-owned Iraqi restaurant housed in a former Alberta Street carriage house fronted by a garden patio. Try the tender shredded chicken over rice, *mezze* platter, sweet cardamom tea, and house-made baklava while watching the fascinating procession of Iraqi photos projected on the flat-screen TV. Most of the menu is vegan and/or gluten free, and there's also a downtown location, which isn't as charismatic but has the same tasty food.

Ya Hala

MONTAVILLA

8005 SE Stark St.

503-256-4484

www.yahalarestaurant.com

$$

A fun and festive member of the close-knit Montavilla community, this family-owned Lebanese restaurant is a good time for kids, who can dip warm, pillowy pita into the delicious house-made hummus and baba ghanouj, nibble skewers, and sink their teeth into soft, gooey cheese pies. Try the generously portioned weekend brunch, a solid value for famished families.

MAC 'N' CHEESE, PLEASE!

SpongeBob and Patrick, Batman and Robin, Bert and Ernie, mac and cheese—this tasty team is up there with the best of them, so save the boxed stuff for another day and hit one of these five fantastic mac 'n' cheese meccas instead.

Cheese & Crack Snack Shop
BUCKMAN
22 SE 28th Ave.
503-206-7315
www.cheeseandcrack.com
$$

As much fun as you can possibly have with cheese and crackers, this clever little snack shop dreams up artful arrangements of these two culinary besties that never fail to elicit oohs and aahs. After polishing off the mac 'n' cheese, get one of the fantastical seasonal sundaes or an espresso-powder-dusted soft-serve cone.

Chkchk
NORTHWEST
1305 NW 23rd Ave.
971-302-6368
www.chkchk.com
$

While fried-chicken sandwiches are the main attraction at this bright and cheery "fast-casual" concept on NW 23rd Avenue, the Chkchk mac has its own fan club, and rightfully so—made with white cheddar and crusted with deep gold garlic bread crumbs, it's as decadent as the homemade funfetti Twinkies.

Herb's Mac and Cheese
SUNNYSIDE
4255 SE Belmont St.
503-622-9090
$

It's mac 'n' cheese your way at this Belmont Street food cart, where kids get to pick their toppings from a long list that includes everything from hot dogs and bacon to broccoli and blue cheese crumbles. In the summer, the cart also breaks out its shave ice machine.

Le Bistro Montage
BUCKMAN
301 SE Morrison St.
503-234-1324
www.montageportland.com

$$

Just this once, *don't* clean your plate—because at this Southeast Industrial district institution, servers weave leftovers into elaborate foil animal sculptures that kids won't stop talking about for days. More adventurous eaters might want to try the alligator bites, frog legs, or crawfish hush puppies; most will probably stick to one of the nine kinds of mac 'n' cheese, all of which can be made gluten free.

Vita Café
CONCORDIA
3023 NE Alberta St.
503-335-8233
www.vita-cafe.com

$

This funky Alberta Street vegetarian café says those three little words so near and dear to a thrifty parent's heart: kids' dollar menu. From 5 to 7 p.m. every day, kids have their choice of a dozen healthy dollar dishes, from veggie burgers and corn cakes to bean burritos and mac 'n' cheese. Plus they can color on the menu. Score!

PIZZA

If there's one food the whole family can agree on (most of the time), it's pizza. New Haven, Neapolitan, cat-shaped—it doesn't really matter how you slice it, everyone's going to love these delicious dough slingers.

Apizza Scholls

SUNNYSIDE

4741 SE Hawthorne Blvd.

503-233-1286

www.apizzascholls.com

$$

Baking big, New Haven–style pies, this boisterous Hawthorne Boulevard pizza joint really packs in a crowd, so go right when they open to sidestep the wait. Don't expect to see much of the family Pac-Man lover upon arrival; the arcade room has regular *and* Ms., plus Donkey Kong, Defender, and Gorf.

East Glisan Pizza Lounge

MONTAVILLA

8001 NE Glisan St.

971-279-4273

www.eastglisan.com

$

If feeding a big pizza-devouring family, try to make happy hour at this modern Montavilla pizzeria—from 4 to 6 p.m. Monday through Saturday, slices are only $2, salads are $3, and pepperoni rolls are two for $3.

Hot Lips Pizza

BUCKMAN	GOOSE HOLLOW
2211 SE Hawthorne Blvd.	*633 SW 18th Ave.*
503-234-9999	*503-517-9354*
CONCORDIA	HOLLYWOOD
5440 NE 33rd Ave.	*4630 NE Sandy Blvd.*
503-445-1020	*503-284-4046*
DOWNTOWN	PEARL DISTRICT
1909 SW 6th Ave.	*721 NW 9th Ave.*
503-224-0311	*503-595-2342*
www.hotlipspizza.com	

$$

Fast and unfussy, this prolific Portland chain uses local, organic ingredients in its food and house-made fruit sodas; has a location in pretty much every corner of the city; and does takeout, eat-in, *and* delivery, making for an easy-breezy family pizza night. On a side note, one of the best, simplest summer desserts ever is a Hot Lips berry soda and vanilla ice-cream float.

Ken's Artisan Pizza
KERNS
304 SE 28th Ave.
503-517-9951
www.kensartisan.com
$$

Sister to Northwest pastry paragon Ken's Artisan Bakery (page 185), this *very* popular Southeast Portland pizzeria packs in the neighborhood regulars nightly, creating a steady buzz that conceals cries and squeals. The wood-fired pies take mere minutes to cook, so once you get a table, the food arrives quickly, and don't pass up the seasonal fruit crisp for dessert.

Life of Pie
BOISE
3632 N. Williams Ave.
503-719-7321
www.lifeofpiepizza.com
$

Besides being fast and friendly, this Boise pizzeria has one more major ace in the pizza hole—every day from 11 a.m. to 6 p.m., they offer generously sized $5 happy hour *margherita* pizzas (and $4 beer and wine), so hustle everyone over right after school/work.

Lovely's Fifty Fifty
BOISE
4039 N. Mississippi Ave.
503-281-4060
www.lovelysfiftyfifty.com
$$

Sister act Sarah and Jane Minnick turn out some of the best pies in town, if not the world, including a special kids-only cheese pizza (ask nicely enough, and they may even make you an elusive off-menu "pizza cat"). They also churn some of the best ice cream around; try the salted caramel with fudge sauce.

Mississippi Pizza Pub

BOISE

Contact information on page 43

$$

The whole family will have a ball at this popular pizza pub, where you can down slices of pizza while tapping your toes along with the nightly live music. Popular local acts like Red Yarn, Tallulah's Daddy, and Mr. Ben play frequently, so check the calendar.

Old Town Pizza

OLD TOWN/CHINATOWN

226 NW Davis St.

503-222-9999

www.oldtownpizza.com

$$

For pizza with a side of possible resident ghost sighting, hit up this allegedly haunted Old Town pizza joint, which also delivers via bike to most of the west side.

Pizza Jerk

CULLY

5028 NE 42nd Ave.

503-284-9333

www.pizzajerkpdx.com

$$

Funky and fun, this Cully pizzeria is a family favorite thanks to the generously sized pies, laid-back service, and kids' play area. In fair weather, the big back patio is a neighborhood magnet.

Pizzeria Otto
ROSEWAY
6708 NE Sandy Blvd.
971-373-8348
www.pizzeriaotto.com
$$

Located a mile from the Grotto (page 31), making it the perfect stop before/after your family Christmas visit, this Northeast Portland pizzeria makes some creative moves, whether it's putting tangerines on a pie, pairing garlic knots with cheese fondue, or serving a Nutella calzone for dessert.

Red Sauce Pizza
CONCORDIA
4935 NE 42nd Ave.
503-288-4899
www.redsaucepizza.com
$$

Stop into this mellow neighborhood pizza parlor for the excellent Caesar salad and a Boo Boo the Bandit or Porkland pie (on the cheery patio, if the weather's agreeable), then get dessert next door at delightfully old-fashioned Rose's Ice Cream (page 141).

Scottie's Pizza Parlor
HOSFORD-ABERNETHY
2128 SE Division St.
971-544-7878
www.scottiespizzaparlor.com
$$

Friendly staff and big, New York–style pies make this laid-back Division Street pizzeria a perfect pick for a family meal. Order a whole pie for pickup or delivery, or just drop in for a round of garlic knots and $2 slices. For dessert, try the lemon Italian ice, made by nearby Fifty Licks (page 230).

Tastebud
MULTNOMAH VILLAGE
7783 SW Capitol Hwy.
503-234-0330
www.tastebudpdx.com
$$

There's no pizza like a Tastebud pizza—these tip-top wood-fired pies are covered in gorgeous produce straight from the farmers' market (Tastebud also has a stand at the PSU, Shemanski, and Pioneer Courthouse Square markets), and once you've devoured your pizza, there's homemade ice cream for dessert.

SANDWICHES, SALADS & SOUPS

These bread-and-filling aficionados turn out superb sandwiches, spanking fresh salads, and nourishing soups, and maybe—just maybe—homemade chocolate chip cookies too.

Addy's Sandwich Bar
DOWNTOWN
911 SW 10th Ave.
503-267-0994
www.addyssandwichbar.com
$

A couple blocks from the grand Central Library (page 95), this simple sandwich shop is a relaxed spot to sit with your babes 'n' baguettes, or take lunch to nearby Director Park, a grassy PSU knoll, or a South Park Blocks bench.

Breken Kitchen
NORTHWEST
1800 NW 16th Ave.
503-841-6359
www.brekenkitchen.com
$

Perhaps due to its proximity to the Montessori school, this airy Northwest café's a kid's haven, with a petite play area and simple menu that starts at 7 a.m. with fried-egg breakfast sandwiches and granola bowls, and segues into lunch with hearty salads and grilled cheese 'n' tomato soup.

East Side Deli

DOWNTOWN	PORTSMOUTH	RICHMOND
1438 SW Park Ave.	*4823 N. Lombard St.*	*4626 SE Hawthorne*
503-243-3354	*503-247-3354*	*Blvd.*
		503-236-7313

www.pdxdeli.com

$

Big, fresh, and fast, these standard-issue deli sandwiches are just the ticket for a band of picky eaters—pluck a laminated card and a pen from the basket by the door, check off what you want, and minutes later you'll have a custom sandwich at a very nice price.

Elephants Delicatessen

DOWNTOWN, DIRECTOR PARK, LAKE OSWEGO, NORTHWEST, PORTLAND
AIRPORT, SOUTH WATERFRONT, AND SOUTHWEST

www.elephantsdeli.com

$

Part European-style café, part feast for the senses, these fun delis delight with an impressive array of sandwiches, salads, soups, and snacks all packaged for easy grab-and-go if eating in isn't on the agenda. If planning a group picnic, take advantage of the online sack-lunch order form.

Lardo

DOWNTOWN	HOSFORD-ABERNETHY
1205 SW Washington St.	*1212 SE Hawthorne Blvd.*
503-241-2490	*503-234-7786*

www.lardosandwiches.com

$

Most of the sandwiches at these busy shops are pretty sophisticated, but that won't stop the adventurous eater from mowing through a pork meatball *banh mi*, then cramming in as many pork-scrap-strewn dirty fries as possible, followed by a hearty helping of bacon- and pineapple-studded mac salad.

Downtown has sidewalk seating, but for a patio with some serious wiggle room, head to the Hawthorne shop.

The Portland Soup Company
DOWNTOWN
1941 SW 4th Ave.
503-987-0217
www.portlandsoup.com
$

A strong contender for cutest cart in Portland, with its country house aesthetics and hanging planters, this sweet PSU soup cart makes some of the most flavorful from-scratch soups, salads, and sandwiches in town. Don't miss the house-made chocolate chip cookies, either.

SWEETS

Whether you are craving banana cupcakes with peanut-butter-fudge icing, homemade coconut cotton candy, or deep-fried deliciousness—be it Nutella-drizzled mini doughnuts or chocolate-covered churros—this list's going satisfy *all* the family sweet teeth.

CANDY & CHOCOLATE

Cacao
DOWNTOWN (HEATHMAN)   DOWNTOWN (WEST END)
712 SW Salmon St.   *414 SW 13th Ave.*
503-274-9510   *503-241-0656*
www.cacaodrinkchocolate.com
$

Widely worshipped for their incomparable selection of bars and confections, these stunning downtown chocolate shops also carry the closest thing to ambrosia—their three European-style drinking chocolates, which you can sip separately or as a tasting trio, or have poured over Salt & Straw olive-oil ice cream for the ultimate affogato.

Candy Babel

KING

1219 NE Alberta St.

503-867-0591

www.candybabel.com

$

Sure, candy isn't exactly intended to be healthy, but this eclectic little sweet shop supplies the highest-quality sugar high by sourcing sustainably made, mostly European sugar snacks that eschew GMOs and high-fructose corn syrup. Don't leave without a cloud of house-made cotton candy, preferably coconut.

Hattie's Sweet Shop

MULTNOMAH VILLAGE

7828 SW Capitol Hwy.

503-293-0088

www.hattiessweetshop.com

$

Named after the owner's candy-loving grandmother, this pretty-in-pink Multnomah Village candy shop sells all sorts of sweet delights, from homemade fudge, nostalgic candies, and nearly forty kinds of licorice to Umpqua ice cream. They're also very conveniently located next to Annie Bloom's Books (page 37) and Thinker Toys (page 92).

Moonstruck Chocolate Café

BEAVERTON

11705 Beaverton-Hillsdale Hwy.

503-352-0835

DOWNTOWN

608 SW Alder St.

503-241-0955

NORTHWEST

526 NW 23rd Ave.

503-542-3400

ST. JOHNS

6600 N. Baltimore Ave.

503-247-3448

www.moonstruckchocolate.com

$

Since 1993 this Portland chocolate chain's been churning out whimsical treats like milk chocolate Labrador truffles and peanut-butter-cream cones, plus a line of chocolate bars and barks. It's also renowned for its rich hot cocoa and decadent chocolate milkshakes. The St. Johns shop is located inside its NoPo chocolate factory, and until 2:30 p.m., watch the chocolatiers in action through the viewing window.

Quin
DOWNTOWN
1025 SW Stark St.
971-300-8395
www.quincandy.com
$

Founded by endlessly imaginative sweet-dreams queen Jami Curl, who reworks classic candies with a distinctly local twist, this wee Downtown sugar shop is stocked with Oregon honey and hazelnut caramels, cherry Dreams Come Chew, Water Avenue Coffee lollipops, and seed-specked blackberry gumdrops.

CREPES

Flapjak
BOISE
4220 N. Mississippi Ave.
503-889-0195
www.flapjakpdx.com
$

From classic banana Nutella to pistachio-cardamom cream, this Mississippi Avenue creperie will fold just about anything into a crepe, each combination more delicious than the last. Gluten-free and vegan options are available, and watch for seasonal specials like huckleberry.

CUPCAKES

Cupcake Jones
KING
1405 NE Alberta St.

PEARL DISTRICT
307 NW 10th Ave.

Phone number for both: 503-222-4404
www.cupcakejones.net
$

Good luck buying just one at these Pearl District and Alberta cupcake shops, where flavors like peach cobbler and strawberry shortcake will likely tempt you into a whole dozen, and the full-size cupcakes all have gooey centers filled with something divine, be it lemon curd or chocolate-peanut-butter ganache.

Saint Cupcake

BOISE
4200 N. Williams Ave.
503-287-3344
DOWNTOWN
1138 SW Morrison St.
503-473-8760
www.saintcupcake.com
$

NORTHWEST
740 NW 23rd Ave.
971-888-4937
SUNNYSIDE
3300 SE Belmont St.
503-235-0078

Try not to drool on the glass case while ogling the neat rows of everything from good old vanilla cupcakes with cream-cheese frosting to the Fat Elvis–banana chocolate chip cake topped with peanut-butter-fudge icing and a crisp banana chip.

DOUGHNUTS & OTHER FRIED DELIGHTS

180

SULLIVAN'S GULCH
2218 NE Broadway St.
503-477-9163
www.180pdx.com
$

Even from a very young age, most kids know intuitively that fried dough is a good thing, and this Spanish-style *xurreria* takes it a step further by teaching them that fried dough is even better when it's dusted in cinnamon sugar, dipped in *dulce de leche*, and submerged in molten chocolate.

Blue Star Donuts

BOISE
3753 N. Mississippi Ave.
971-254-4575
DOWNTOWN
1237 SW Washington St.
503-265-8410
NORTHWEST
921 NW 23rd Ave.
503-265-8659
www.bluestardonuts.com
$

SOUTH WATERFRONT
0672 SW Gaines St.
503-954-3672
SUNNYSIDE
3549 SE Hawthorne Blvd.
503-477-9635

Made to order, these big, beautiful brioche doughnuts are relatively guilt-free, crafted with sustainably sourced ingredients, and fried in rice oil before being drenched in innovative glazes like blueberry basil, passion fruit, and *horchata*. Lines are the norm and sellouts are not uncommon, so make this an early stop.

Pip's Original Doughnuts

CULLY
4759 NE Fremont St.
503-206-8692
www.pipsmobile.com
$

This friendly Fremont doughnut shop commands a fierce following, and rightfully so—it fries up some of the most marvelous made-to-order mini doughnuts around, and if it happens to be your birthday, the first dozen's on them (mark the calendar!). You can't go wrong with the basic honey and sea salt or cinnamon-sugar doughnuts, but be sure to scope out the seasonal specials—from Meyer lemon pear butter to blueberry wild rose. Or request the secret menu's Tropical Wu, adorned with cinnamon sugar, Nutella, honey, and toasted coconut.

Voodoo Doughnut

22 SW 3rd Ave.
503-241-4704
www.voodoodoughnut.com
$

KERNS
1501 NE Davis St.
503-235-2666

Some will argue that the lengthy lines aren't worth the wait, but if only an authentic Voodoo Doll doughnut will do, line up along the glitter-painted brick walls and pay your doughnut dues. Early mornings are best for beating the crowd, although the day's last customers are sometimes sent home with a free bucket of leftovers.

ICE CREAM & GELATO

Cloud City Ice Cream
WOODSTOCK
4525 SE Woodstock Blvd.
503-719-4603
www.cloudcityicecream.com
$

Follow the scent of fresh-made waffle cones to this Woodstock ice-cream parlor, where classic flavors like pistachio and butter pecan share the case with extra-super-fun flavors like Unicorn (red velvet cake and strawberry jam) and Sasquatch Tracks (peanut-butter cups, chocolate shavings, and house-made fudge).

Cool Moon Ice Cream
PEARL DISTRICT
1105 NW Johnson St.
503-224-2021
www.coolmoonicecream.com
$

It's all about location, location, location at this Pearl District ice-cream shop just across the street from Jamison Square (page 49), a city park that transforms from serene town square to writhing mass of splish-splashing, ice-cream-devouring children come summer. Choose from dozens of ice-cream flavors, Moon Pop fruit popsicles, ice-cream sandwiches, and chocolate-dipped frozen bananas.

Eb & Bean

IRVINGTON
1425 NE Broadway St.
503-281-6081
www.ebandbean.com
$

RICHMOND
3040 SE Division St.
971-242-8753

Kids love these fabulous fro-yo shops because they get a sky-high swirl of rosemary caramel or mango coconut frozen yogurt heaped with toppings like cocoa crumbles, salted vanilla caramel corn, and organic gummy bears. Parents love them because the menu's natural, local, and organic, and accommodates all dietary sensitivities. Everyone wins!

Fifty Licks

BUCKMAN
2742 E. Burnside St.
503-395-3333
www.fifty-licks.com
$

HOSFORD-ABERNETHY
2021 SE Clinton St.

Working with a homemade custard base and local ingredients, these cute Southeast ice-cream shops sling some of the creamiest scoops in town, in simple, sublime flavors like caramelized honey, chocolate malt, and blood-orange creamsicle. Adults will love the Affogato Cubano, and the 21 and up chocolate porter float.

Pinolo Gelato

RICHMOND
3707 SE Division St.
503-719-8686
www.pinologelato.com
$

Specializing in flavors so fresh you'd swear your pluot or peach gelato was just picked off a tree, this unassuming Division Street shop has lines out the door come summer, when the always-changing menu's crowded with local berry and stone-fruit gelatos and sorbets.

Ruby Jewel

BOISE	DOWNTOWN	SUNNYSIDE
3713 N. Mississippi Ave.	428 SW 12th Ave.	4703 SE Hawthorne Blvd.
503-954-1978	971-271-8895	503-954-1345
www.rubyjewel.com		

$

From farmers'-market pushcart to multiple locations around town, these sister-owned scoop shops proudly use Pacific Northwest–sourced dairy, fruit, spices, nuts, coffee, and salt in their ice creams and ice-cream sandwiches, which you can find at grocery stores all over town if you don't happen to be within range of a scoop shop when a craving hits.

Salt & Straw

DOWNTOWN	RICHMOND
126 SW 2nd Ave.	3345 SE Division St.
503-384-2150	503-208-2054
NORTHWEST	VERNON
838 NW 23rd Ave.	2035 NE Alberta St.
971-271-8168	503-208-3867
www.saltandstraw.com	

$

If brunch has long passed and you spy a suspiciously long line, it's probably one of these relentlessly popular ice-cream shops, where people consider it sport to wait for their shot at a scoop of chocolate gooey brownie or sea salt with caramel ribbons. If the natives are restless and you need pints to go, you can jump the line. FYI: Salt & Straw's soft-serve spin-off, the Wiz Bang Bar, sits just inside downtown's bustling Pine Street Market food hall (page 96).

Staccato Gelato
KERNS
232 NE 28th Ave.
503-231-7100
www.staccatogelato.com
$

_____

It's hard to know where to run first upon entering this color-splashed dessert den—the case full of homemade gelatos ready for sampling, the stacks of fresh, fragrant cake doughnuts, or the toy-strewn play area. It will take time to do it all, so parents, order a latte and stay awhile.

What's the Scoop?

BOISE	SOUTH WATERFRONT
3540 N. Williams Ave.	*0664 SW Gaines St.*
971-266-1787	*503-719-5308*
www.whatsthescooppdx.com	

$

_____

From both a science and tastiness standpoint, this scoop shop's pretty cool, using nitrogen to rapidly deep-freeze its from-scratch ice creams, creating an incredibly creamy scoop. Flavors both static and seasonal range from chocolate and coffee to blueberry ribbon, lavender honey, and Peaches and Scream, and there are always a few vegan sorbets on the menu.

PIE

Lauretta Jean's
DOWNTOWN AND RICHMOND
Contact information on page 186
$

_____

Good luck picking your pie from the glossy glass case at these darling Downtown and Division Street pie shops, because how do you choose between salted caramel apple, blackberry raspberry streusel, honey hazelnut, chocolate banana cream, and s'mores pie? Clearly, the best course of action is to bring the whole family along and get a slice of each.

Pacific Pie Company
HOSFORD-ABERNETHY AND NORTHWEST
Contact information on page 189
$-$$

Whether your taste in pie skews sweet or savory, these smart Australian-style pie shops have things covered—dishing up everything from crisp-crusted personal-size chicken pot pies and spinach-feta pasties to wedges of key lime, chocolate peanut butter, and Oregon mixed-berry pie for dessert.

Pie Spot
KERNS
521 NE 24th Ave.
503-913-5103
www.pie-spot.com
$

Purveyors of the beloved "pie hole," this sweet little pie shop is part of the Ocean microrestaurant complex that includes 24th & Meatballs (page 213) and Slowburger (page 202), making it the ideal dessert stop after a mini-restaurant crawl. Besides nearly a dozen kinds of pie holes, including marionberry, brown butter pecan, and s'more, the shop also sells savory potpies, gluten-free pies by the slice, pie-crust cinnamon rolls, and an assortment of scones and cookies.

PART 4

DAY TRIPS & WEEKEND GETAWAYS

As much fun as there is to be had in the city, sometimes you gotta get out of town, and endless adventures await beyond Portland's urban fringes—from **salt-licked seaside cities** and **huckleberry-dotted mountain hamlets** to **Central Oregon ski towns**.

Divided into day trips and weekend getaways, and spanning cities all over the state, the following section will help you suss out the best eats, sleeps, shops, playgrounds, and activities wherever you may wander (most day trips include hotel info, just in case you decide to stay awhile).

Follow in the footsteps of legendary explorers Lewis and Clark near **Astoria** (page 242), take a waterfall shower in **Silverton** (page 241), get up close and personal with bobcats and bald eagles in **Bend** (page 260), and munch on marionberry hand pies as you wind through the Applegate Valley on your way to **Ashland** (page 268).

So dig out the bikes and hiking boots, pack *lots* of snacks, mediate any existing backseat border disputes, plug in your "Ticket to Ride" playlist, and put the rubber to the road!

DAY TRIPS

ONE HOUR OR LESS AWAY

COLUMBIA RIVER GORGE

One of the most classic Pacific Northwest day trips, the Columbia River Gorge refreshes with rushing waterfalls, lush forest canopies, and vast vistas (so hang on tight to wiggly ones at all times!). If time allows, couple this adventure with the **Hood River & the Fruit Loop** day trip (page 244).

Get There

From Portland proper, I-84 is the speediest route to the Gorge, but it's well worth it to turn off in Corbett at exit 22, slow down, and explore the **Historic Columbia River Highway**'s gorgeous twists and turns at a leisurely pace.

Eat, See & Do

To start the day like a local, dig into stacks of butter-drenched pancakes and chicken fried steak at homey **Sweet Betty's Bistro** (1000 N. Main Ave.; 503-665-5052; www.sweetbettysbistro .com) in Gresham, then continue on to the historic highway via SE Stark Street. A few miles before the Vista House, stop at charming **Corbett Country Market** (36801 Historic Columbia River Hwy.; 503-695-2234) for road snacks and/or picnic provisions. Wind your way up to the landmark **Vista House at Crown Point** (40700 Historic Columbia River Hwy.; 503-695-2230; www.vistahouse.com), a marble-and-sandstone masterpiece built in 1927 as a rest stop for road-weary Gorge travelers. Take in the breathtaking views, read up on the monument's fascinating history, visit the downstairs gift shop and espresso bar, and make any necessary potty stops.

A couple miles up the highway, find the first of the Columbia Gorge Scenic Waterfalls—**Latourell Falls** (43240 Historic Columbia River Hwy., Corbett), a lovely and less-crowded alternative to famous Multnomah Falls if you aren't in the mood for the tourist throngs. Cross historic **Shepperd's Dell Bridge**, the second ever built along the highway, waterfall-hop your way to mighty **Multnomah Falls** (53000 Historic Columbia River Hwy., Corbett), and then continue on to the **Bonneville Dam** (70543 NW Herman Loop; 541-374-8393; www.dfw.state.or.us/resources /visitors/bonneville_hatchery_more.asp) to tour the visitor center and feed the trout at the fish hatchery (bring quarters).

Drive across the famous **Bridge of the Gods** and back ($2 toll each way), then dig into burgers, fries, and mile-high soft serve at **East Wind Drive-In** (395 NW Wanapa St.; 541-374-8380) in Cascade Locks before doubling back toward home. Or head west to nostalgic **Tad's Chicken 'n Dumplins** (1325 E. Historic Columbia River Hwy.; 503-666-5337; www.tadschicdump.com) for the kid-size versions of the namesake dish, and marionberry cobbler à la mode.

End the day at **McMenamins Edgefield** in Troutdale (page 22), a former county poor farm turned 74-acre family resort, complete with a nine-hole golf course, movie theater, and soaking pool.

WILLAMETTE VALLEY

While the Willamette Valley wine country may seem like a decidedly adult destination, it's full of family-friendly happenings, from a state park that transports you to the pioneer days to an aviation-themed museum and water park with a full-size Boeing 747 on top. Which isn't to say you can't stop for some sipping and swilling—this guide includes a few wineries that warmly welcome families.

Get There
From Downtown Portland take I-5 South to exit 282A, then follow Arndt Road NE and Champoeg Road NE to **Champoeg State Park** (8239 Champoeg Rd. NE; 503-678-1251; www.champoeg.org).

Eat, See & Do
Before you set out for the day, pack a picnic breakfast to eat at your first stop, Champoeg State Park, a historic site situated along the southern shores of the Willamette River. At Champoeg,

tour the visitor center, Robert Newell House Museum, Pioneer Mothers Memorial Cabin museum, and 1860s-style garden. Walk or ride the flat, gentle path to the **Butteville General Store** (which rents bikes, if you didn't bring yours; 10767 Butte St. NE, Aurora; 503-678-1605; www.champoeg.org/attractions/historic -butteville-store.html).

Post-Champoeg, pass through the tiny town of Newberg, with a pit stop at **Chapters Books and Coffee** (701 E. 1st St.; 503-554-0206; www.chaptersbooksandcoffee.com), a lively local bookshop that serves Coava coffee, smoothies, bagels, and pastries. Continue into Dundee for lunch at **Red Hills Market** (155 SW 7th St.; 971-832-8414; www.redhillsmarket.com), a community café and specialty market with a kids' menu, chalkboard-walled play area, and corn hole and bocce courts. Eat in or get lunch to go, and spread a blanket in the grassy pastures of family-friendly **Stoller Family Estate** winery (16161 NE McDougall Rd., Dayton; 503-864-3404; www.stollerfamilyestate.com).

After lunch visit the **Evergreen Aviation & Space Museum** (page 66) and adjoining **Wings & Waves Waterpark** (page 51), where kids will lose their minds over the main attraction—a waterslide emerging from a full-size Boeing 747 parked on the roof. On Saturdays, visit the **Yamhill Valley Heritage Center**, which houses a large collection of antique farm equipment (11275 SW Durham Ln., McMinnville; 503-434-0490; www .yamhillcountyhistory.org).

Make your way to Downtown McMinnville and walk the main street, where you'll find **Hopscotch Toys** (103 SE Baker St.; 503-472-3702; www.hopscotchtoys.com), **Honest Chocolates** (575 NE 3rd St.; 503-474-9042; www.honestchocolates.com), **Red Fox Bakery** (328 NE Evans St.; 503-434-5098; www.redfoxbakery .com), and on Thursday afternoons from May through October, the **McMinnville Farmers Market** (www.downtownmcminnville .com). If the adults in the group want to indulge in some in-town wine tasting, stop into darling **R. Stuart & Co.** wine bar (528 NE 3rd St.; 866-472-8614; www.rstuartandco.com). For dinner, hit **3rd Street Pizza Company** (433 NE 3rd St.; 503-434-5800; www.3rdstreetpizza.com), which has a second-run movie theater inside, then get cones at old-fashioned **Serendipity Ice Cream** (502 NE 3rd St.; 503-474-9189). FYI: if you happen to stay overnight, perhaps in a vintage Airstream at **the Vintages Trailer Resort** (16205 SE Kreder Rd., Dayton; 971-267-2130; www .the-vintages.com) nearby, have a big breakfast at bright, busy **Community Plate** (315 NE 3rd St.; 503-687-1902; www .communityplate.com). If more family-friendly winery-hopping is in order, head north to **Willakenzie Estate** in Yamhill (19143 NE Laughlin Rd.; 503-662-3280; www.willakenzie.com), then take in the big valley views at **Bald Peak State Scenic Viewpoint** (www .oregonstateparks.org/index.cfm?do=parkpage.dsp_parkpage &parkid=77) before finishing the day at venerable **Ponzi Vineyards** in Sherwood (19500 SW Mountain Home Rd.; 503-628-1227; www.ponziwines.com). Head home via State Route 210 through Tigard, or for a very happy ending, set course for the **Family Fun Center** (page 16) and a gripping game of mini golf.

SALEM

In the spring visit Salem, a.k.a. Cherry City, a.k.a. the state capital, for the blooms and blossoms that blanket the city (okay, *and* for the riverfront carousel). In the summer go for the popular Oregon State Fair (page 115) held at the Oregon State Fairgrounds.

Get There

From Portland city center, it's a straight forty-five-minute shot down I-5 to Salem.

Eat, See & Do

Just before town pull off at exit 263 and visit **Antique Powerland** (3995 Brooklake Rd. NE; 503-393-2424; www.antiquepowerland .com), a unique volunteer-led collection of independent museums that restore and exhibit historic farm machinery and equipment—members include the Caterpillar Museum and Trolley Interpretive Center. Then hop back on I-5 or take the back roads to Willamette-River-hugging **Keizer Rapids Park**; kids will love the innovative 15,000-square-foot **Big Toy** playground (1900 Chemawa Rd. N), designed with input from thousands of local schoolchildren.

Continue to Downtown Salem for corned beef hash and cinnamon-roll pancakes with the locals at **Word of Mouth**

Bistro (140 17th St. NE; 503-930-4285; www.wordofsalem.com), then walk it all off en route to the **Willamette Heritage Center** (1313 Mill St. SE; 503-585-7012; www.willametteheritage.org), a grouping of fourteen historic buildings and exhibits that give kids a sense of what early settlers' iPhone-free nineteenth-century lives were like.

Admire the regal state capitol building (free weekday tours available) while strolling through the **Oregon State Capitol State Park** (155 Waverly St. NE; www.oregonstateparks.org /index.cfm?do=parkpage.dsp_parkpage&parkid=187), then continue west to the **Riverfront Park Playground** (200 Water St. NE). Here you'll find the painstakingly hand-carved and hand-painted **Riverfront Carousel** (101 Front St. NE; 503-540-0374; www.salemcarousel.org) and grand **Willamette Queen Sternwheeler** (503-371-1103; www.willamettequeen.com)—book the hour-long cruise to experience what was once the region's main means of transportation.

At the north end of Riverfront Park, kids can explore the hands-on exhibits and tromp through the all-natural outdoor adventure playground at the beautiful **Gilbert House Children's Museum** (116 Marion St. NE; 503-371-3631; www.acgilbert.org), then stop for a lemon bar or almond swirl at **Cascade Baking Company** (229 State St.; 503-589-0491; www.cascadebaking .com), or get a serious sugar high at quirky **Ricky's Bubbles and Sweets Shoppe** (102 Liberty St. NE; 971-599-5678; www .rickyssweetshoppe.wixsite.com/candy) or sleek **Sugar Sugar** (335 State St.; 503-385-1225; www.sugarsugarboo.com).

After lunching on burgers and sweet potato fries at beloved **Wild Pear** (372 State St.; 503-378-7515; www .wildpearcatering.com), brick oven pizzas at **Ritter's** (102 Liberty St. NE; 503-339-7928; www.ritterseatery.com), spicy mac 'n' cheese and pork belly ramen at eclectic **Table Five 08** (508 State St.; 503-581-5508; www.tablefive08.com), or classic Mexican fare at lively **La Margarita** (545 Ferry St. SE; 503-362-8861; www.lamargaritasalem.com), hike around beautiful 90-acre **Bush's Pasture Park** (600 Mission St. SE), stopping to smell the two-thousand-plus roses in the botanical garden, tour the **Bush Barn Art Center** and **Bush House Museum** (www.salemart.org), and patronize the playgrounds. In the summer months, pick up cheap tickets to see the **Salem-Keizer Volcanoes** minor league baseball team (www.milb.com/index.jsp?sid=t578).

On the way home, take a detour into the country, driving northeast to the **Willamette Valley Pie Company** (2994 82nd Ave. NE; 503-362-8857; www.wvpie.com) for a slice of marionberry pie and a factory tour (e-mail beforehand to schedule), then continue on to quaint, small-town **Silverton**, where you can tour the **Gordon House** (869 W. Main St.; 503-874-6006; www.thegordonhouse.org), the only building in Oregon designed by Frank Lloyd Wright (kids are free); dig for dinosaur bones and crawl through the Hobbit House at the **Oregon Garden** (879 W. Main St.; 503-874-8100; www.oregongarden.org); or hike behind a waterfall along the Trail of Ten Falls at **Silver Falls State Park** (20024 Silver Falls Hwy. SE; 503-873-8681; www.oregonstateparks.org/index.cfm?do=parkpage.dsp_parkpage&parkid=151), about a twenty-minute drive from downtown Silverton.

Continue 5 miles north to Bavarian-accented **Mount Angel**, where you can admire the four-story-tall glockenspiel and gobble authentic German bratwurst, *bockwurst*, and knockwurst (with cherry strudel for dessert) at beloved **Mt. Angel Sausage Company** (105 S. Garfield St.; 503-845-2322; www.ropesausage.com).

If visiting in the spring or fall, make a petal pit stop in Woodburn at the **Wooden Shoe Tulip Farm** (33814 S. Meridian Rd.; 503-634-2243; www.woodenshoe.com) for its spectacular spring **Tulip Fest**, which features fields full of flowers, train rides, food and games, and a kids' carnival, or fall **Pumpkin Fest**.

ONE TO TWO HOURS AWAY

ASTORIA/WARRENTON

Sitting pretty at the mouth of the Columbia River, small-town Astoria has been forever immortalized by *The Goonies*, and while the owners of Mikey's iconic house have disavowed visitors, there's still tons to do—toss gliders off a 125-foot column, follow in Lewis and Clark's famous footsteps, and see firsthand how Warrenton's infamous stretch of surf earned its unnerving nickname "Graveyard of the Pacific."

Get There
From Downtown Portland, take US Route 26 West, a busy thoroughfare best tackled first thing in the morning to beat the sea-seeking rush. At the US Route 101 junction, veer north toward Seaside, and skim the coast until you reach Warrenton, which takes about two hours.

Eat, See & Do
In Warrenton, get out and stretch little legs at **Fort Stevens State Park** (100 Peter Iredale Rd.; 503-861-3170; www.oregonstate parks.org/index.cfm?do=parkpage.dsp_parkpage&parkid=129), a former coastal-defense fort. Tumble down dunes, tour an underground gun battery, and investigate the bony wreckage of the *Peter Iredale*, a four-masted steel ship that met its fate on the treacherous Clatsop Spit. If you trust your travel partners not to fall in the water, have a floating breakfast picnic at picturesque (and less windy) **Coffenbury Lake**, then continue on to the **Lewis and Clark National Historical Park** (92343 Fort Clatsop Rd.; 503-861-2471; www.nps.gov/lewi) for a tour of the visitor center and **Fort Clatsop** replica (don't forget to claim your junior ranger packet!) and a peaceful walk along the **Fort to Sea Trail**. Two miles away lies the **High Life Adventures** zip-line park (92111 High Life Rd.; 503-861-9875; highlife-adventures.com) where eight zip lines crisscross forests, ponds, and even a 7-acre lake (dunking optional).

Next, cross Youngs Bay and drop in to quaint Astoria. If brunching, try **Blue Scorcher Bakery and Café** (1493 Duane St.; 503-338-7473; www.bluescorcher.coop); otherwise, it's all about the fish 'n' chips at darling boat-bound **Bowpicker** (1634 Duane St.; 503-791-2942; www.bowpicker.com). For old-fashioned burgers 'n' chocolate shakes, try cheery little **Custard King** (1597 Commercial St.; 503-325-5464; www.custardkingastoria.com). Tour the **Columbia River Maritime Museum** (1792 Marine Dr.; 503-325-2323; www.crmm.org), then catch the **Astoria Riverfront Trolley** (www.old300.org) right outside. Kids will also dig the **Uppertown Firefighter's Museum** (2968 Marine Dr.; 503-325-0920; www.cumtux.org) and upstairs **Children's Museum**, a half mile east on Marine Drive. Continue east on the **Astoria Riverwalk** to visit the free **Hanthorn Cannery Museum** at Pier 39 (100 39th St.; 503-325-2502; www.canneryworker.org). If the weather's particularly nasty, sail for **Captain Gray's Port of Play** indoor play center (785 Alameda Ave.; 503-325-8669; www.astoriaparks.com/parks/port_of_play.aspx) or the **Astoria Aquatic Center**, home to four indoor pools, a lazy river, and a waterslide (1997 Marine Dr.; 503-325-7027; www.astoriaparks .com/parks/astoria_aquatic_center.aspx).

Try the signature honeycomb-candy-studded Hokey Pokey ice cream at **Frite & Scoop** (175 14th St.; 503-468-0416; www .friteandscoop.com), then take the family film buffs to the **Oregon Film Museum** (732 Duane St.; 503-325-2203; www .oregonfilmmuseum.com), formerly the historic Clatsop County Jail, as seen in *The Goonies*. A block away, find the stunning Queen Anne architecture and ornate gardens of the landmark **Flavel House Museum** (441 8th St.; 503-325-2203; www.cumtux .org), former home of community pillar Captain George Flavel. Afterward trek to the resplendently restored **Astoria Column** (1 Coxcomb Dr.; 503-325-2963; www.astoriacolumn.org); before climbing the spiral staircase to take in the 360-degree views, stop in to the gift shop and buy biodegradable gliders to toss off the top. If time allows, drive north to Long Beach Peninsula's **Cape Disappointment State Park** (244 Robert Gray Dr., Ilwaco, WA; www.capedisappointment.org) to visit the **North Head Lighthouse** and **Lewis and Clark Interpretive Center**.

Come supper time, parents will love the house taps and river views at **Buoy Beer Company** (1 8th St.; 503-325-4540; www .buoybeer.com), and kids will love the glass panel in the floor for sea-lion watching. Pub grub, patio tables, and kid-friendly vibes also abound at popular **Fort George Brewery** (1483 Duane St.; 503-325-7468; www.fortgeorgebrewery.com).

Stay

Affordable, comfortable, and convenient lodging can be found at the **Holiday Inn Express** (204 W. Marine Dr.; 503-325-6222; www.ihg.com/holidayinnexpress/hotels/us/en/astoria/astor /hoteldetail) or **Hampton Inn** (201 39th St.; 503-325-8888; www.hamptoninn3.hilton.com/en/hotels/oregon/hampton-inn-and-suites-astoria-astorhx/index.html), both of which have complimentary breakfast, pools, and loaner bikes for riding along the riverwalk trail. For more luxe digs (with DIY waffles in the morning), stay at the beautiful **Cannery Pier Hotel** (10 Basin St.; 503-325-4996; www.cannerypierhotel.com), where ships steam right past your riverfront balcony, and the front desk keeps copies of the *The Goonies* on DVD.

HOOD RIVER & THE FRUIT LOOP

Wind, waves, and waterfalls meet fruit 'n' flowers in this picturesque stretch of Oregon, where you'll skip from the dramatically rugged basalt cliffs of the Columbia River Gorge to the gently meandering meadows and orchards of the Hood River Fruit Loop, with a little cherry picking, river stomping, rhubarb-pie eating, and stand-up paddleboarding in between.

Get There

The quickest route from Portland to Hood River is to get on I-84 and go east, young man (or woman), but if you've got a couple extra hours for vistas and waterfalls, hop on the **Historic Columbia River Highway** and fold in the **Columbia River Gorge** day trip (page 236).

Eat, See & Do

If the family consensus is that the first sight they'd like to see in Hood River is a hearty breakfast, try the gargantuan Grandma's cinnamon rolls and Pigs in a Blanket at family-friendly **Bette's Place** (416 Oak St.; 541-386-1880; www.bettesplace.com), or head uptown to lively local hub **Pine Street Bakery** (1103 12th St.; 541-386-1719; www.pinestreetbakery.com) for bacon, cheddar, and egg biscuit sandwiches and bricks of blueberry molasses cornbread. Or, for Stumptown coffee, great house hot chocolate, and a kids' play area, line up with the locals at **Dog River Coffee** (411 Oak St.; 541-386-4502; www.facebook.com /dogrivercoffee).

Poke around the Downtown Hood River shops, particularly the **Waucoma Bookstore** (212 Oak St.; 541-386-5353; www .waucomabookstore.com) and **G. Williker's Toy Shoppe** (202 Oak St.; 541-387-2229; www.gwtoyshoppe.com), and most definitely the darling and wildly popular **Mike's Ice Cream** (504 Oak St.; 541-386-6260). If it's Saturday, head down to the **Hood River Farmers Market** (5th St. and Columbia St.; www.gorgegrown.com), then have lunch across the street at **Full Sail Brewing Company** (506 Columbia St.; 541-386-2247; www.fullsailbrewing.com), where the salmon fish 'n' chips and Imperial Stout brownies come with gorgeous Gorge views off the back deck. Or grab pizza and Oh Man! draft root beer at buzzy **Double Mountain Brewery** (8 4th St.; 541-387-0042; www.doublemountainbrewery.com).

Take State Street to State Route 35, then follow the **Hood River Fruit Loop** (www.hoodriverfruitloop.com) through a vibrant valley filled with u-pick fruit orchards, farm stands, and wineries set against a backdrop of cerulean skies and majestic Mt. Hood. Kids will love picking their own blueberries and picnicking alongside the u-cut flower fields at the **Gorge White House** (2265 SR 35; 541-386-2828; www.thegorgewhitehouse .com), chowing down on cinnamon rolls and cherry hand pies at **Packer Orchards and Bakery** (3900 SR 35; 541-234-4481; www .packerorchardsandbakery.com), feeding the furry residents of **Cascade Alpacas of Oregon** (page 155), and snipping their own bouquet at ethereal **Hood River Lavender Farm** (3801 Straight Hill Rd.; 541-354-9917; www.hoodriverlavender.com), which hosts the **Lavender Daze** festival every July. On your way back to town, take the Odell Highway over to the **Hood River U-Pick Organic** farm (4320 Royal Anne Dr.; 541-359-4481; www .hoodriverupick.com; cash/check only) to stock up on fresh organic cherries, berries, apples, and flowers. For a unique peek at the valley sans car—hop the **Mount Hood Railroad** (110 Railroad St.; 800-872-4661; www.mthoodrr.com) and explore the valley via historic locomotive (box lunch available for purchase).

Back in town, if the weather's sizzling and beach time's in order, let little ones romp on the riverfront beach or playground at the **Hood River Waterfront Park** (650 Portway Ave.; www .hoodriverwaterfront.org), also a prime vantage point for watching windsurfers. Or sign the family adventurer up for stand-up paddleboarding lessons at **Big Winds** (207 Front St.; 541-386-6086; www.bigwinds.com). If the weather's not so nice, spend a couple of hours admiring the lovingly restored relics at the **Western Antique Aeroplane and Automobile Museum** (1600 Air Museum Rd.; 541-308-1600; www.waaamuseum.org).

If you've got extra time and a touch of wanderlust, cross the Hood River Bridge (you'll need a dollar per axle for the toll) and wind up into scenic Downtown **White Salmon**, stopping for organic, locally sourced picnic provisions at **Feast Market and Delicatessen** (320 E. Jewett Blvd.; 509-637-2530; www .feastmarket.org) and sweet treats at **White Salmon Baking Company** (80 NE Estes Ave.; 509-281-3140; www .whitesalmonbaking.com). Continue east along the Washington side of the Columbia until you reach the **Catherine Creek Trailhead** (www.wta.org/go-hiking/hikes/catherine-creek); with over ninety varieties of wildflowers, it's a must-see spring stop, plus there's a mile-long paved loop that's perfect for strollers. Continue east for 17 miles, cross The Dalles Bridge, and make your way back down to the **Columbia Gorge Discovery Center and Museum** (5000 Discovery Dr.; 541-296-8600; www .gorgediscovery.org), then pause at the **Tom McCall Nature Preserve** (www.gorgefriends.org/hike-the-gorge/tom-mccall -nature-preserve.html) for the 1-mile Rowena Plateau hike and breathtaking views from **Rowena Crest Viewpoint**.

End the day by stuffing yourselves with local-produce-topped wood-fired pies at **Solstice** (501 Portway Ave.; 541-436-0800; www.solsticewoodfirecafe.com), or burgers 'n' (root) beer at **pFriem Family Brewers** (707 Portway Ave.; 541-321-0490; www.pfriembeer.com) before heading home with windswept hair and cherry pits in your pockets.

Stay
For big views on a budget, book the riverfront **Best Western Plus Hood River Inn** (1108 E. Marina Way; 541-386-2200; www .hoodriverinn.com), or bunk down in the heart of Downtown at

the cheery historic **Hood River Hotel** (102 Oak St.; 541-386-1900; www.hoodriverhotel.com).

MT. HOOD

Snow or shine, Portland's favorite pointy white peak is a kids' paradise. Scarf huckleberry short stacks and deep-fried Snow Balls in Government Camp, paddle around Trillium Lake, snuggle up by the stone fireplace at Timberline Lodge, and go night-tubing to a disco beat—then end the day with s'mores, obviously.

Get There
Taking the scenic route to Mt. Hood through the **Hood River Fruit Loop** (page 244) makes for delicious detours, but the most direct route to the mountain is via US Route 26 East through small-town Sandy, where, speaking of delicious detours, you happen to drive right past **Joe's Donuts** (39230 Pioneer Blvd.; 503-668-7215; www.joes-donuts.com). If you're staying between Sandy and Timberline and would rather outsource the driving, take advantage of TriMet's **Mt. Hood Express** (www.mthoodexpress .com) bus service, which includes bike trailers and ski boxes for your gear.

Eat, See & Do
When Mt. Hood's in winter-wonderland mode, there's endless fun to be had in the snow. Besides the major ski resorts—**Mt. Hood Meadows** (14040 SR 35; 503-337-2222; www.skihood .com), **Mt. Hood Skibowl** (87000 US 26; 503-222-2695; www .skibowl.com), and **Timberline** (27500 E. Timberline Rd.; 503-272-3311; www.timberlinelodge.com)—tubing, snowshoeing, and snowmobiling options abound. At **Skibowl** kids can ride the Tubing Carousel, clown around in Frosty's Playland, ride mini snowmobiles, race the snow tube runs, or stay high and dry in the indoor Super Play Zone. On weekend nights plan on staying up late for **Cosmic Tubing**, a wild evening of after-dark tubing featuring over six hundred thousand LED lights, laser light shows, black lights, and fun music. (Just a note: many of the activities have a height restriction, so check the website before you go.) For a smaller, quieter, cheaper ski experience, try **Summit Ski Area** (90255 Government Camp Loop Rd.; 503-272-0256; www.summitskiarea.com), or if you're sticking to the Hood

River area, the **Cooper Spur Mountain Resort** (10755 Cooper
Spur Rd.; 541-352-6692; www.cooperspur.com).
    To explore the area on snowshoes or snowmobiles, visit
Mt. Hood Adventure (88661 Government Camp Loop Rd.; 503-
715-2175; www.mthoodadventure.com) for rentals, trail advice,
and guided tours. And if all you really want is a snowy slope to
break out the sleds, pick up a $4 sno-park permit and hit the
White River Sno-Park (www.fs.usda.gov/recarea/mthood/null
/recarea/?recid=53332&actid=88).
    Although Timberline *is* the country's only year-round ski
resort, in the summer skis and snowboards take a backseat to
hiking, biking, swimming, rafting, and fishing, not to mention
the awesome **Magic Mile Sky Ride** (www.timberlinelodge.com
/magic-mile-sky-ride). Down the mountain, Mt. Hood Skibowl
opens its **Adventure Park** (www.skibowl.com), where purchased
passes give the kids varying levels of access to over twenty
attractions, from mountain biking and zip-lining to the Freefall
Bungee Tower and Alpine Slide.
    If communing with nature's on the agenda, paddle or
hike around kid-friendly **Trillium Lake** (www.recreation.gov
/camping/trillium/r/campgroundDetails.do?contractCode
=NRSO&parkId=71614), kayak lovely **Mirror Lake** (www.fs.usda
.gov/recarea/mthood/recreation/recarea/?recid=53566), get
the fly fishing 411 at **the Fly Fishing Shop** in Welches (67296
E. US 26; 503-622-4607; www.flyfishusa.com), then claim a
spot along the Sandy River, or hike the **Little Zigzag Falls Trail**
(www.fs.usda.gov/recarea/mthood/recarea/?recid=53414) or **Old
Salmon River Trail** (www.fs.usda.gov/recarea/mthood
/recarea/?recid=53442). From Government Camp, it's about an
hour's drive to Maupin, renowned for its Deschutes River rafting;
book a half- or full-day trip with **Deschutes River Adventures**
(602 Deschutes Ave.; 541-395-2238; www.800-rafting.com) or **All
Star Rafting** (405 Deschutes Ave.; 541-395-2201; www.asrk.com).
    All this activity will leave the family famished, and most
of the area's eats are in Government Camp. For a hearty
breakfast of steak 'n' eggs and huckleberry short stacks, try
the nostalgic **Huckleberry Inn** (88611 Government Camp Loop
Rd.; 503-272-3325; www.huckleberry-inn.com). For pub grub
and a solid kids' menu, there's **Mt. Hood Brewing Company**

(87304 E. Government Camp Loop Rd.; 503-272-3172; www
.mthoodbrewing.com), while **Glacier Haus Bistro** (88817 E.
Government Camp Loop Rd.; 503-272-3471; www.glacierhaus
.com) breaks out the Bavarian bites with hearty Hungarian beef
goulash and schnitzel, plus a half dozen or so house pizzas.
Also working the après-ski bar theme is **the Ratskeller**
(88335 E. Government Camp Loop Rd.; 503-272-3635; www
.ratskellerpizzeria.com), where kids will plow through The Rat
pizza to get back to the arcade games. **Timberline Lodge** (page
106) also offers a variety of eateries throughout the property,
from the lively **Ram's Head Bar** to the cozy **Cascade Dining
Room**, where kids 11 and under eat free during the first hour of
dinner service, with an adult entrée purchase.

Stay

If money's no object, **Timberline Lodge** (page 106) is the
consummate room with a view—plus kids will love the heated
year-round outdoor pool, game room, and board-game- and
DVD-lending libraries. When you book, add on the Campfire
S'mores upgrade, and put your room's fireplace to good use.
To stay close to the Government Camp action, book the **Best
Western Mt. Hood Inn** (87450 Government Camp Loop Rd.; 503-
272-3205; www.bestwesternoregon.com/hotels/best-western
-mt-hood-inn). For full-service adult amenities like a spa and
golf course, spread out in one of the roomy studios or Sunrise
suites at lushly landscaped **the Resort at the Mountain** (68010 E.
Fairway Ave., Welches; 503-622-3101; www.mthood-resort.com),
located about a fifteen-minute drive from Mt. Hood (or take its
free shuttle to the Mt. Hood Express bus stop).

WEEKEND TRIPS

TWO TO THREE HOURS AWAY

CANNON BEACH/SEASIDE

Light on the rich historical sights and landmarks enjoyed by Astoria, the central Oregon coast towns of Cannon Beach and Seaside are all about, well, the beach. Explore the teeming tide pools of Haystack Rock, race sit-down "funcycles" along the water's edge, picnic with panoramic Pacific views, and eat your weight in saltwater taffy before packing up the pails, dusting the sand off your toes, and heading home.

Get There

Once on US Route 26 West, it's tempting to put the pedal to the metal until you hit Cannon Beach (especially if trying to beat the traffic), but **Camp 18** (42362 US 26, Elsie; 503-755-1818; www .camp18restaurant.com) is worth the stop for the fun log-cabin ambience, tire-size cinnamon rolls, and a wiggles-banishing walk along pretty Humbug Creek. Not to mention the clean, warm, *indoor* bathrooms.

Eat, See & Do

If you don't want to backtrack later, veer north at the US Route 101 fork and visit Seaside first—while this well-worn sea town's atmosphere trends more carnie than classy, kids (particularly flirty teens) think it's the bee's knees, especially if you head straight for the **Seaside Carousel Mall** (300 Broadway St.; 503-738-6728; www.seasidecarouselmall.com) for a carousel spin, arcade games, and **Flashback Malt Shoppe** banana split. School everyone at Skee-Ball at the **Funland Entertainment Center** (201 Broadway St.; 503-738-7361; www.funlandseaside .com), walk or pedal a surrey along the highly social 1.5-mile **Seaside Promenade**, and visit the **Seaside Aquarium** (200 N. Prom; 503-738-6211; www.seasideaquarium.com), a former 1920s salt-water bathhouse and oldest privately owned aquarium on the West Coast. If spending some time in town, teen girls (ages 14 and up) may enjoy the surfing and stand-up paddlebboarding lessons or day camps offered by **NW Women's Surf Camps** (www.nwwomenssurfcamps.com). Before you leave, slurp scoops at **Sea Star Gelato** (8 N. Columbia St.; www.seastargelato.com), and browse the boggling array of sweets at **Schwieter's Cones & Candy** (406 A Broadway St.; 503-717-8808; www.schwieterts.com).

En route to Cannon Beach, follow the signs to ruggedly beautiful **Ecola State Park** ($5 parking permit required; www.oregonstateparks.org/index.cfm?do=parkpage.dsp_parkpage&parkId=136), a popular hiking and picnicking spot. Follow in Captain William Clark and the Corps of Discovery's footsteps as you hike the Clatsop Loop Trail, take in the sweeping views of Tillamook Head, and poke around the Indian Beach tide pools.

In **Cannon Beach**, join the brunch crowds clamoring for bay shrimp omelets and gingerbread waffles at **Lazy Susan Café** (126 N. Hemlock St.; 503-436-2816; www.lazy-susan-cafe.com), or just have a quiet cup of Stumptown, an açai bowl, and a sticky bun at **Sea Level Bakery** (3116 S. Hemlock St.; 503-436-4254; www.sealevelbakery.com). Then hit the downtown shops—kids will love picking out a kite at **Once Upon A Breeze** (240 N. Spruce St.; 503-436-1112), toy testing at **Geppetto's Toy Shoppe** (200 N. Hemlock St.; 503-436-2467) and **Voyages Toy Co.** (172 N. Hemlock St.; 503-436-0266), browsing beach reads at **Cannon Beach Book Company** (130 N. Hemlock St.; 503-436-1301; www.cannonbeachbooks.com), picking up Haystack Rock-shaped macaroons at **Cannon Beach Bakery** (240 N. Hemlock St.; 503-436-0399; www.cannonbeachbakery.com), and blowing their allowance at iconic pink-and-white-striped **Bruce's Candy Kitchen** (256 N. Hemlock St.; 503-436-2641; www.brucescandy.com). For lunch or dinner, pile into fast, unfussy **Ecola Seafood Restaurant and Market** (208 N. Spruce St.; 503-436-9130; www.ecolaseafoods.com) for everything from clam strips to cod burgers to corn dogs, or dig into chowder bread bowls at old school **Driftwood Restaurant** (179 N. Hemlock St.; 503-436-2439; www.driftwoodcannonbeach.com).

Come low tide, rent sit-down bikes for the whole gang at **Family FUNcycles** (1160 S. Hemlock St.; 503-440-6942; www.facebook.com/cannonbeachfamilyfuncyles) and speed along the sand, then head down to **Tolovana Beach State Park** (S. Hemlock St. and W. Warren Way) and spend some time exploring the teeming tide pools of hallowed **Haystack Rock** (see if you can spot a nesting tufted puffin). Continue ten minutes south on US Route 101 to **Hug Point State Recreation Site** (www.oregonstateparks.org/index.cfm?do=parkpage.dsp_parkpage&parkid=137), and trace the old stagecoach wheel ruts carved into the rocks, then move on to **Oswald West State Park** (www.oregonstateparks.org/index.cfm?do=parkpage.dsp_parkpage&parkid=139) and walk the half-mile trail to beautiful **Short Sand Beach.** Moving south toward the quaint seaside town of Manzanita, you'll pass stunning Neahkahnie Mountain—the trail to the top is relatively strenuous, but be sure to stop at the viewpoint for breathtaking views.

In Manzanita, brake for **Bread and Ocean**'s lauded cardamom cinnamon rolls and a cup of Sleepy Monk coffee (154 Laneda Ave.; 503-368-5823; www.breadandocean.com); stock up on chocolate-covered Swedish fish and birthday-cake-flavored taffy at **Manzanita Sweets** (310 Laneda Ave.; 503-368-3792; www.manzanitasweets.com); and find the perfect kite, book, or puzzle at the aptly named **Toylandia** toy shop (320 Laneda Ave.; 503-368-3792). Twenty minutes further south, in **Rockaway Beach**, get schooled in the art of crabbing (and crab eating) at **Kelly's Brighton Marina** (29200 US 101 N; 503-368-5745; www.kellysbrightonmarina.com), or munch on stellar crab cakes, cod 'n' chips and clam chowder at the laid-back **Old Oregon Smokehouse** fish shack (120 US. 101; 503-355-2817).

After a pit stop at beautiful **Kilchis Point Reserve**, arrive in Tillamook, ready for softball-size ice-cream cones and a free self-guided tour at famous **Tillamook Cheese Factory** (4175 US 101; 503-815-1300; www.tillamook.com). Just down the way, challenge the family to eighteen holes at **Bay Breeze Golf** putting course (2325 Latimer Rd. N; 503-842-1166; www.baybreezegolf.com), visit the petting farm and do some Brie sampling and shopping at **Blue Heron French Cheese Company** (2001 Blue Heron Dr.; 800-275-0639; www.blueheronoregon.com), and tour the

Tillamook County Pioneer Museum (2106 2nd St.; 503-842-4553; www.tcpm.org), a rich resource for learning about early life in Tillamook County. From here, take State Route 131 to **Cape Meares State Park** (www.oregonstateparks.org/index.cfm?do=parkpage .dsp_parkpage&parkid=131) to tour the nineteenth-century lighthouse; hike to the Octopus Tree; and try to spot a whale, bald eagle, sea lion, or common murre seabird colony. Afterward visit the engine room and examine aviation artifacts at the **Tillamook Air Museum** (6030 Hangar Rd.; 503-842-1130; www.tillamookair. com), then make the fifteen-minute trip to **Munson Creek Falls State Park** (www.oregonstateparks.org/index.cfm?do=parkpage. dsp_parkpage&parkid=175) to see the tallest waterfall in the Coast Range (319 feet!). Driving back to Portland on State Route 6, visit the **Tillamook Forest Center** (45500 Wilson River Hwy.; 503-815-6800; www.tillamookforestcenter.org) to explore the hands-on exhibits, watch a fifteen-minute film about the Tillamook Burn, climb a 40-foot-tall replica of a forest-fire lookout tower, and cross a 250-foot-long suspension bridge to the Wilson River Trail.

Trip tip: if visiting in June, mark your calendar for the annual **Cannon Beach Sandcastle Contest and Fun Run** (www .cannonbeach.org), which draws thousands of competitors and onlookers alike. The **Cannon Beach Farmers Market** (www .cannonbeachmarket.org) also runs every Tuesday afternoon, June through September.

Stay

With its oceanfront location, complimentary cookies and beach cruisers, weekend weenie roasts and ice-cream socials, and nightly bonfires (with s'mores, of course), Cannon Beach's **Surfsand Resort** (148 W. Gower Ave.; 855-632-6744; www .surfsand.com) will please the whole family. The **Inn at Cannon Beach** (3215 S. Hemlock St.; 800-321-6304; www .innatcannonbeach.com) curries favor with free sand pails and taffy at check-in, not to mention having a particularly prolific wild rabbit population, while the **Blue Gull Inn** (632 S. Hemlock St.; 503-436-2714; www.bluegullinn.net) is a cheap and charming pick.

CENTRAL OREGON COAST

Stuffed with salty, sandy seaside to-dos, this guide will take you through the Central Coast towns of Lincoln City, Depoe Bay, Newport, and Yachats, where you can hunt for blown-glass treasure, run rampant in the dragon-guarded Sandcastle Playground, marvel at the geological wonder that is the ominously named Devil's Punchbowl, sit in on an octopus feeding, and chomp on fresh fish 'n' chips.

Get There

From Portland take State Route 99 West through McMinnville (if you have an extra day, fold in the **Willamette Valley** day trip, page 237, and stay the night in a vintage Airstream at **the Vintages Trailer Resort**, page 239), then continue following State Route 18 West to US Route 101 South, which drops you right into Lincoln City.

Eat, See & Do

In Lincoln City, after blueberry French toast and crab Benedict at cozy **Wild Flower Grill** (4250 NE US 101; 541-994-9663; www .thewildflowergrill.com), continue less than a half mile southwest on US Route 101, turn north at Logan Road, and follow it to **Roads End State Recreation Site** (www.oregonstateparks.org /index.cfm?do=parkpage.dsp_parkpage&parkid=163); you'll find a beautiful and blissfully nontouristy stretch of sand perfect for a beach romp (or picnic, if you brought your own breakfast). Roads End is also a good spot to hunt for one of the nearly three thousand handcrafted glass floats the city plants along the public beaches each year as part of its **Finders Keepers** program (www .oregoncoast.org/finders-keepers).

Continue south along US Route 101 to the **Connie Hansen Garden**, a gorgeous 1-acre botanical garden that's free to stroll through from dusk to dawn (1931 NW 33rd St.; 541-994-6338; www.conniehansengarden.com). If your fellow travelers are more into railslides than rhododendrons, just down the road is the **Lincoln City Skate Park** (NE 22nd St. and NW Devil's Point Dr.; www.lincolncity.org/index.asp?sec=2cf768db-81f6-4778 -8b05-0df8e2d577ef&type=b_basic), once dubbed the country's gnarliest skate park by *Thrasher* magazine. From here, loop toward Devil's Lake to **Regatta Grounds Park**, where little ones (and even not-so-little ones) will go nuts over the wooden **Sandcastle Playground**, complete with a giant metal-and-repurposed-rubber dragon, a.k.a. Sparky the Wish Guardian. There's also a lovely lakefront beach and dock area for picnicking, swimming, fishing, and kayaking. As you continue south, stop at **D River State Park** (www.oregonstateparks.org/index.cfm?do=parkpage.dsp_parkpage&parkid=154) to see the shortest river in the world as it flows into the Pacific, and watch the kites . . . or fly your own—**Northwest Winds Kites and Toys** (130 SW US 101; 541-994-1004; www.nwwinds.biz) is just across the road. Three miles farther, brush up on local lore while kids play in the children's corner at the **North Lincoln County Historical Museum** (4907 SW US 101; 541-996-6614; www.northlincolncountyhistoricalmuseum.org), then visit neighboring **Jennifer Sears Glass Art Studio** (4821 SW US 101; 541-996-2569; www.jennifersearsglassart.com) to watch local artisans deftly craft works of blown-glass art; for an unforgettable family art activity (age 8 and up), book a half-hour session and create your own one-of-a-kind keepsakes. If catching your own crab or clam feast at nearby **Siletz Bay** is on your bucket list, the city offers free summer clinics (www.oregoncoast.org/crabbing-and-clamming-clinics). Pick up gear at Bi-Mart or Ace Hardware, or if you have your traps and bait already, stop into **Eleanor's Undertow** (869 SW 51st St.; 541-996-3800) for a license . . . and blueberry cobbler à la mode.

A half hour south in **Depoe Bay**, whale watch for free from beautiful **Boiler Bay State Scenic Viewpoint** (www.oregonstateparks.org//index.cfm?do=parkpage.dsp_parkpage&parkid=153), or for an up-close-and-personal whale tale, book an hour-long excursion with **Dockside Charters** (270 Coast Guard Dr.; 541-765-2545; www.docksidedepoebay.com)—its thirty-four-passenger boat has a heated cabin and bathrooms, and kids under 5 sail free. Afterward head up Bay Street toward **Gracie's Sea Hag** (58 N. US 101; 541-765-2734; www.theseahag.com) for bowls of the famous clam chowder, then stop into **Ainslee's Salt Water Taffy** (66 SE US 101; 541-765-2431; www.ainslees.com) to watch taffy being made in the glassed-in kitchen. After a stop at **Rocky Creek State Scenic Viewpoint** (www.oregonstateparks.org//index.cfm?do =parkpage.dsp_parkpage&parkid=184), detour along the **Otter Crest Loop** for spectacular views, access to the **Devil's Punchbowl**, and more whale-watching opportunities from **Otter Crest State Scenic Viewpoint.** Also not to be missed is the **Yaquina Head Outstanding Natural Area**, about ten minutes south—visit the interpretive center, spot harbor seals and whales, and take the forty-five-minute tour of **Yaquina Head Lighthouse** (www.yaquinalights.org; kids must be at least 42 inches tall to take the tour). And if you've seen one lighthouse, you *haven't* seen them all, so drive fifteen minutes south to the **Yaquina Bay Lighthouse** (www.yaquinalights.org); rumored to be haunted, it's Newport's oldest structure and the only historic wooden Oregon lighthouse still remaining.

From the **Yaquina Bay State Recreation Site**, make your way east to Newport's bustling **Bay Boulevard**, and put your name on the list at ever-popular **Local Ocean Seafoods** (213 SE Bay Blvd.; 541-574-7959; www.localocean.net), or drop into funky, flotsam- and jetsam-draped **Ocean Bleu at Gino's** (808 SW Bay Blvd.; 541-265-2424; www.oceanbleuseafoods .com) for popcorn shrimp and hand-dipped fish 'n' chips, then browse the main drag's kitsch and candy shops. Kids will be enthralled by the gently bobbing floats piled with sea lions, whose uncouth antics and ceaseless squabbling ensure a rapt audience. Or get your fish 'n' chips and smoked salmon candy fix at funky **South Beach Fish Market** (3640 S. Coast Hwy.; 541-867-6800; www.southbeachfishmarket.com), before spending a few hours at the nearby **Oregon Coast Aquarium** (page 12), then stop in to the visitor center at neighboring **Hatfield Marine Science Center** (2030 SE Marine Science Dr.; 541-867-0100; www.hmsc.oregonstate.edu), where kids can handle sea animals, engineer a tsunami-proof Lego house, and watch the octopus feeding. Come dinnertime, slurp spaghetti 'n' meatballs and *margherita* pizzas at Nye Beach's lively **Sorella** (526 NW Coast St.; 541-265-4055; www.sorellanyebeach.com), before getting your fudge fix at **Nye Beach Sweets** (314 NW Coast St.; 541-574-1963; www.nyebeachsweets.com). If bunking here for the night, book at the beachfront **Hallmark Resort** (744 SW Elizabeth St.; 855-391-2484; www.hallmarkinns.com) or

Inn at Nye Beach (729 NW Coast St.; 541-265-2477; www
.innatnyebeach.com)—the kids' suite has bunk beds, board
games, and beautiful ocean views.
Keep moving south, pausing at **Seal Rock State Park** (10032
NW Pacific Coast Hwy.; www.oregonstateparks.org/index
.cfm?do=parkpage.dsp_parkpage&parkId=147) to prowl around
the tide pools, find the elephant outline in Elephant Rock,
observe the eponymous residents from a safe distance, and do
some agate hunting. End up in tiny, cheery **Yachats**, where you
can crack crab at funky **Luna Sea Fish House** (153 NW US 101;
541-547-4794; www.lunaseafishhouse.com), stock up on taffy and
Tillamook ice cream at **Topper's** (153 US 101; 541-547-3273), or
warm up with hot chocolate and orange-blossom honey buns at
Green Salmon (220 US 101; 541-547-3077; www.thegreensalmon
.com). End your explorations at **Cape Perpetua Scenic Area**
(www.fs.usda.gov/recarea/siuslaw/recarea/?recid=42265)—tour
the visitor center's interpretive exhibits; hike the 23-mile trail
system; see a 600-year-old Sitka spruce; and visit Devil's Churn,
Thor's Well, and Cook's Chasm.

Stay
It's worth the extra drive south to stay at the marvelous
Heceta Head Lighthouse B&B (www.hecetalighthouse.com), a
technology-free, turn-of-the-century lighthouse-keeper's house
complete with ocean views, roaring fire, board games, lavish
multicourse breakfast, and famous ghost story.

EUGENE
Sure, happy hippy Eugene is the state's biggest college town,
but there's still plenty to do for the preuniversity set. Spend a
weekend playing pioneer-style in a history-themed riverfront
park, getting eye to eye with owls and ospreys, and riding *bikes*
around the solar system.

Get There
It's about two hours from Portland to Eugene on I-5 South,
but this itinerary features a few fun back-road pit stops—like
a mysterious forest theme park outside of Salem, a carousel-
museum tour in Albany, and a farm-stand lunch in the fields
of Philomath.

Eat, See & Do

If you've seen the signs but haven't yet experienced the **Enchanted Forest** (8462 Enchanted Way SE; 503-371-4242; www.enchantedforest.com), located about ten minutes south of Salem, now's the time. Tucked into the trees just off I-5, this uniquely quirky vintage kiddie theme park has a dozen or so rides and attractions based on classic fairy tales, from log runs and bobsled rides to kiddie bumper boats and a haunted house. Pan for treasure, watch live shows, and gobble corn dogs and chicken strips at Gretel's Grill (outside food is allowed too).

Continue south to Albany, a pleasant rural river town where you can tour the **Historic Carousel and Museum** (250 SW Broadalbin St.; 541-791-3340; www.albanycarousel.com), then run around the playground at nearby **Monteith Riverpark**. From there, hop on US Route 20 and drive a half hour to Philomath's **Gathering Together Farm** (25159 Grange Hall Rd.; 541-929-4270; www.gatheringtogetherfarm.com), an organic farm with a sweet little farm stand and restaurant that turns out true farm-to-table salads, soups, and pizza (open March–November; reservations strongly recommended).

Continue on to Eugene, then stretch little legs at the epic **RiverPlay Discovery Village** (248 Cheshire Ave.; www.eugene-or.gov/facilities/facility/details/45) at Skinner Butte Park. One of the largest playgrounds in the state, this hands-on park-meets-history-lesson features a pioneer village, fossil dig, stagecoach and ferry replicas, mini version of the butte's basalt climbing columns, and a rain circle for summer day splashing (pack a swimsuit and towels).

Next cross the Willamette River to the lollipop-striped **Science Factory Children's Museum and Planetarium** (2300 Leo Harris Pkwy.; 541-682-7888; www.sciencefactory.org) in **Alton Baker Park**, where kids explore economics in the interactive "city" of Moneyville, act out sea stories with ocean-animal puppet characters, and learn about landfills via the Recyclotron. Break out the bikes and pedal through Alton Baker Park, stopping at each planet in the park's 1:1 billion scale model of the solar system (some planets are located along bike paths outside park boundaries). If it's Saturday, shop over two hundred farmers'-market and arts-and-crafts vendors at the nearby **Eugene Saturday Market** (126 E. 8th Ave.; 541-686-8885; www.eugenesaturdaymarket.org), and then continue on to the University of Oregon's **Museum of Natural and Cultural History** (1680 E. 15th Ave.; 541-346-3024; natural-history.uoregon.edu). From the museum, it's a fifteen-minute drive south to the **Cascades Raptor Center** (32275 Fox Hollow Rd.; 541-485-1320; www.cascadesraptorcenter.org), a nature center and wildlife hospital where nearly fifty birds of prey are housed in outdoor aviaries. Cross town to take a guided nature walk at **Mount Pisgah Arboretum** (34901 Frank Parrish Rd.; 541-747-3817; www.mountpisgaharboretum.com), then stop at **Dorris Ranch** (205 Dorris St.; 541-736-4544; www.willamalane.org/park/dorris-ranch), Oregon's first filbert farm. Experience log-cabin life in the Living History Village, take a walk through the old orchards, and picnic by the river.

If it's hot and all anyone really wants to do is play in the pool, visit the **Amazon Pool** (2600 Hilyard St.; 541-682-5350; www.eugene-or.gov/3223/amazon-pool) or **Splash! At Lively Park** (6100 Thurston Rd.; 541-736-4244; www.willamalane.org /facility/splash-at-lively-park), a year-round indoor water park with a wave pool, kiddie pool, and waterslide.

Shopping-wise, visit the **Fifth Street Public Market** (296 E. 5th Ave.; 541-484-0383; www.5stmarket.com), a marvelous mini mall of shops and restaurants; kids will zero in on **Goody's Chocolates** and **Elephant's Trunk Toy Company**. Pop into **Provisions Market Hall** (www.provisionsmarkethall.com) for a light lunch or picnic, then eat on the patio. For organic coffee and fresh pastries, try funky **Wandering Goat Coffee Co.** (268 Madison St.; 541-344-5161; www.wanderinggoat.com), and for pretty pastries and fresh-baked breads, visit **Noisette Pastry Kitchen** (200 W. Broadway; 541-654-5257; www.noisettepk.com). Other family-friendly eateries include the covered-sandbox-endowed **Hideaway Bakery** (3377 E. Amazon Dr.; 541-868-1982; www.hideawaybakery.com), funky **Morning Glory Café** (450 Willamette St.; 541-687-0709; www.morninggloryeugene.com), and **Falling Sky Brewery** (1334 Oak Alley; 541-505-7096; www.fallingskybrewing.com).

For dinner, kids will dig popular **Roaring Rapids Pizza Company** (4006 Franklin Blvd.; 541-988-9819; www .roaringrapidspizza.com), with its riverfront patio, game room, merry-go-round, and proximity to **Camp Putt Adventure Golf Course** (www.willamalane.org/facility/camp-putt). If your tweens and teens prefer pinball to putt putt, hit buzzy **Blairally Vintage Arcade** (245 Blair Blvd.; 541-683-1721; www.facebook .com/blairallyarcade). In summertime, make the most of the long warm nights with tickets to a **Eugene Emeralds** minor league baseball game (www.milb.com/index.jsp?sid=t461), or check the city's **Movies in the Park** calendar (www.willamalane .org/movies-in-the-park) for a fun alfresco flick.

Stay

For superb service, thoughtful details, and easy access to the adjoining Fifth Street Public Market, book at the **Inn at the Fifth** (205 E. 6th Ave.; 541-743-4099; www.innat5th.com). Budgeteers, try the clean and modern **Hilton Garden Inn** (3528 Gateway St.; 541-736-3000; www.hiltongardeninn3.hilton.com), or the all-suites **Residence Inn** (25 Club Rd.; 541-342-7171; www.marriott .com), just a short walk from the river and Alton Baker Park.

THREE TO FOUR HOURS AWAY

BEND & BEYOND

For those who live in the deep green Portland canopy, a trip to the high desert is a refreshing change of scenery. Regardless of what time of year you go, the outdoor adventure quotient is off the charts, and kids on the go will love the Bend life—dogsled riding, ice skating, river floating, lizard petting, mountain biking, lava cave spelunking, and all.

Get There

There are two main routes to Bend, both roughly three hours—either take US Route 26 East over Mt. Hood (if you have an extra day or two, knock a few things off the **Mt. Hood** day trip on page 247), then drop down through Madras and Redmond; or drive south on I-5 to Salem (**Salem** day trip on page 239), then cut east on US Route 20 through **Sisters** (page 264). If time isn't of the essence, you can also drive east to **Hood River**, then wind along scenic State Route 35 through the **Hood River Fruit Loop** (page 244) until you intersect US Route 26 at Mt. Hood.

Eat, See & Do

In the winter Bend is a serious snow-sports destination. And rightfully so, especially considering that at **Mt. Bachelor** kids 12 and under ski free with advance online adult ticket purchase (13000 SW Century Dr.; 800-829-2442; www.mtbachelor.com). If skiing isn't your jam, the resort also offers snowmobiling, snowshoeing, and dogsled rides led by a former Iditarod contender. Or tube the day away at nearby **Wanoga Snow Play Area** (www.fs.usda.gov/recarea/deschutes/recreation/hiking/recarea/?recid=38542&actid=88). In town, slip on your skates and hit the skating rink at **the Pavilion** (1001 SW Bradbury Way; 541-389-7588; www.bendparksandrec.org/the-pavilion), which morphs into a fair-weather fun zone come spring, with a skate park, rock wall, and court games and lawn games galore.

During summer Bend's an outdoor adventure lover's paradise. Start your day with lemon ricotta pancakes at **McKay Cottage** (62910 O. B. Riley Rd.; 541-383-2697; www.themckaycottage.com), biscuits 'n' gravy and cardamom French toast at homey **Jackson's Corner** (845 NW Delaware Ave.; 541-647-2198; www.jacksonscornerbend.com), bacon breakfast sandwiches and the legendary Ocean Rolls at **the Sparrow Bakery** (50 SE Scott St.; 541-330-6321; www.thesparrowbakery.net), or buttermilk knots and Bigfoots at **Sweetheart Donuts** (210 SE 3rd St.; 541-323-3788; www.sweetheartdonuts.com). Then hike it off—pick up the **Deschutes River Trail** in Farewell Bend Park or the Old Mill District (1000 SW Reed Market Rd.; www.bendparksandrec.org/parks_trails/trail_list), stroll along Tumalo Creek at lovely 650-acre **Shevlin Park** (18920 NW Shevlin

Park Rd.; www.bendparksandrec.org/parks/shevlin-park), or embark on the seven-stop **Bend Heritage Walk** starting at the **Deschutes Historical Museum** (129 NW Idaho Ave.; 541-389-1813; www.deschuteshistory.org), located in a historic downtown schoolhouse. The family artist will love the **Roundabout Art Route**—pick up a map at the **Bend Visitor Center** (750 NW Lava Rd.; 541-382-8048; www.visitbend.com), visit at least ten of the more than twenty eclectic sculptures that dot Bend's famous traffic roundabouts, then return for a prize.

A surefire kid pleaser is to float the **Deschutes River**—the city runs a summer "floater shuttle" service from Riverbend Park to Drake Park (www.bendparksandrec.org/bend-whitewater -park/passageway-channel), and if you don't already have tubes, rent them from **Sun Country Tours** (531 SW 13th St.; 541-382-6277; www.suncountrytours.com), which also offers free kids' life-jacket rentals all summer at its Riverbend Park trailer. Or pay a visit to **Tumalo Creek Kayak and Canoe's** rental shop (805 SW Industrial Way; 541-317-9407; www.tumalocreek.com), then paddle the Deschutes. If your wee one isn't quite ready for the river, stick to the **Juniper Swim & Fitness Center** (800 NE 6th St.; 541-389-7665; www.bendparksandrec.org/parks/juniper -swim-fitness-center). And while admission to the **Sunriver Homeowners Aquatic and Recreation Center** (57250 Overlook Rd.; 541-585-5000; www.sunriversharc.com), a.k.a. SHARC, doesn't come cheap, kids will love the 22-acre complex with indoor/outdoor pools, a tot pool, sand play area, playground, ball courts, and a picnic area.

The family naturalist will find lots to love around these parts—learn about prescribed forest burns, pet a lizard, and hang out with Vivi the bobcat at the renowned **High Desert Museum** (59800 S. US 97; 541-382-4754; www .highdesertmuseum.org), then continue ten minutes down the highway to the **Lava Lands Visitor Center** (58201 S. US 97; 541-593-2421; www.fs.usda.gov/recarea/deschutes/recreation /recarea/?recid=38394) and spelunk in the **Lava River Cave** before continuing to explore the **Newberry National Volcanic Monument** (www.bit.ly/1eTrazM); be sure to snap a few shots from the breathtaking **Paulina Peak Overlook**. From the Lava Lands Visitor Center, it's fifteen minutes southeast to the

Sunriver Nature Center (57245 River Rd.; 541-593-4394; www .sunrivernaturecenter.org), where kids can examine native animal habitats, handle bones and fur, commune with their favorite reptiles in the Creature Cave, and spot wetlands wildlife on the Sam Osgood Nature Trail.

This is hiking country, so lace up your boots and hit the trail—easy kid hikes include **Tumalo Falls** (www.fs.usda.gov /recarea/deschutes/recarea/?recid=38526), where you'll see stunning scenery whether you walk a few steps or a few miles; the **Ray Atkeson Loop Trail** (www.fs.usda.gov/recarea /deschutes/recreation/hiking/recarea/?recid=38964&actid=50) at Sparks Lake; and the longer but gorgeous **Green Lakes Trail** (http://www.fs.usda.gov/recarea/deschutes/recreation/recarea /?recid=38870), which can get crowded, so go early or on a weekday. Don't miss spectacular **Smith Rock State Park** (www .smithrock.com) in Terrebonne, less than an hour from Bend and well worth the drive. And as long as you're out in Terrebonne, hunt down the scenic **Steelhead Falls**, a peaceful hike with plenty of picnicking opportunities. If your group would rather be on the water than look at it, book a rafting trip with **Sun Country Tours** or **Ouzel Outfitters** (www.oregonrafting.com), or tote rafts, canoes, or kayaks to one of the area's lovely lakes— popular stops along the **Cascade Lakes Scenic Byway** include **Sparks Lake**, **Devil's Lake**, and **Hosmer Lake**. For two-wheeled wanderings, rent bikes or take the half-day family bike tour at **Cog Wild** (255 SW Century Dr.; 541-385-7002; www.cogwild. com), and if you want something else to do the heavy lifting, book a horseback riding tour at **Flyspur Ranch** (64460 Research Rd.; 541-389-4995; www.flyspur.com) or **Diane's Riding Place** (65535 Cline Falls Hwy.; 541-408-1731; www.bendhorseride.com).

For family-friendly eats, slip into a booth for burgers, mac 'n' cheese, and milkshakes at Downtown's cheerful **Drake** (801 NW Wall St.; 541-306-3366; www.drakebend.com); graze the food carts at **The Lot** cart pod (745 NW Columbia St.; 541-610-4969; www.facebook.com/thelotbend); let kids loose on a make-your-own-pizza adventure at **Flatbread Neapolitan Pizzeria** (375 SW Powerhouse Dr.; 541-728-0600; www.flatbreadpizza.com) in the Old Mill District; or enjoy the crayons, kids' menu, *and* craft beer at Downtown's **Deschutes Brewery & Public House**

(1044 NW Bond St.; 541-382-9242; www.deschutesbrewery
.com). For dessert, indulge in sweet treats from **Powell's Sweet
Shoppe** (818 NW Wall St.; 541-617-9866; www.powellsss.com),
or a banana split at **Goody's** (957 NW Wall St.; 541-389-5185;
www.goodysgoodies.com). End the night with some backcountry
stargazing–at **Oregon Observatory** at Sunriver (57245 River Rd.;
541-598-4406; www.oregonobservatory.org) or the University
of Oregon–operated **Pine Mountain Observatory** (56100 Pine
Mountain Rd.; 541-382-8331; pmo.uoregon.edu).

As far as side trips go, a half hour from Bend sits **Sisters**,
a charming Old West–themed town. Get hot chocolate and do
a little front-porch sittin' at **Sisters Coffee Company** (273 W.
Hood Ave.; 541-549-0527; www.sisterscoffee.com), browse
Paulina Springs Books (252 W. Hood Ave.; 541-549-0866;
www.paulinasprings.com), and dig into old-fashioned burgers,
fries, and shakes at **Sno Cap** (380 W. Cascade Ave.; 541-549-
6151; www.facebook.com/sno-cap-drive-in-269793833045140).
After catching a family flick at the **Sisters Movie House** (720
Desperado Ct.; 541-549-8800; www.sistersmoviehouse.com),
bunk at the clean and cozy **Best Western Ponderosa Lodge** (500
US 20; 541-549-1234; www.bestwesternsisters.com), which has a
sparkling outdoor pool and a 5-acre llama corral. Or splurge and
rent a condo at **Black Butte Ranch** (13899 Bishops Cap; 866-901-
2961; www.blackbutteranch.com), where kids can splash around
the pool, ride bikes or horses through the meadow, and sign up
for classes and camps at the family activity center.

Kids will also love the rec room, trout pond, and sparkling
pool at **Lake Creek Lodge** (13375 SW Forest Service Rd.; 541-
516-3030; www.lakecreeklodge.com) in **Camp Sherman**, a tiny
town on the edge of the magical Metolius River. They'll also
get a kick out of the old-timey **Camp Sherman Store** (25451 FS
Rd. 1419; 541-595-6711; www.campshermanstore.com), where a
dollar goes a long way at the candy counter. Get sandwiches and
snacks, then hike up the **Metolius River Trail** and have a picnic.
On the way home, stay at the rustic-chic **Suttle Lodge** (13300
US 20; 541-638-7001; www.thesuttlelodge.com), a lakefront
resort with all the makings of unforgettable summer memories—
including cabins, canoes, and an awesome on-site restaurant,
the Boathouse.

Stay

For downtown Bend digs with family-friendly touches (hello, fresh-baked organic chocolate chip cookies and complimentary loaner bikes), book at modern, eco-chic **the Oxford Hotel** (10 NW Minnesota Ave.; 541-382-8436; www.oxfordhotelbend.com); or go the resort route at **Sunriver Resort** (17600 Center Dr.; 855-420-8206; www.sunriver-resort.com). A half hour northeast of town, hide out at luxe **Brasada Ranch** (16986 SW Brasada Ranch Rd.; 866-373-4882; www.brasada.com), which caters to kids with the Hideout game and movie room, cowboy cookouts, and nightly s'mores roasts around the fire pit.

SOUTHERN OREGON

The road less traveled leads to Southern Oregon, a breathtakingly beautiful stretch of the state that's largely free of the tourist hordes found at the coast or Columbia River Gorge. Here, kids can travel via tree, jet-boat down remote rivers, trolley their way around gold-rush towns, visit wildlife sanctuaries, and eat a *lot* of homemade berry pie.

Get There

Once on I-5 South, set the cruise control; it's about a five-hour trip, including a pit stop in **Rice Hill** for cones at **K & R Drive-In** (201 John Long Rd., Oakland; 541-849-2570), home of the famous fifteen-scoop Pig-Out (and *not* home to any bathrooms, unfortunately; cross to the other side of the freeway for those).

Eat, See & Do

Start the festivities in Downtown Grants Pass with a hearty chicken 'n' waffles brunch/lunch at **Ma Mosa's** (118 NW E St.; 541-479-0236; www.mamosas.com). If it's Saturday, walk to the **Grants Pass Growers Market** (4th and F St.; www.growersmarket.org), a mix of farmers'-market vendors and local artisans. A mile away, on the north side of the Rogue River, take **Hellgate Jet Boat Excursions'** two-hour, 36-mile jet-boat ride (966 SW 6th St.; 541-479-7204; www.hellgate.com) through historic Hellgate Canyon. Or drive up to tiny Merlin and take the ninety-minute guided tour of the **Wildlife Images Rehabilitation Center** (11845 Lower River Rd.; 541-476-0222;

www.wildlifeimages.org), an animal sanctuary, clinic, and education center, where kids will meet bears, bald eagles, coons, and cougars. An hour southeast, pass through Cave Junction to reach the **Oregon Caves National Monument** (19000 Caves Hwy.; 541-592-2100; www.nps.gov/orca), where kids can become junior rangers (all ages) and take the ninety-minute ranger-led tour through the narrow passageways of the Oregon Caves (42 inches and taller only). For an unforgettable overnight, drive forty-five minutes to the remote **Out 'n' About Treehouse Treesort** (300 Page Creek Rd.; 541-592-2208; www.treehouses.com) to spend the night in a bona fide treehouse (day trippers also welcome to participate in the resort's many "activitrees").

From Grants Pass, take State Route 238 into the beautiful **Applegate Valley**, stopping for fresh fruit hand pies at **Pennington Farms** (11341 Williams Hwy.; 541-846-0550; www.penningtonfarms.net), organic produce and locally made treats at **Whistling Duck Farm** (12800 Williams Hwy.; 541-761-6772; www.whistlingduckfarm.com), and perhaps some wine tasting along the **Applegate Valley Wine Trail** (www.applegatewinetrail.com)—**Schmidt Family Vineyards** (330 Kubli Rd.; 541-846-9985; www.sfvineyards.com) and **Red Lily Vineyards** (11777 Williams Hwy.; 541-846-6800; www.redlilyvineyards.com) are particularly picturesque *and* picnic friendly. After lunch in funky **Peace of Pizza**'s secret garden (15090 SR 238; 541-702-4420; www.peaceofpizza.com), go for a dip in the Applegate River at **Cantrall Buckley County Park** (154 Cantrall Rd.; 541-774-8183; www.jacksoncountyor.org/parks/day-use/cantrall-buckley), which also sports a picnic area, playground, and potty. Continue down the road to **Sanctuary One** (13195 Upper Applegate Rd.; 541-899-8627; www.sanctuaryone.org), a working care farm with a marvelous mission; book the $10 tour online before you go (April–October).

At the southeastern end of the Applegate Valley, pop into the perfectly preserved gold-rush town of **Jacksonville**. Stroll the two-block downtown, poking into antique shops, old-timey **Scheffel's Toys** (180 W. California St.; 541-899-7421; www.scheffels.com), and **the Scoop Shoppe** (235 E. California St.; 541-613-3909). Hop aboard the **Historic Jacksonville Trolley Tour** (www.jacksonvilleoregon.org/directory/4101), tiptoe around the tombs (some nearly 200 years old) at the **Jacksonville Pioneer Cemetery** (www.friendsjvillecemetery .org), and pick up one of the **Jacksonville Woodlands Trails** in the **Britt Gardens** (www.jvwoodlands.org). Run around **Doc Griffin Park**'s playground and splash pad (298 S. 5th St.), then have dinner on the patio at festive, family-owned **Las Palmas** (210 E. California St.; 541-899-9965) or at **Onyx** restaurant (635 N. Oregon St.; 541-702-2700; www.onyxjvilleor.wixsite.com /onyx), part of the beautiful historic Nunan Estate. Bunk down at pleasant, affordable **Wine Country Inn** (830 N. 5th St.; 541-899-2050; www.countryhouseinnsjacksonville.com), dreaming of the next day's pancake (and cinnamon roll) breakfast at darling **Mustard Seed Café** (130 N. 5th St.; 541-899-2977).

Check to see if your Jacksonville visit coincides with a summertime show at the internationally acclaimed **Britt Fest** (www.brittfest.org), especially the free children's concerts in August and/or the **Storytelling Guild's Annual Children's Festival** (www.storytellingguild.org), also held at the Britt Pavilion (350 S. 1st St., Jacksonville) every July.

From Jacksonville head northeast to downtown Central Park. Stop at **Rogue Creamery Cheese Shop** (311 N. Front St.; 541-665-1155; www.roguecreamery.com) for cheese sampling and shopping, then neighboring **Lillie Belle Farms** chocolate shop (211 N. Front St.; 541-664-2815; www.lilliebellefarms.com), which doesn't skimp on the samples either and always has a few daily dollar chocolate specials. For a cheap and speedy lunch, hit up the Medford **In-N-Out Burger** (1970 Crater Lake Hwy.; 800-786-1000; www.in-n-out.com), the first one ever to grace Oregon soil. Just down the way, little ones will love the **Kid Time! Discover Experience** museum (106 N. Central Ave.; 541-772-9922; www.kid-time.org), where they can stock and shop a miniature grocery store, tend the Discovery Farm garden, and X-ray their favorite stuffed animal in the vet's clinic. Just down the road, take an hour-long factory tour at the **Harry & David** factory (1314 Center Dr.; 541-864-2278; www.harryanddavid.com; e-mail or call for tour reservations)—kids get to ride the tour bus, watch Moose Munch caramel popcorn being made, and receive a tasty gift at the end. Then have family recess on the big wooden play structure at beautiful **Bear Creek Park** (1520 Siskiyou Blvd.; www.ci.medford.or.us/page.asp?navid=3997).

Continue down State Route 99 to **Ashland**, Southern Oregon's cultural epicenter. Walk the main street, popping into **Paddington Station** (125 E. Main St.; 541-482-1343; www.paddingtonstationashland.com) for trinkets galore, magical **Tree House Books** (15 N. Main St.; 541-482-9616) for books and whimsy (don't be surprised if the staff is in costume); and **Mix Bakeshop** (57 N. Main St.; 541-488-9885; www.mixashland.com) for scoops, scones, and Stumptown coffee. Then walk along Ashland Creek and into **Lithia Park**; hit the playground, feed the ducks, take a dip in the swimming hole or Fairy Ponds, and, in the winter, ice skate on the **Ashland Rotary Centennial Ice Rink** (www.ashland.or.us/page.asp?navid=14057). From March through October, Ashland runs two farmers' markets (www.rvgrowersmarket.com)—a Saturday market downtown and a larger Tuesday market at the **National Guard Armory**. Buy fresh local berries, greens, and baked goods, and don't leave without a scrumptious freshly fried **Daddy's Doughnut**. A short walk from the armory is the **ScienceWorks Hands-On Museum** (1500 E. Main St.; 541-482-6767; www.scienceworksmuseum.org), a local favorite where kids take on various art and science activities like painting with a pendulum, creating stop-motion animation movies, and tinkering with technology in Da Vinci's Garage. The family thespian should experience Ashland's famous **Oregon Shakespeare Festival** (15 Pioneer St.; 800-219-8161; www.osfashland.org), and most of the shows are appropriate for teens and mature tweens, so check the calendar to see what's playing.

On the Ashland dining front, get coffee and carrot muffins at bright, busy **Noble Coffee Roasting** (281 4th St.; 541-488-3288; www.noblecoffeeroasting.com) in the railroad district (then walk two blocks to the **Railroad Park** playground), then dig into some of the best buttermilk pancakes around at worth-the-wait **Morning Glory** (1149 Siskiyou Blvd.; 541-488-8636). Come lunchtime, sink your teeth into the house-cured pastrami and house-poached tuna sandwiches at **Sammich** (424 Bridge St.; 541-708-6055; www.sammichashland.com), or hit the **Ashland Co-op** (237 N. 1st St.; 541-482-2237; www.ashlandfood.coop), a lively local hangout with a fully stocked deli, juice bar, and dine-in area. If anyone's veggie, vegan, or gluten free, **Northwest Raw** (370 E. Main St.; 541-708-6363; www.nwraw.com) will meet all the family smoothie, salad, and bowl needs. And for dinnertime views, brews, and an excellent kids' menu served 'til 10 p.m., head out to **Caldera Brewery** (590 Clover Ln.; 541-482-4677; www.calderabrewing.com) located just off I-5, about a ten-minute drive from Downtown.

Hotel-wise, if you're trying to get off I-5 and into a pool as quickly as possible, try the **Best Western Windsor Inn** (2520 Ashland St.; 541-488-2330; www.bestwestern.com) or **Holiday Inn Express and Suites Ashland** (565 Clover Ln.; 541-201-0202; www.ihg.com/holidayinnexpress/hotels/us/en/ashland/hsaor /hoteldetail), both located southeast of Downtown (and a block from Caldera Brewery). For something near Southern Oregon University, just across the street lies beautifully landscaped, eco-chic motor inn **the Palm** (1065 Siskiyou Blvd.; 541-482-2636; www.palmcottages.com); and for a touch of historic posh with a supremely central location, book at Downtown's stately **Ashland Springs Hotel** (212 E. Main St.; 541-488-1700; www .ashlandspringshotel.com).

In summer take a field trip to **Emigrant Lake** (5505 SR 66; www.jacksoncountyor.org/parks/camping/emigrant-lake), located twenty minutes to the east—picnic, play on the playground, fish for rainbow trout, water ski, and ride the awesome 280-foot twin flume waterslide. In winter make the half-hour drive to **Mt. Ashland** (11 Mt. Ashland Ski Rd.; 541-482-2897; www.mtashland. com), a laid-back, family-friendly ski resort where kids under 6 ski for free.

Before heading home to Portland, take a scenic detour to Crater Lake via Dead Indian Memorial Road. En route, schedule a tour or farm stay at 440-acre **Willow-Witt Ranch** (658 Shale City Rd.; 541-890-1998; www.willowwittranch.com), then spend a few hours (or days) at **Lake of the Woods** (950 Harriman Route, Klamath Falls; 541-949-8300; www.lakeofthewoodsresort.com), a historic lakefront resort with an old-fashioned general store, wide array of activities, and cozy cabins outfitted with Pendleton blankets and locally crafted myrtlewood lamps. Continue on to **Crater Lake National Park** (541-594-3000; www.nps.gov/crla)—

marvel at the world-famous indigo waters, pick up your junior ranger packet at either the Steel or Rim Village Visitor Centers, take a historic trolley tour, hike the easy Sun Notch Trail or up to the supercool Watchman Lookout Station, and reserve a cruise to Wizard Island, which includes a swim in the cold, pure water.

Back on State Route 62, make a hamburger and huckleberry-pie pit stop at **Beckie's Café** at **Union Creek Resort** (56484 SR 62, Prospect; 541-560-3565; www.unioncreekoregon. com), then head northeast to pretty **Diamond Lake** for a hike or bike ride along the 11-mile **John Dellenback Trail** (rent bikes at Diamond Lake Resort in summer). Move on to nearby **Watson Falls** (www.blm.gov/or/districts/roseburg/recreation/Thundering _Waters/watson_falls.html), the tallest waterfall in southwest Oregon—you can see the falls from the parking lot, but make the 0.3-mile trip up the trail for a closer look. End your loop through **Umpqua National Forest** in Roseburg, where you can visit the **Wildlife Safari** (1790 Safari Rd., Winston; 541-679-6761; www .wildlifesafari.net), a 600-acre drive-thru wild animal park. Then back to Portland you go, with a car full of sand, pine needles, and Moose Crunch, and phones full of Crater Lake selfies.

SOUTHERN OREGON COAST

While a Southern Oregon Coast sojourn does require considerable family car time, the distance also means less crowds, which can be a refreshing contrast to its northern neighbors. As you explore the towns of Florence, Coos Bay, Bandon, Port Orford, Gold Beach, and Brookings, bask in the strikingly rugged terrain and breathtaking views, race across the sands in a giant dune buggy, catch your own crabs, and seeing as this is cranberry country, sample cranberry *everything*.

Get There
Routes vary—start up north and end here (see the **Cannon Beach/Seaside** and **Central Oregon Coast** guides on pages 250 and 254, or take I-5 South to **Eugene** (page 257), then follow State Route 126 West to **Florence**.

Eat, See & Do

Upon reaching Florence, a former mill town nestled into a crook of the Siuslaw River, head for charming historic Old Town. Grab hot chocolate and a cranberry scone at **Siuslaw River Coffee Roasters** (1240 Bay St.; 541-997-3443; www.coffeeoregon.com), then sit out on the lovely river-facing patio. Walk the historic Old Town's waterfront boardwalk and admire the fishing boats, embark on a historic walking tour from the **Siuslaw Pioneer Museum** (278 Maple St.; 541-997-7884; www.siuslawpioneermuseum.com), and visit **Given Back Bird Houses** (1300 Bay St.; 541-590-9108; www.givenbackbirdhouses.com), where you can watch a woodworking poet/artist husband-and-wife team craft uniquely magical birdhouses. For chowder, burgers, and Hippie Pie, try **Homegrown Public House** (294 Laurel St.; 541-997-4886; www.homegrownpub.com), then mosey over to **BJ's Ice Cream Parlor** (1495 Bay St.; 541-902-7828) for Bing Cherry cones and over one hundred flavors of saltwater taffy.

North of Florence visit the seasonal and extremely popular (try to go off-season) **Sea Lion Caves** wildlife preserve and bird sanctuary (91560 US 101; 541-547-3111; www.sealioncaves.com), hike the **Heceta Head Lighthouse Trail** (www.oregonstateparks.org/index.cfm?do=parkpage.dsp_parkpage&parkid=86), and channel your inner Frodo and Sam on the **Washburne State Park Hobbit Trail** (www.oregonstateparks.org).

South of Florence book the one-hour giant dune buggy tour with **Sandland Adventures** (85366 US 101; 541-997-8087; www.sandland.com) and zoom up and down 8 miles of the **Oregon Dunes National Recreation Area**; hike the **John Dellenback Dunes Trail** (www.fs.usda.gov/recarea/siuslaw/recarea/?recid=42607) through round, rolling sand dunes; and visit the totem-pole-fronted **Umpqua Discovery Center** in Reedsport (409 Riverfront Way; 541-271-4816; www.umpquadiscoverycenter.com), where kids will love the interactive natural history exhibits, like the slide that drops them into a bear den, where they learn about hibernation.

Drive south to **Coos Bay** and dig into fish tacos and clam chowder at **Shark Bites Café** (240 S. Broadway; 541-269-7475; www.sharkbites.cafe), then poke around **Waxer's Surf &**

Skate shop next door (242 S. Broadway; 541-266-9020; www
.surfwaxers.com). If you caught your own crab lunch, the
Fisherman's Wharf (63534 Kingfisher Rd. D-Dock; 541-888-8862;
www.fishermenswharforegon.com) in nearby Charleston will
clean and cook your catch.

Head west along Cape Arago Highway, which leads to
three state parks in a row, starting with **Sunset Bay State
Park** (89814 Cape Arago Hwy.; www.oregonstateparks.org
/index.cfm?do=parkpage.dsp_parkpage&parkid=70) where
you can book a yurt and stay awhile, then **Shore Acres State
Park** (89039 Cape Arago Hwy.; www.shoreacres.net), a former
timber baron's estate with some serious scenery, both man-
made and natural. Stroll the beautifully manicured Japanese
garden and rose gardens before walking the winding path
down to secluded Simpson Beach. End at **Cape Arago State
Park** (www.oregonstateparks.org/index.cfm?do=parkpage.
dsp_parkpage&parkid=66), where you can whale watch, explore
the tide pools, and picnic.

Next stop: **Bandon**, a.k.a. the Cranberry Capital of Oregon,
home to the widely attended annual September **Cranberry
Festival** (www.bandon.com/cranberry-festival). En route, stop at
the **Bandon Marsh National Wildlife Refuge** (www.fws.gov
/refuge/bandon_marsh), whose mudflats are a crucial stopover
for tens of thousands of shorebirds each spring and fall. A mile
west, at **Bullards Beach State Park** (www.oregonstateparks.
org/index.cfm?do=parkpage.dsp_parkpage&parkid=50), visit the
Coquille River Lighthouse. Although the tower is inaccessible,
from May through September visitors can tour the fog-signal
room, then walk or bike the 4.5 miles of shoreline.

If you've worked up an appetite, stop into **Face Rock
Creamery** (680 2nd St. SE; 541-347-3223; www.facerockcreamery
.com) to nibble samples, stock up on Vampire Slayer cheese
curds, and dig into ginormous "kid"-size scoops of ice cream.
Continue on to Old Town Bandon's cozy, kitschy **Tony's Crab
Shack** (155 1st St. SE; 541-347-2875; www.tonyscrabshack.com) for
grilled oysters, crab sandwiches, and whole steamed Dungeness
crabs (if you caught your own crab, they'll clean and cook it for
you). For dessert cross the street to **Cranberry Sweets & More**
(280 1st St. SE; 541-347-9475; www.cranberrysweets.com) for

the signature cranberry jellies and cranberry walnut fudge, or walk around the block for chocolate-covered cranberries and old-timey candies at **Bandon Sweets & Treats** (255 2nd St. SE; 541-347-7072; www.bandonsweetsandtreats.com), then check out darling toy shop **the Toy Room** (295 2nd St. SE; 541-347-9783). If you'd rather sip your dessert, try a drinking chocolate (or drinking *caramel*) flight at **Coastal Mist** (210 2nd St. SE; 541-347-3300; www.coastalmist.com).

Ten minutes southwest of Downtown, find **Face Rock State Scenic Viewpoint** (www.oregonstateparks.org/index.cfm?do =parkpage.dsp_parkpage&parkid=47), then try to find the namesake face in the rock. Continue south on Beach Loop Road to **Bandon Beach Riding Stables** (54629 Beach Loop Rd.; 541-347-3423; cash and check only) and saddle up for a leisurely surfside ride that will delight the family horse fanatic. Back on US Route 101, head south to **West Coast Game Park Safari** (46914 US 101; 541-347-3106; www.westcoastgameparksafari .com), a well-established walk-through safari park with over 75 species and 450 animals, from goats and peacocks to lions and tigers and bison, oh my!

For a Bandon beachfront slumber party, the cute family cottages at **Windermere on the Beach** (3250 Beach Loop Dr.; 541-347-3710; www.windermereonthebeach.com) sleep up to six; the clean and cozy **Bandon Beach Motel** (1090 Portland Ave. SW; 541-347-9451; www.bandonbeachmotel.com) has budget-friendly rates and million-dollar Coquille Point views; and the **Bandon Inn** (355 US 101; 541-347-4417; www.bandoninn.com) is right in the middle of the Old Town action.

A half hour south, the fishing village of **Port Orford** is both the oldest town on the Oregon Coast *and* the most westerly town in the forty-eight contiguous states. On your way into town stop at **Cape Blanco State Park** to tour the **Hughes Historic House** (91816 Cape Blanco Rd.; 541-332-0248; www.enjoyportorford .com/hugheshouses; April–October) and lighthouse. Then grab fish 'n' chips, tuna melts, and razzleberry pie at **the Crazy Norwegian's Fish & Chips** (259 6th St.; 541-332-8601).

Visit the **Port Orford Lifeboat Station** museum at **Port Orford Heads State Park** (www.oregonstateparks.org), where you can pick up the scenic Cove, Tower, and Headland. If you've got bikes, explore as much of the 60-mile **Wild Rivers Coast Scenic Bikeway** (www.rideoregonride.com) as the kids can handle.

Keep driving down the coast to the **Battle Rock Park** (www.enjoyportorford.com/battlerockpark.html), named after a particularly contentious clash between the Native Americans and early European settlers. Stop in to the visitor center, then hike up the rock for breathtaking views and perhaps even a gray whale sighting. Ten minutes south pull over at **Humbug Mountain State Park** (www.oregonstateparks.org/index.cfm?do=parkpage.dsp_parkpage&parkid=40) to watch the windsurfers, or tackle the **Humbug Mountain Trail** (or just stroll the mostly paved Old Highway 101 Trail). And finally, another 10 miles south or so, let the future family paleontologist loose in the **Prehistoric Gardens** (36848 US 101; 541-332-4463; www.prehistoricgardens.com), a stroller-friendly, self-guided, twenty-minute forest walk peppered with life-size dinosaur replicas.

If the family's into jet-boat thrill rides and giant myrtlewood trees, **Gold Beach** is where it's at. On the way into town, stop at **Otter Point State Recreation Site** (www.oregonstateparks.org/index.cfm?do=parkpage.dsp_parkpage&parkid=41) for big views of Bailey Beach and beyond (hang onto little ones). Continue south to **Jerry's Rogue Jets** (29985 Harbor Way; 800-451-3645; www.roguejets.com), where the Historic Mail Boat Route jet-boat tour zooms 64 miles up the scenic Rogue River along the same route the pioneers would have taken before roads . . . with just a *bit* more engine power. Posttrip, stop at **Gold Beach Books** (29707 Ellensburg Ave.; 541-247-2495; www.oregoncoastbooks.com), the largest bookstore on the Oregon coast. Browse the wordy wares, have hot chocolate and a homemade cranberry muffin at the café, and ask a local for directions to the **Myrtle Tree Trail**. After you've found and hugged the state's largest myrtle tree (www.fs.usda.gov/recarea/rogue-siskiyou/recreation/recarea/?recid=69554), continue down the coast to 1,400-acre **Cape Sebastian State Scenic Corridor** (www.oregonstateparks.org/index.cfm?do=parkpage.dsp_parkpage&parkid=52), where the spectacular views start right in the parking lot—on a clear day, visibility is upwards of 50 miles.

Finish your tour in quaint **Brookings**, known for its temperate climate, historically significant azaleas, summer kite festival, and breathtaking coastline. Ten minutes north of town, stop at **Samuel H. Boardman State Scenic Corridor** (www.oregonstateparks.org/index.cfm?do=parkpage.dsp _parkpage&parkid=56), named after the first Oregon Parks superintendent. Hiking and picnicking options abound throughout the 12-mile state park; see if you can spot **Arch Rock** and catch the vivid views at **Cape Ferrelo**, one of the coast's best vantage points for migrating gray whales. If you've seen one park, you *haven't* seen them all, so about ten minutes south, visit **Harris Beach State Park** (www.oregonstateparks.org/index .cfm?do=parkpage.dsp_parkpage&parkid=58) for a look at the coast's largest island, **Bird Island** (or Goat Island, depending who you ask), a national wildlife sanctuary that hosts scores of nesting seabirds.

In Brookings, go the chowder and fish 'n' chips route at **Fat Irish Kitchen & Pub** (16403 Lower Harbor Rd.; www.fatirishpub .com), or tuck into pretzel bites with pub cheese, burgers, and the local catch fish tacos at jovial **Oxenfrē Public House** (631 Chetco Ave.; 541-813-1985; www.oxenpub.com), then snap a selfie with the angel/devil wings painted on the wall. Or try the Extreme Mac & Cheese pizza at **Zola's Pizzeria** (16362 Lower Harbor Rd.; 541-412-7100; www.zolaspizzeria.com), where kids don't just get to doodle on the paper tablecloths, they're also given pizza boxes to decorate. For dessert hit **Slugs 'n Stones 'n Ice Cream Cones** (16360 Lower Harbor Rd.; 541-469-7584) for scoops, then continue the rhyming lesson at neighboring **Whale's Tail Candy & Gifts** (16350 Lower Harbor Rd.; 541-469-5750; www.whalestailcandyandgifts.com), which stocks over fifty kinds of taffy.

Don't miss **Azalea State Park** (640 Old County Rd.; 541-469-1103; www.brookings.or.us/facilities/facility/details/azalea -park-5), which boasts both the **Kidtown Playground** *and* some serious history—some of the park's ancient azaleas were around when Lewis and Clark wintered on the Oregon Coast in the early 1800s. From here it's about a twenty-minute drive northeast to **Alfred A. Loeb State Park** (www.oregonstateparks.org/index .cfm?do=parkpage.dsp_parkpage&parkid=51)—spot wildlife, fish for salmon and steelhead in the Chetco River, and hike the nearby **Redwood Nature Trail** to the country's northernmost redwood grove.

Retrace your steps to US Route 101, then head toward the **Chetco Valley Historical Society Museum** (15461 Museum Rd., Harbor; 541-469-6651; www.chetcomuseum.org), set in the mid-nineteenth-century Blake House, which at one point was a trading post and stagecoach stop and is the oldest standing building in the valley. Wander through the sewing room and parlor and examine the historic photographs and artifacts. A few miles south, end your travels less than a half mile from the California border at the **Crissey Field State Recreation Site** (www.oregonstateparks.org/index.cfm?do=parkpage.dsp _parkpage&parkid=53). Visit the handsome 4,500-square-foot welcome center (which has excellent restrooms), find the mouth of the Winchuk River, then walk to California and back via the long, flat sandy beach.

If visiting in July, don't miss Brookings' acclaimed **Southern Oregon Kite Festival** (www.southernoregonkitefestival.com), one of the best in the country. Kids will dig the free kite-making, fun food, and kite demonstrations.

Stay
For a good night's rest before heading home, bunk at the Brookings **Best Western Plus Beachfront Inn** (16008 Boat Basin Rd.; 541-469-7779; www.bestwestern.com), a clean and pleasant property with ocean views, free breakfast, an outdoor pool and hot tub, and easy beach and harbor access.

ACKNOWLEDGMENTS

To Portland, for the endless adventures

To Mom, Dad, Michael, Christopher, Cherish, and Lance, the
Stevenson squad, for being the best research team ever

To Jeff, for being the funniest (big) kid of all

To Marnie Hanel Superstar, for always having the most
insightful insights

ANNUAL EVENTS

Mark your calendars for these annually occurring favorites.

JANUARY

GREAT TRAIN SHOW
Dates vary each year
Portland Expo Center in
North Portland
www.trainshow.com/portland

ROSE CITY CLASSIC DOG SHOW
Dates vary each year
Portland Expo Center in
North Portland
www.rosecityclassic.org

FEBRUARY

BRICKS CASCADE LEGO CONVENTION
Dates vary each year
Oregon Convention Center in
the Lloyd District
www.brickscascade.com

CHINESE NEW YEAR AT LAN SU CHINESE GARDEN
*Dates vary each year,
spanning the 15 days of
Chinese New Year*
Old Town/Chinatown
www.lansugarden.org

KIDFEST NORTHWEST
Dates vary each year
Portland Expo Center in
North Portland
www.kidfestnw.com

MARCH

KELL'S ST. PATRICK'S DAY FESTIVAL
*Dates vary each year, but
always close to the St. Patrick's
Day holiday*
Old Town/Chinatown
www.kellsportland.com

SHAMROCK RUN
*Sunday nearest of St.
Patrick's Day*
Tom McCall Waterfront Park
www.shamrockrunportland.com

SELLWOOD-MORELAND ST. PATRICK'S DAY PARADE & FESTIVAL
*Weekend of or before the St.
Patrick's Day holiday*
Sellwood-Moreland
www.stagathaschoolpdx.us

APRIL

BABYFEST NW
Dates vary each year
Portland Expo Center in
North Portland
www.babyfestnw.com

EASTER EGG HUNTS
(see page 111)

WOODEN SHOE TULIP FEST
*Dates vary each year, from late
March to early May*
Woodburn
www.woodenshoe.com

MAY

CINCO DE MAYO FIESTA
*Dates vary each year,
near May 5*
Tom McCall Waterfront Park
www.cincodemayo.org

EAST PORTLAND SUNDAY PARKWAYS
Dates vary each year
East Portland
www.portlandoregon.gov
/transportation/58929

JUNE

NORTH PORTLAND SUNDAY PARKWAYS
Dates vary each year
North Portland
www.portlandoregon.gov
/transportation/58929

PORTLAND ROSE FESTIVAL
*Third Sunday in May through the
second weekend in June*
Locations vary, mostly held in
Downtown Portland and the Lloyd
District
www.rosefestival.org

JULY

MISSISSIPPI STREET FAIR
Second Saturday of July
Mississippi Avenue
www.mississippiave.com/streetfair

NORTHEAST PORTLAND SUNDAY PARKWAYS
Date varies each year
Northeast Portland
www.portlandoregon.gov
/transportation/58929

AUGUST

ALBERTA STREET FAIR
Second Saturday of August
Alberta Street
www.albertamainst.org/whats-happening
/street-fair

BITE OF OREGON
Dates vary each year
Tom McCall Waterfront Park
www.biteoforegon.com

FESTA ITALIANA
Dates vary each year
Pioneer Courthouse Square
www.festa-italiana.org

PROVIDENCE BRIDGE PEDAL
Date varies each year
Ride begins near Tom McCall
Waterfront Park
www.providence.org/bridge-pedal

SOUTHEAST PORTLAND
SUNDAY PARKWAYS
Date varies each year
Southeast Portland
www.portlandoregon.gov
/transportation/58929

SEPTEMBER

PORTLAND POLISH FESTIVAL
Dates vary each year
North Portland
www.portlandpolonia.org

SELLWOOD-MILWAUKIE
SUNDAY PARKWAYS
Date varies each year
Sellwood and milwaukie
www.portlandoregon.gov
/transportation/58929

OCTOBER

THE GREAT PUMPKIN PATCH
(see page 121)

PORTLAND PET EXPO
Dates vary each year
Portland Expo Center in
North Portland
www.portlandpetexpo.com

NOVEMBER

OREGON ZOO TURKEY TROT
Thanksgiving Day
Oregon Zoo
www.oregonzoo.org

DECEMBER

CHRISTMAS FESTIVAL OF LIGHTS
AT THE GROTTO
*Friday after Thanksgiving through
December 30*
The Grotto
www.thegrotto.org

CHRISTMAS SHIP PARADE
Early to mid-December
Portland waterfront
www.christmasships.org

ZOOLIGHTS
*Friday after Thanksgiving through
January 1*
Oregon Zoo
www.oregonzoo.org

RESOURCES

Here are the best local resources for fresh kid-friendly Portland content, including the tourism office, family magazines, websites, and blogs.

CASCADIA KIDS
www.cascadiakids.com

NW KIDS MAGAZINE
www.nwkidsmagazine.com

PDX PARENT
www.pdxparent.com

PORTLAND FAMILY
www.portlandfamily.com

RED TRICYCLE
www.redtri.com/portland-kids

TRAVEL OREGON
www.traveloregon.com

TRAVEL PORTLAND
www.travelportland.com

INDEX